The Investors' Guide to the United Kingdom 2010/11

in association with UK TRADE & INVESTMENT

The Investors' Guide to the United Kingdom 2010/11

Edited by

Jonathan Reuvid

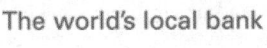
The world's local bank

Watson, Farley & Williams

WILDER COE
CHARTERED ACCOUNTANTS

ARTAIUS LIMITED
BUSINESS OUTSOURCE SOLUTIONS

Legend Business

Independent Book Publisher

Legend Business, 2 London Wall Buildings,
London EC2M 5UU
business@legend-paperbooks.co.uk
www.legendpress.co.uk

British Library Cataloguing in Publication Data available.

ISBN 978-1-9074611-8-7

Set in Times
Printed by JF Print, Sparkford / Lightning Source, Milton Keynes.

Cover designed by EA Digital, Leicester
www.eadigital.com

Publisher 's note

Legend ⬛ Business
Independent Book Publisher

Contents

Rocked in Hollywood.
Made in Borehamwood.

It may sound like a quiet little town but Borehamwood is home to Orange Amps, which has been supplying the world's music industry for the past 40 years.

At HSBC we believe that a local business doesn't have to stay local. By thinking about your business from a global perspective, we can help you thrive both locally and internationally.

If you would like to find out more about how HSBC can help you establish and develop your business in the UK speak to one of our Inward Investment Managers on +44 (0) 207 991 0538* or email us at inwardinvestmentuk@hsbc.com

HSBC Business

HSBC ◆

The world's local bank

A multi-faceted firm of
Chartered Accountants
helping **Overseas Business** to address their **accountancy** and **taxation** needs

We provide a professional, pro-active service with a personal touch and we care passionately about meeting our clients' goals.

Our services include:

- **Accounts Preparation**
- **Audit and Business Assurance**
- **Business Risk and Advisory Services**
- **Buying, Selling or Floating a Business**
- **Company Formation**
- **Company Secretarial**

- **Due Diligence and Viability Reviews**
- **Litigation Support and Forensic Accounting**
- **Tax Planning**
- **Tax Returns and Compliance**
- **Transfer Pricing**
- **Turnaround, Restructuring and Business Recovery**

INTEGRA⊕INTERNATIONAL®
Your Global Advantage

Wilder Coe is proud to be a member of Integra International, an interactive global association of over 100 local independent Accounting and Consulting firms dedicated to exchanging information and advising growing businesses and professionals.

"As we continue to grow, I can rely on Wilder Coe for more services, they have the ability to grow with us and be a trusted adviser in the UK or Europe, should we expand." **Christopher Holden** Eze Castle Integration Inc.

Contact us
t 020 7724 6060
e advice@wildercoe.co.uk

Wilder Coe
233-237 Old Marylebone Road
London NW1 5QT

www.wildercoe.co.uk

Ten years experience in assisting overseas business
set up in the UK

Artaius provides a one-stop service for inward investment companies to the UK. We take care of all the administration, compliance and back office functions, freeing your management team to run and expand the business.

Our expertise includes:

- **Company formation**
- **Company secretarial services**
- **Bank account set up**
- **Tax registration**
- **Bookkeeping**
- **VAT**
- **Payroll**
- **Management accounts**
- **Online accounting**
- **Credit control**
- **Budgetary control**
- **Cash flow forecasting**

Our worldwide client portfolio covers many industry sectors and we work closely with UK Trade and Investment.

"From setting up the company, opening bank accounts and finding solicitors, to signing leases and hiring staff, Artaius has been providing advice and contacts. Now the company is established and the store is about to open, Artaius will continue to provide bookkeeping, tax preparation and company services."

Janelle O'Connell, Calleija Jewellers, Australia

Contact **Melanie Troiano**
t **01438 758 100**
e melanie.troiano@artaius.com

Artaius Limited
Southgate House
St George's Way
Stevenage SG11HG

www.artaius.com

ARTAIUS LIMITED

Helping overseas business with complex **VAT issues**

- **Do you plan to import goods to the UK?**
- **Do you plan to sell goods or services internationally from the UK?**

As well as providing a one-stop service for inward investment companies to the UK, Artaius offers specialist VAT advice for business involved with international trade.

Our expertise includes:

- **Specialist VAT services**
- **Company formation**
- **Company secretarial services**
- **Bank account set up**
- **Tax registration**
- **Bookkeeping**

- **Payroll**
- **Management accounts**
- **Online accounting**
- **Credit control**
- **Budgetary control**
- **Cash flow forecasting**

Our worldwide client portfolio covers many industry sectors and we work closely with UK Trade and Investment.

"Artaius have been an excellent source of information and they have contacts for everything. If I need to know anything, I just give them a call and they provide good guidance. It is the perfect service."

Asil Tan, Director UK operation, Cimstone, Turkey

Contact **Melanie Troiano**
t 01438 758 100
e melanie.troiano@artaius.com

Artaius Limited
Southgate House
St George's Way
Stevenage SG1 1HG

www.artaius.com

ARTAIUS LIMITED

Dundee - Discovering Life Sciences

Discovery is a word never far from one's lips when talking about Dundee today. It has always been a city full of life, energy and endeavour but these days it has transformed itself into a dynamic modern city with an international reputation as a centre for arts and culture, creative industries and life sciences.

Discover Dundee

Steeped in history, Dundee commands a breathtaking position on the banks of the River Tay. The City boasts excellent communication links through road, rail, air and sea, being 90 minutes drive from 90% of the Scottish population including Edinburgh and Glasgow, on the main UK east-coast rail line, and having a city-centre airport with daily direct London flights. The scenic location gives rise to a high quality of living offering beautiful countryside and a wide range of sporting and recreational activities. As a student city, Dundee also offers a lively hub of contemporary art and culture, with a vibrant music scene and all the advantages of city life but in a compact package. Lifestyle rewards include short commuting times and low cost living. The average house price in Dundee is 42% lower than that of Edinburgh, and 12% lower than Glasgow (April 2010). According to the Lonely Planet Guide to Scotland, the people of Dundee are 'among the friendliest, most welcoming and most entertaining people you'll meet anywhere in the country'.

Life Sciences in Dundee

Outside of Oxford and Cambridge, Dundee is home to the most significant biomedical and life sciences communities in the UK, boasting a larger medical research complex than the National Institute for Medical Research in London. With world-class companies, Universities, research institutions and scientists all within a three mile radius, the area offers a wide range of expertise from drug discovery, through medical devices and diagnostics to ag-biotech and environmental biotechnology. Around 20% of the life sciences companies in Scotland are based in or around Dundee, making the area a major player in the UK and European life sciences industry. With 22 core life sciences companies (and a similar number of support organisations) and an internationally renowned academic sector, Dundee currently employs over 4,000 people in the sector, with the sector accounting for 16% of the local economy.

"The world's best scientists are coming to Dundee and the two main reasons are - one is the quality of the work being carried out here and the other is the quality of life on offer. People are often fed up living in big cities and spending all their time commuting. I always talk about the fact it takes me a whole eight minutes to travel between my home and my office! Then there's the fact that there are dozens of golf courses within 20 minutes of the city. I tell them that I have a garden that backs on to the Tay and that, as a keen ornithologist, I've spotted 120 different species of birds from there. People want to enjoy their non-scientific lives, as well as working hard."

- Sir Philip Cohen,
Director, MRC Protein
Phosporylation Unit

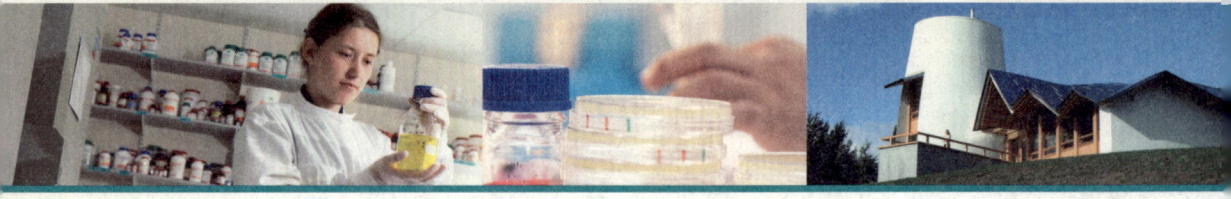

Commercial Success

A key factor in Dundee's rapid rise to the status of a life sciences hub is the close relationship between academic institutions, private companies and the public sector. Many of the city's most successful biotechnology and medical device companies were set up to commercialise technology developed at institutions such as the University of Dundee. Strong links between the private and academic sectors have made it possible to establish unique projects such at the University of Dundee's Division of Signal Transduction Therapy, a £23M partnership with six of the world's leading pharmaceutical companies and the Medical Research Council to develop novel industry ready targets for the pharmaceutical sector. The City has also been named as the lead institute for translational biology by SULSA (Scottish Universities Life Sciences Alliance), the £77million collaboration between six Scottish universities which will attract the best researchers and more investment to the area.

Strategic Infrastructure

Dundee offers 3 research parks, each strategically positioned in close proximately to key sites, including the University of Dundee, and Ninewells Hospital and Medical School. The majority of the core life science companies in Dundee are accommodated in fit-for purpose premises in each of these three main locations across the city. The Dundee Technopole is the centre of the city's biomedical research community, strategically positioned in walking distance to the Wellcome Trust Biocentre and University of Dundee's main campus. The site is home to two of the city's most successful life sciences companies - Cyclacel and CXR Biosciences as well as the Dundee Incubator facility which offers suitable accommodation for new technology companies. The Dundee Medipark is located on a 25 arce greenfield site adjacent to Ninewells Hospital and Medical School, and is purposely built to support cross communication between the clinical, business and research communities. At the west of the city, the Dundee Technology Park is designed for companies in the high growth technology sector and provides a campus style environment with high quality landscaping and prestigious buildings. Companies within the Park include Axis-Shield, W.L Gore and Millipore.

Business Support

Business support is available for companies locating to Dundee through Dundee City Council and Scottish Enterprise. All companies positioned within the area will also benefit from services offered by BioDundee - a partnership between public, private and academic sectors to promote the growth of life sciences in the Dundee area. BioDundee also offers seminars, networking and social events to all, as well offering marketing support through use of the internationally recognised brand, at exhibitions, through newsletters and at the BioDundee International Conference.

The growth of life science excellence in Dundee shows no signs of stopping. The city's success is a magnet for investment, entrepreneurial talent, ambitious young scientists and renowned academics. A superb location, world class academic base, and strong focus on networking and collaboration make Dundee a force to be reckoned with on a global scale.

For further information please contact us at:
BioDundee, 3 City Square, Dundee DD1 3BA
Email: info@biodundee.co.uk
Tel: 01382 434913
Web: www.biodundee.co.uk

EUROPE & SCOTLAND
European Regional Development Fund
Investing in your Future

FOREWORD

I am delighted to provide this foreword to the 2010 edition of the *Investors' Guide to the United Kingdom*. UK Trade & Investment is pleased to have contributed to the content for this independent book. I hope you find it useful.

The UK's success at attracting Foreign Direct Investment remains outstanding and all the signs are that this trend will continue in the coming year. Indeed, the United Kingdom is rated the most attractive location for investment in Europe (European Attractiveness Survey 2010, Ernst & Young). And at US$1.0 trillion our stock of foreign direct investment is equalled by only one other country globally, and exceeded only by the USA (World Investment Report 2009, UN Conference on Trade and Development).

Offering a solid framework in which companies can prosper, the UK is at the heart of global business. That is why the Government has made a clear commitment to creating the best environment for business, attracting enterprise and supporting entrepreneurialism. And our actions in our first weeks in office – for example announcing significant reductions in corporation tax – signal a strong intent to ensure that the United Kingdom, as a balanced, diverse and highly competitive economy, leads the world as a location of choice for business and global investment.

For companies to grow they need outstanding support networks and the UK has well established clusters of business services that are truly world class. As well as boasting a large market and quality suppliers, the UK also offers global business leaders the opportunity to interact with the very best of their international peers. In short, it plugs companies into a vital international network of connections.

Just like the most successful global businesses, UK Trade & Investment is constantly looking at ways to improve its offering. To this end, the organisation is committed to building strategically on the strengths of its overseas network and improving its services to customers.

All this will help to ensure that the UK – and the overseas companies that invest here – stay ahead of the game.

In the UK, companies, including many of the world's major corporations, are connected directly into the heart of global finance, global creative and professional services, global media and global talent. They enjoy access to world-class science and academia and link into a wide-ranging network of smaller enterprises, many of which are also world leaders in their fields.

A unique, multicultural and entrepreneurial economy, the UK is at the heart of global business, bringing the world to every company's door.

Mark Prisk MP
Minister of State for Business and Enterprise

INTRODUCTION

Jonathan Reuvid

This new edition of *Investors' Guide to the United Kingdom* is published as the UK emerges from the recession that gripped almost all developed economies from the last quarter of 2008 and in the wake of the global financial crisis to which it was the sequel. The previous third edition was published in 2007 before these traumatic events disrupted the pattern of world trade and investment.

However uncomfortable the experience of the past three years has been, it has caused UK industry, commerce and government to overhaul development strategies, to focus on strengths and opportunities and to address structural weaknesses and threats to future prosperity. The Coalition Government which has been in office since May 2010 has grasped firmly the need to shrink the structural elements of the UK fiscal deficit and to help business to regain competitiveness. An outcome of these major shifts in policy has been to enhance the attractiveness of the UK as a destination for inward investment.

This book reflects the improving business environment for both foreign investors and resident UK enterprises and has been organised to provide business readers who are appraising the UK as a target for their investment funds and corporate development with the information that they need.

Part One provides an overview of the economy and business environment including identification of the grants and incentives that are available to businesses in the UK. In Part Two, the key elements of the regulatory environment which are most relevant to inward investors are addressed by major contributors to the book: Watson, Farley & Williams, Artaius and Wilder Coe.

Part Three reviews 10 industry sectors of business opportunity where the UK has particular innovative skills and is established as a global leader; in these sectors growth prospects outpace those of the economy as a whole. In Part Four, the emphasis returns to regulation and business practice in operating a company in the UK with the same Part One contributors and associates providing clear explanations in the areas of accounting, taxation, employment law, pensions and benefits and commercial property.

Part Five focuses on banking and finance for companies with contributions from HSBC, and provides overviews of the AIM, the UK's second tier stock market, mergers and acquisition and venture capital and private equity. Further key investment sectors of the UK economy are featured in Part Six, the final section of the book, with location related chapters on Science Parks and Business Incubators, commercial and agricultural property investment and London itself as a premier investment location. The full contact details of all contributors and some useful websites for supplementary research are listed in Appendix.

As always, I am grateful to the many authors who have written chapters and to Mark Prisk, Minister of State for Business and Enterprise, for his Foreword. I also express the thanks of the publisher Legend Business, to the sponsors of the book, HSBC, Watson, Farley & Williams and Wilder Coe and Artaius, without whose engagement publication would not have been possible.

List of Contributors

Watson, Farley and Williams LLP Corporate

Christina Howard is a partner in the International Corporate Group of Watson, Farley & Williams LLP, dealing with a wide range of corporate and commercial work including corporate finance transactions, mergers and acquisitions, joint ventures and restructurings.

Tanvir Dhanoa is an associate in the International Corporate Group of Watson, Farley & Williams LLP. Tanvir's areas of practice include public and private mergers and acquisitions, equity capital markets and joint ventures, as well as general corporate and commercial work across a range of sectors.

Ravinder Sandhu is an associate in the International Corporate group of Watson, Farley & Williams LLP, specialising in a broad range of domestic and international general corporate and corporate finance transactions including mergers and acquisitions, equity fundraisings, group reorganisations, joint ventures and regulatory matters.

Gareth Burge is an associate in the International Corporate Group at Watson, Farley & Williams LLP specialising in corporate and commercial transactions including corporate finance, strategic alliances (joint ventures and private equity fundraisings), mergers and acquisitions and group reorganisations.

Energy and Project

Mark Evans is a partner in the International Corporate Group of Watson, Farley & Williams LLP, specialising in a range of transactional and financing work in the natural resources and energy sectors, including energy project financing and trading. His trading and structured transaction experience encompasses gas, LNG, power, carbon, coal, freight and uranium.

Neil Budd is an associate at Watson, Farley & Williams LLP, specialising in energy and clean technology. He has worked on a number of renewable energy projects, both in the UK and internationally (including onshore and offshore windfarms, biomass and waste to energy plants and solar installations) and has advised sponsors and funders with regard to investments in the clean technology sector.

Employment

Liz Buchan is a partner of Watson, Farley & Williams LLP, specialising in employment law and employee incentives. She heads WFW's Employment Group and is a former member of the Law Society's Employment Law Committee.

Asha Kumar is a senior associate at Watson, Farley and Williams LLP specialising in employment law and advises on a range of employment law issues affecting those looking to invest in the UK.

Rhodri Thomas is an associate at Watson, Farley and Williams LLP, specialising in employment law and a contributor to *Discrimination in Employment – Law and Practice*, 2006, Law Society Publishing.

Property

Gary Ritter is a partner at Watson, Farley & Williams LLP. Gary specialises in advising on a broad range of residential and commercial property matters, including development, investment and landlord and tenant. He acts for substantial companies as well as for individual investors.

Felicity Jones is a partner in the International Corporate Group at Watson, Farley & Williams LLP. Felicity is head of WFW's Hotel and Leisure Group and specialises in sales, purchases, funding, shareholders agreements and management structures in the hotel, leisure and technology sectors.

Competition & Regulatory Law

Emanuela Lecchi is head of WFW's London Competition & Regulatory Group. She focuses in particular on competition law and regulation of communications and utilities. Fluent in Italian and French, Emanuela also has a Masters in International and Comparative Business Law, a Masters in Information Technology and Telecommunications Law, and a MSc in Economic Regulation and Competition.

Jason Logendra is an associate at Watson, Farley & Williams LLP. Jason is based in London and practices in WFW's Competition & Regulatory group, with a specific focus on communications and utilities. Jason advises companies and regulators and has complemented his experience with secondments to a FTSE 100 communications company and an overseas communications regulator.

Immigration

Angharad Harris is a partner at Watson, Farley & Williams LLP, specialising in all aspects of employment and immigration law and is a member of the Law Society's Employment Law Committee.

Devan Khagram is an associate at Watson, Farley and Williams LLP specialising in employment and immigration law. His immigration practice includes advising on all aspects of the Points Based Immigration System including investors, entrepreneurs and application for settlement and naturalisation.

Intellectual Property

Mark Tooke is a partner in the International Corporate Group at Watson, Farley & Williams LLP. Mark is head of WFW's London intellectual property department, and has a particular focus on the corporate and commercial aspects of IP, including assisting clients in the communications, media and technology sectors.

Wilder Coe LLP and Artaius Ltd.

Michael Bordoley has been with Wilder Coe since 1991 and is an audit partner. In this role he is responsible for advising clients on budgetary control and forecasts. Although working across a broad sector range, Michael specialises in SMEs, family businesses, travel agencies and insurance brokers and charities. He advises clients on all aspects of furthering a business from the day-to-day running to specialist areas and dealing with legislation.

Robert Coe is senior partner at Wilder Coe with responsibility for corporate tax and corporate finance. He has acted as non-executive director for numerous public companies. Robert has also been a non-executive director of Dowgate Capital Advisers, a corporate adviser and Nomad, and now advises Cairn Financial Advisers, also Nomad.

Bee-Lean Chew has been a partner at Wilder Coe since 2005. Her main areas of expertise lie in the corporate arena where she focuses on financial reporting, auditing, internal controls and valuation work. Bee is also a non-executive director of Bromley NHS Trust.

Mark Saunders is a partner at Wilder Coe Chartered Accountants. Mark works chiefly in the corporate sector and performs audit and assurance assignments, as well as providing pro-active tax advice. He is the firm's Money Laundering Reporting officer and lectures on the subject. Mark is also chairman of Integra International.

Robin Berry is Managing Director of Artaius Ltd. Artaius specialises in helping businesses set up in the UK. In particular, Artaius' comprehensive service includes accounting and tailored financial management reporting. Artaius also provides VAT and payroll services. Artaius are fully accredited by SAGE.

Jitendra Pattani is an experienced General Practice Partner at Wilder Coe. He has a varied portfolio of corporate and personal tax clients covering many business sectors. Jitendra has particular expertise in the hotel and retail fashion sectors. He also has technical expertise in corporate finance transactions work, including due diligence assignments for clients, and carried out Reporting Accountants work for a main market flotation of a client in the health and fitness sector. In addition, Jitendra has co-responsibility for monitoring the firm's compliance with audit regulations and ensuring that work is carried out to the highest professional standards.

Neil Warren is a specialist VAT consultant. He is also a lecturer and author, and was the winner of the 2008 Taxation Awards Tax Writer of the Year competition. He worked for HM Customs and Excise for 14 years and is also the author of Tolley's annual *VAT Planning* book.

Ian Saunders is a Chartered Secretary and Director of Artaius Ltd. He helps clients to maintain statutory records for Companies House and the Stock Market. He performs registrar work, and is a company formation agent and nominee. He also advises on corporate restructuring.

Tim Cook joined Wilder Coe in 1996 and heads the firm's tax department. Tim handles tax returns, capital gains tax, trusts, inheritance tax and HM Revenue and Customs investigations. His areas of expertise include tax planning, pensions, emigration and trusts. He works primarily with entrepreneurs and families.

HSBC Bank plc

James Roberts has been working for HSBC for 13 years and has undertaken a variety of roles, most recently being a Senior Commercial Manager in London.

Other Contributors

Nasima Ahmed joined Jones Lang LaSalle in 2005, working in the EMEA Capital Market Strategy team, and has recently obtained an MSc in Real Estate Investment from Cass Business School. As well as undertaking strategic work for core clients such as USS, Lend Lease and the Crown Estate, Nasima has published a number of articles including "Market Transparency, Liquidity and Volatility / risk management & diversification" for Freeman.

Richard Binning is a Director of Savills. Savills are International Property Consultants covering the full range of property matters. Richard heads the Farm and Estate Agency team for Central England. Savills sell more than any other Agent in the UK and are the recognised market leaders. Properties which have been dealt with by the team in the last year range from bare blocks of farmland to large agricultural and sporting Estates and specialist equestrian training yards.

Michael Charlton is Chief Executive of Think London, the official foreign direct investment agency for London. He directs the team responsible for world-wide promotion and business development. He has a great deal of experience working across global markets and sectors and in developing business opportunities in Asia Pacific, North Americas and Europe.

Think London is a not-for-profit private-public partnership and the experts on doing business in the Capital. It connects international businesses in London, helping them set up, succeed and grow. The service is comprehensive, confidential and funded.

Belinda Clarke is the Life Sciences Manager for the East of England in the UK, developing and implementing the sector strategy for the health and life sciences sector in the region. She has been a member of the UK Life Sciences Marketing Strategy Workstream to develop the marketing messages for the UK and is Chair of the UK Life Sciences Network. Previously, Belinda was the Regional International Trade Adviser for Biotechnology and Pharmaceuticals for the east of England. She has a first degree in Natural Sciences from the University of Cambridge and a PhD from the John Innes Centre in Norwich.

Alan Eastwood spent most of his career with ICI, first in the Paints Division and then as a member of the Planning and Economics team at head office in London. At the beginning of 2000 he was seconded to the Chemicals Unit of the Department of Trade and Industry. Since 2005, he has been with the Chemical Industries Association (CIA) and has been involved with a wide range of economic and commercial issues affecting the industry. He is also the chairman of the Economic Outlook group at CEFIC, the European chemical industry association.

Neil Harvey has been Head of International Trade at the UK Chemical Industries Association (CIA) for nearly 8 years. He joined the CIA in 1998 after 24 years in the Department of Trade and Industry, covering UK trade relations with Central and Eastern Europe in the early 1990s and Government's relationship with the UK chemicals industry in the mid-1990s. The mission of the CIA is to represent the interests of the UK chemical and allied industries sector in regulatory, economic and social affairs. Neil oversees international trade promotion activities and trade policy issues. He also manages the group of experts within the European chemicals association , Cefic, which advises on trade regulations relating to the precursor chemicals that have the potential for illicit use. The CIA has produced a Code of Conduct for companies dealing with chemicals that are subject to UK, EU and International trade controls, including a chapter covering CWC precursor chemical.

Nick Hood is a Partner within Carter Jonas, a Director of St. John's Innovation Centre Ltd, The City of Cambridge Education Foundation, and is a Chartered Surveyor. Nick leads the Carter Jonas Technology Team which specialises in the development and marketing of Science Parks and Innovation Centres. Carter Jonas is one of the leading property consultants in the Science Park sector. The Technology Team offers a broad spectrum of services to both public and private sector clients including feasibility studies, demands and needs studies, development agreements, marketing strategy reports, lettings and acquisitions of incubators, laboratory and/or R&D buildings.

Maxine J Horn is founder and CEO of British Design Innovation (BDI). Maxine began her careers in design media publishing before taking on new business development roles at board level within strategic design consultancies. She launched British Design Initiative Ltd in 1993 to assist exporting design firms to share market knowledge and costs – the first membership organization to put the commercial design sector on the UKTI export map – and launched the national online Design Directory in 1996. In 2005, she licensed the assets of British Design Initiative to BDI as a spin-out. The independent not-for-profit trade association is owned and driven by six national board directors supported by 24 regional directors, with further input from over 500 directors and its member companies, each with more than 10 years business and sector experience.

Mark Littlewood is the founder of the BLN, the UK's leading forum for CEOs, founders and investors in high growth businesses. Before that, he was a founder at Library House, an investment research business serving the global venture capital and banking communities. He led the business development activities for the organization, created and managed a network of angels, early stage, venture and corporate investors. Previously, Mark worked with university spin outs; ran a 40 person consultancy business and founded a web portal for the CAD community. He has also worked in the publishing and information sectors and attended Trinity College, Cambridge.

Mark Norcliffe has been closely involved, for over 15 years, in promoting business partnerships between British and overseas automotive companies – formerly as

Head of International Services at the Society of Motor Manufacturers and Traders and latterly as a specialist adviser to UK Trade & Investment. He is now Managing Director at TheSourcingSolutions Ltd.

Tony Rawlinson is a Chartered Accountant who has around 25 years experience advising quoted companies on a broad range of transactions. Tony was a founder of Dowgate Capital plc, a specialist AIM Market Nominated Adviser and Broker. He was appointed Chief Executive on 2004 and led the successful development of the Group until its sale in summer 2009. Since then, Tony and his team from Dowgate have successfully established Cairn Financial Advisers LLP, an AIM Nominated Adviser, Plus Adviser and Takeover Code specialist. Tony is a member of the AIM Advisory Group of the London Stock Exchange.

Jonathan Reuvid is an editor and author of business books and a partner in Legend Business. He has edited all four edition of *The Investors' Guide to the United Kingdom* and has more than 30 titles to his name as editor and part-author including *The Handbook of International Trade, The Handbook of World Trade*, *Managing Business Risk* and business guides to China, the 10 countries that joined the EU in 2004 and, more recently, Morocco. Before taking up a second career in business publishing Jonathan was Director of European Operations of the manufacturing subsidiaries of a Fortune 500 multinational. From 1984 to 2005 he engaged in joint venture development and start-ups in China.

Simon Sacerdoti is a Chartered Accountant. He has worked in the transaction support team of BDO Stoy Hayward where he advised on a number of corporate transactions on AIM and the Official List, later joining the Entrepreneurial Services team and Ernst & Young where he led a number of capital market transactions both in the UK and overseas. Simon joined Dowgate in 2007 and was involved in IPOs, reverse takeovers, fundraisings and acquisitions. Following the sale of Dowgate, Simon helped establish Cairn Financial Advisers LLP where he is a partner.

Chris Wilshaw is the Managing Director of PNO Consultants Limited (part of the PNO Group - Europe' largest and most successful full service grants consultancy). Chris has been involved in the Grant funding arena since 2001 and together with his team help businesses successfully optimise the uptake of funding for their future projects.

Part One

1.1 THE UK ECONOMY AND INVESTMENT ENVIRONMENT

Jonathan Reuvid
Legend Business

Having suffered the full force of the global financial crisis in 2008, the UK economy slid into recession towards the end of that year. The 'credit crunch' caused the UK government to inject investment capital into much of the banking industry and to initiate an extensive and prolonged programme of quantitative easing throughout 2009 to stimulate the economy. As a result, the public sector deficit more than doubled and the UK was plunged into its most serious debt crisis for more than 80 years. The quantitative easing gave only a modest boost to the economy as banks concentrated on rebuilding their balance sheets and a temporary reduction in value added tax had only a limited effect in raising consumer spending.

THE POST-RECESSION INVESTMENT CLIMATE
Nevertheless, a fragile recovery took root from the beginning of 2010 and there are indications that GDP growth will return to more than 2% in 2011. The new Coalition Government that took office in May 2010 took rapid corrective action to reduce the national debt and encourage the private sector and inward investment

through an Emergency Budget in June and by lowering corporation tax over four years to 24% by equal annual reductions of 1%.

The tough budget, which included a hike in value added tax to 20%, also gave notice of deep cuts in government spending to be finalised in the autumn. At the same time, many planned public sector investment projects are being put on hold or curtailed.

Regulation of the banking sector is also under reform with responsibility for the monitoring and control functions, previously dispersed between the Bank of England, the Financial Services Authority (FSA) and the Treasury, now restored to the Bank of England. A new Office for Budget Responsibility has been set up to provide independent growth and fiscal forecasts.

The government's firm action to rebalance the economy, endorsed in July by the OECD, resonates within the EU where other large economies plan to introduce cutbacks, however unpopular domestically. Of course, there will be an impact on public services during the next few years of necessary austerity as waste is eliminated and low priority expenditure is trimmed.

However, there is nothing in these programmes to deter foreign investors. Indeed, the enhanced focus on the private sector where activity is already rising should encourage foreign investors seeking to expand their international reach by developing a business base in a leading global economy which continues to offer an environment that is both stable and open. The UK is very much open to inward investment.

BASICS OF THE UK ECONOMY

Population
The population of the UK stands at an estimated 61.3 million, with a labour force of 31.4 million, ranking it 18 in the world. Of the total population 67% are of working age with 16.5% under 15 and 16.4% over 64. Population growth in 2010 is estimated at only 0.28 per cent. Male life expectancy is 76.7 years and female life expectancy 81.8 years.

Dispersion
In 2008 it was calculated that 90% of the population live within urban locations and that the annual rate of urbanization in the previous five years was 0.5%. Nevertheless, with an advanced and highly productive farming industry the UK

produces 60% of its food needs with less than 2% of the labour force.

Ethnicity and education

Of the indigenous population, 83.6% are English, 5.6% Scottish, 4.9% Welsh and 2.9% Northern Irish. According to the 2001 census, 2% of the population were black, 1.8% Indian, 1.3% Pakistani with a further 2.8% of mixed and other nationalities. Immigration rose sharply in the first decade of the millennium, but will now be capped for non-EU entrants.

All but 1% of the population aged 15 and over have completed five years or more of education; primary, secondary and tertiary school leaver expectancy is 16 for males and 17 for females.

Macro-Economic Indicators

Table 1.1.1 highlights the basics of the UK economy, comparing actual and forecast growth rates from 2007 to 2010

Table 1.1.1 Macro-economic indicators

	2007	2008	2009	2010	2011
GDP growth (%)	2.6	0.5	-4.9	1.3	2.1
Household consumption	2.1	0.9	-3.2	0.5	1.5
Investment	7.8	-3.5	-15.0	-1.4	3.2
Total exports	-2.8	1.0	-11.0	5.0	5.6

Sources: 2007 to 2009 (Coface, 15.07.2010); 2010 and 2011 forecasts (HM Treasury, June 2010)

Debt

The Treasury OBR forecasts are based on the median of 22 City of London forecasters and 16 others including the IMF, OECD and EC. UK net debt stood at £903 billion at the end of May 2010, representing 62.2% of annual GDP. However, the public sector net borrowing requirement (PSNB) is expected to decline from £158 billion (2010 – 2011) to £130 billion (2010 – 2011). The budget deficit for 2010 is currently forecast at 10.5 per cent of GDP.

GDP

In terms of purchasing power parity (PPP), UK GDP at £2.15 trillion (2009 est.) ranks 7 in country comparison, while GDP per capita at $35,200 (2009 est.) places the UK in 34th place.

Among the high value added sectors in which the UK is particularly strong are pharmaceuticals, biotechnology, aeronautics and electronics. Hydrocarbon production covers three-quarters of domestic energy needs. Service industries predominate, accounting for approximately 75% of GDP, with industry the source of 23.8% and agriculture of 1.2%.

Inflation

The pressure from domestic consumption is comparatively weak, with demand forecast to increase by only 1.4% in 2010 and 1.7% in 2011. Bank rate has remained historically low at 0.5% since March 2009 and seems likely to stay at that level for the remainder of 2010. Some increase is forecast during 2011 but the government is committed to a low interest rate policy and the median forecast is for no more than 2.0% by the fourth quarter of 2011. Taking these elements into account, the consumer price index (CPI) is expected to rise by about 2.6% towards 2010 year end and by about 1.8% in 2011.

Employment

The three-month unemployment rate had risen to 7.8% by the end of May 2010 and is forecast to increase by 0.6% over the year as a whole before falling back somewhat in 2011. After a period of workforce reductions in 2009, the private sector has started to take on employees, for the time being mainly in part-time jobs. It remains to be seen how much industry will be able to take up the slack as the public sector sheds jobs in 2011.

Foreign trade

While total exports of merchandise and services are forecast to grow by 5.0% and 5.6% per cent respectively in 2010 and 2011, imports are forecast to outgrow exports in 2010 (5.4%) but to grow less strongly in 2011 (3.7%). Therefore, while the current account deficit for the 12 months ended May 2010 was £33.7 billion, representing 1% of GDP, the net trade contribution in 2011 may be positive.

UK INWARD INVESTMENT

The World Investment Report 2009, UN Conference on Trade and Development (UNCTAD), reported that the UK stock of foreign investment at US$1.0 trillion at the end of 2008 was exceeded only by the USA and China including Hong Kong, and at the same level as France. More recently, the Ernst & Young European Attractiveness Survey 2010 found that the UK is the most attractive location for investors in Europe and praised its resilience in securing foreign direct investment (FDI) during the deep recession of the European economy.

The total number of inward investment projects in the year to March 2010 at 1,619 was rather less than the previous year's total of 1,744 projects; however, the number of new jobs secured rose from 35,111 to 53,358.

Sources of new investment

The number of new projects and new jobs secured by investment from countries of source during 2009/2010 is compared with the results of 2008/09 in Table 1.1.2.

Table 1.1.2 Country sources of investment 2008/09 and 2009/10

Country	Projects		Jobs	
	2008/09	2009/10	2008/09	2009/10
USA	621	484	12,888	15,443
Japan	81	107	1,405	2,293
France	101	99	2,765	3,729
India	108	92	4,139	3,271
Germany	86	90	2,304	1,434
China	59	74	607	760
Australia	65	67	943	549
Canada	83	62	754	2,033
Ireland	57	56	2,056	859
Italy	48	55	752	762
Rest of Europe	252	213	4,288	5,360
Rest of World	183	220	2,210	16,865
TOTAL	**1,744**	**1,619**	**35,111**	**53,358**

Source: UK Inward Investment Reports 2008/2009 and 2009/2010, UKTI

Overall, 54 countries invested in the UK in 2009/20010 compared to 53 in 2008/2009. Sweden and Switzerland which featured in the top 12 countries of 2008/2009 investing in the UK are included in the "Rest of Europe" category in the Table. The 53,358 new jobs created in 2009/2010 is an advance of more than 50% on the previous year and is a more than satisfactory result in a difficult investment climate. As in 2008/2009 over 43,000 further jobs were safeguarded.

Accounting for more than 25% of all projects and almost a third of new or safeguarded jobs, the USA remains by far the biggest source of investment projects. The two other countries from which significantly more projects and jobs were generated in 2009/2010 are Japan in second place, where the number of projects increased by 32%, and China from which the number of projects increased by more than 25%. Australia, Canada, France, Germany, India and Italy also maintained consistently high levels of investment.

Composition of investment projects
Inward investment by category
The 2009/2010 proportions of completely new investments, expansions of previous investments and mergers and acquisition (M&As) including joint ventures (JVs) are compared with the 2008/2009 proportions in Table 1.1.3.

Table 1.1.3 UK inward investment by category

	2008/2009	2009/2010
New investments	827	850
Expansions	460	544
M & A (inc. JVs)	457	275
TOTAL	**1,744**	**1,619**

Source: UK Inward Investment Reports 2008/2009 and 2009/2010, UKTI

This analysis reveals that the overall reduction in the number of investments was entirely due to reduced M&A activity, a worldwide phenomenon in cross-border transactions over the period. Both new investments and expansions were increased, the latter by more than 20%, indicating that those who had invested previously maintained confidence in the UK's status as a springboard for global growth.

Inward investment by sector

The comparison of inward investment performance by sector in Table 1.1.4 shows that investment performances were positive across a broad range of sectors, including life sciences and environment technologies, which both attracted increases in project numbers. These sectors of opportunity which are succeeding in areas of cutting edge innovation are profiled individually in Chapters 3.3 and 3.5.

Table 1.1.4 UK inward investment projects by sector

	2008/2009	2009/2010
Software	306	257
Advanced engineering	211	190
Life sciences	140	173
Business services	187	158
Finance	130	110
ICT	152	105
Environmental technology	56	79
Creative & Media	89	69
Other *	473	478
TOTAL	**1,744**	**1,619**

•"Other" includes the food & drink, power and chemicals sectors
Source: UK Inward Investment reports 2008/2009 and 2009/2010, UKTI

Although levels of investment activity were lower in 2009/2010 than previously, ICT, advanced engineering and business and financial services continued to attract substantial investment. In spite of the continuing problems in the banking industry globally, investment in the UK's financial services sector created or safeguarded more than 5,000 jobs in 2009/2010, an increase of over 20% over the previous 12 months, confirming London's continuing role as the world's leading international financial centre.

Inward investment by type of operation

Completing the analysis of 2009/2010 investment, Table 1.1.5 analyses projects by type of operation.

Table 1.1.5 UK Inward Investment by operation type

	2008/2009	2009/2010
Services	830	706
R & D	202	278
HQ	251	277
Manufacturing	327	248
Distribution	59	56
Contact centres	65	49
E-commerce	10	5
TOTAL	**1,744**	**1,619**

Source: UK Inward Investment Reports 2008/2009 and 2009/2010, UKTI

A headline indicator of the UK's attractiveness as a highly advanced economy is the level of activity in research and development where the number of projects increased by 38% over the 2009/2010 period. Chapter 6.3 provides an overview of science parks and business incubators in the UK where much of the private sector R&D is located. The UK continues to be rated as having the strongest research base in Europe and the second strongest globally after the USA in each of the following fields:

● Bioscience
● Health and medical
● Clinical
● Environmental Science

- Engineering
- Business
- Social sciences
- Humanities

In addition the UK was confirmed in October 2009 as having the five top universities in Europe for R&D. Competition to win high value R&D investment is intense with the top 1,000 companies in the world most active in R&D investing £400 billion annually of which 80% is concentrated in the USA, the UK, Germany, France and Japan. As evidence of the benefits to international companies of locating in the UK from accessing its world class R & D base, overseas entities own 37% of patents in the UK, compared with only 11.3% in the USA and 4.4% in Japan.

As a measure of domestic R&D activity, the Department for Business, Innovation and Skills (BIS) published its most recent "R&D Scoreboard" in February 2010 which showed that 59% of the R&D expenditure for the top 1,000 UK companies was concentrated into the five sectors of:

- pharmaceuticals and biotechnology;
- aerospace and defence;
- software and computer services;
- banks; and
- automobiles and autoparts.

The predominant sector is pharmaceuticals and biotechnology generating six times as much investment as the next largest sector and accounting for 36% of the total. The sectors where R&D investment grew fastest were banking and aerospace and defence.

A lesser but also significant indicator of the UK's attractiveness as an investment destination is the 10% registered in 2009/2010 in the establishment of headquarters operations which created and safeguarded over 7,000 jobs. The UK continues to host more European HQs than all the other European economies combined. The more favourable rates of corporation tax introduced in the June 2010 budget should reinforce that position.

THE ROLE OF UK TRADE AND INVESTMENT (UKTI)
In 2009/2010 UKTI was involved in 750 of the investment projects discussed

above, more than 45% of the total and 25% up on the previous year. UKTI has global reach with representation in 96 countries, of which 33 have dedicated professional and readily accessible inward investment teams. These offices, listed in in Appendix II, are the first port of call for international investors seeking quality advice and support in processing investment initiatives.

Recognizing that innovative and growing companies active in business internationalism are the most likely to make positive R&D impact, the attraction of R&D projects to the UK is at the core of UKTI activity. About half the investment projects in which UKTI was involved in 2009/2010 were rated as "high value" with potential to generate significant added value for the UK economy.

Note: The content for the last two sections of this chapter is derived from the 2009/2010 report The UK at the heart of Global Business, *published 14 July 2010 by UK Trade & Investment.*

1.2 OVERVIEW FOR INWARD INVESTORS

Christina Howard
Watson, Farley & Williams LLP

INTRODUCTION

The UK is one of Europe's most favoured jurisdictions for inward investment[1], that is, the investment of money from an external source into a region. Despite global economic uncertainty, inflows of foreign direct investment (FDI) into the UK in 2008 still exceeded 196 billion.[2] Once established in the UK, foreign-owned companies are treated no differently from UK firms. London is seen to be a particularly attractive place to invest and was recently voted the number one destination in Europe for FDI[3], attracting more than one-third more FDI projects over the past five years than any other European City.[4]

There are many reasons for investors and businesses to choose to invest or establish a presence in the UK, including:

- its sophisticated infrastructure and telecommunications;
- its position as a leading financial centre;
- its recognised and respected legal system;
- its financial incentives and tax environment;
- its stable political environment; and
- its skilled workforce.

[1] Reinventing European Growth – Ernst & Young's 2009 European attractiveness survey.
[2] World Investment Report 2009 – Country Fact Sheet – UK. United Nations Conference on Trade and Development.
[3] Think London's Annual Report 2008-2009
[4] European Cities and Regions of the Future 2010/11

Once a business has chosen to establish a presence in the UK, there are a number of factors, in addition to other, broader commercial issues, that need to be considered, including the following:

1. What type of entity should I choose?
2. What will the tax treatment be on my investment?
3. How do I go about employing people in the UK?
4. Which type of premises do I need for my investment?
5. Is the UK a good place to raise finance?
6. What if my business becomes involved in a dispute?

TYPE OF ENTITY TO BE CHOSEN

There are a number of entities or arrangements that may be chosen when establishing a business presence in the UK, including trading partnerships, limited liability partnerships, agency arrangements and European Economic Interest Groupings. However, the most common arrangements chosen for those investing or establishing a presence in the UK are the incorporation of a UK company (which may be a subsidiary of the overseas parent company) or the opening of a UK establishment (a branch or place of business in the UK).

UK companies and establishments are all regulated by UK companies' legislation. Companies House, operated by the Registrar of Companies, is the key government organisation that coordinates the registration and administration of businesses in the UK.

Where a business establishes a presence in the UK through a company or UK establishment, a number of consequences will flow, which will to some extent vary with the form or presence chosen, but will include obligations to file certain documents at Companies House and to submit tax returns to HM Revenue & Customs.

Establishing a UK company

The most common method of establishing a business presence in the UK is through the incorporation of a limited liability company. The company may be incorporated as a wholly owned-subsidiary of a non-UK parent entity, or by one or more individuals. The company will have its own legal personality as an entity separate from its parent undertaking or individual shareholders, and will be able, therefore, to enter into contracts and operate in its own name.

In certain cases, the best way to develop a presence in the UK may be to partner experienced and established local representatives or undertakings through cooperation or joint venture arrangements, which will often be structured through a UK company as the joint venture vehicle. For further discussion on joint ventures, reference should be made to chapter 5.5 of this book entitled "Mergers and Acquisitions and Joint Ventures".

In order to establish a UK company, certain documents must be filed with Companies House, including the company's constitutional documents (namely, the Memorandum and Articles of Association). Depending on the nature of the company's business going forward, standard documents may be adopted, or these can be tailored to specific requirements (for which a solicitor's advice should be sought). Once the constitutional documents have been finalised, these and other incorporation documents are filed at Companies House, and a certificate of incorporation and an incorporation number are issued. It can take as little as a day to register a company at Companies House.

Opening a UK establishment

As an alternative to incorporating a UK company, a non-UK business may simply open a UK establishment either by way of a branch or place of business in the UK. An overseas company will be required to register its UK establishment at Companies House and will also be subject to certain on-going accounting requirements and requirements to deliver returns. In simple terms, if an overseas company has a presence in the UK from which it regularly conducts business or premises in the UK where it may be contacted, this will constitute a UK establishment requiring registration.

Under previous legislation, the UK had separate registration regimes dependent on whether an overseas company set up a branch or a place of business in the UK. From 1 October 2009, however, the two regimes were merged such that a single regime now applies for all overseas companies that carry on business in the UK through a UK establishment whether it is a place of business or a branch.

THE TAX TREATMENT ON INVESTMENT

The format chosen for establishing a business presence in the UK will vary according to the taxation implications as well as the commercial considerations and objectives of the investors involved. The basic principles of UK corporation tax and the taxation consequences of each format are briefly set out below.

When deciding which entity would be most suitable for an inward investor, it should be noted that the tax implications of establishing a company, branch or a place of business/representative office in the UK may vary significantly from entity to entity depending on, for example, the size of the business or the nature of the trade that is being undertaken.

Since the taxation implications of any investment will vary from case to case and may be complex, it is advisable to seek more detailed tax advice from a solicitor specialising in UK tax before establishing any sort of UK presence.

Companies resident in the UK

A company incorporated in the UK will generally be regarded as resident in the UK for tax purposes and will consequently be liable to pay UK corporation tax on its worldwide profits (subject to double taxation relief for foreign taxes).

In the UK, local and foreign-owned UK resident companies are taxed alike. Inward investors may have access to certain regional grants and incentives that are designed to attract industry to particular areas of the UK, but no tax concessions are granted.

The main corporation tax rate is currently 28 per cent., with a small profits rate (previously the small companies' rate) of 21 per cent. Following the emergency budget announced by the new coalition government on 22 June 2010, the headline rate of corporation tax will be reduced to 27 per cent. from 1 April 2011 and thereafter, the rate will reduce by 1 per cent. per year until it reaches 24 per cent. from 1 April 2014. The small profits rate of corporation tax will be reduced to 20 per cent. from 1 April 2011. These reforms were introduced with a view to increasing the UK's competitiveness from a tax perspective.

The UK has a fairly simple system of personal income tax, with a basic rate of 20 per cent. for income up to £37,400 (excluding personal allowances), a higher rate of 40 per cent. for income between £37,401 and £150,000 and an additional rate of 50 per cent. for income over £150,000. There is also a National Insurance system into which taxpayers and their employers make mandatory payments. This funds social security and retirement benefits.

Companies that are not resident in the UK

Companies that are not resident in the UK but that have UK source profits are subject to corporation tax on their UK source profits, only if the company trades through a branch or permanent establishment in the UK and derives its UK source profits through that branch / permanent establishment.

A non-UK resident company that does not have a branch or permanent establishment in the UK, although not liable to corporation tax, will be liable to income tax on its UK source profits (eg. rents from a UK property) at, generally, the basic rate of 20%.

Where a company is resident or has a permanent establishment in a country with which the UK has a double taxation treaty, the impact of that treaty must be considered.

EMPLOYING PEOPLE IN THE UK

Businesses wishing to establish a presence in the UK have various options in relation to their staff. These, along with connected immigration issues, are discussed in more detail in chapters 2.5 and 4.6 of this book entitled "UK Immigration" and "UK Employment Law".

Due to the challenging economic conditions, there has been some downturn in the UK's employment data; however, between January and March 2010, the number of people in work in the UK was still 28.83 million although the unemployment rate was at 8 per cent.[5]

Much of the employment legislation currently affecting the UK workforce originates from the European Commission in Brussels. EU regulations affect working patterns, wage structures and employee protection rights in the UK; for example, the European Working Time Directive creates an entitlement to minimum daily and weekly rest periods, an average working week limit of 48 hours, and restrictions on night work. As it has implemented the EU directives, the UK government has been proactive in trying to maintain its flexibility and competitiveness; for example, it has currently negotiated a special provision under the Working Time Directive that allows employees to opt out of the 48-hour working week limitations.

Whilst citizens of EEA Member States can usually enter the UK to live and work without restriction, migrants from other countries will usually require a visa. Individuals from certain countries can enter as business visitors for up to six months without applying for a visa in advance but their activities whilst in the UK are restricted. The UK immigration regime is dealt with in more detail in the chapter of this book entitled "UK Immigration".

RAISING FINANCE

The City of London is widely regarded as one of the leading financial centres in the

5 Office for National Statistics – Labour Market Statistics (May 2010).

world. London offers a huge variety of financial services, including:

- commercial and investment banking;
- insurance;
- venture capital;
- stock and currency brokering;
- fund management;
- commodity dealing;
- accounting and legal services;
- electronic clearing and settlement systems; and
- bank payments systems.

Notwithstanding the challenging global economic conditions, London remains attractive to inward investors because of its solid regulatory, legal and tax environment, a supportive market infrastructure and a dynamic and highly skilled workforce.

UK government policies are intended to facilitate the free flow of capital and to support the flow of resources in the product and services markets. The principles involved in legal, regulatory and accounting systems in the UK are transparent, and they are consistent with international standards. In all cases, regulations have been published and are applied on a non-discriminatory basis by a single regulatory body: the Financial Services Authority.

The London Stock Exchange (LSE) is one of the most active equity markets in the world, combining its robust and liquid nature with a high degree of integrity. An increasingly popular forum for inward investment into the UK, particularly for smaller companies, is the LSE's AIM market, which is examined in the chapter 5.3 of this book entitled "The AIM Market of the London Stock Exchange".

REAL ESTATE

The UK has one of the most dynamic and transparent property markets in the world, with a wide range of property options and flexible short-lease arrangements. For inward investors in the UK, one of the first decisions to make regarding real estate is whether to rent premises (known as 'leasehold') or to buy premises (known as 'freehold'). There are no restrictions on overseas companies either buying or renting property in the UK.

Renting or leasing

Companies can either rent premises that are already available or enter into what is known as a "pre-let". This is an agreement with a developer to lease premises before construction is completed, enabling prospective tenants to specify the design, layout and fittings of the building. Commercial leases in the UK typically run for 15 years with reviews every 5 years, although shorter terms are becoming more common. It may be possible to negotiate break clauses at set times through-out the lease (enabling the occupier to serve notice to vacate the premises).

The majority of leases on commercial premises in the UK are let on "full repair-ing and insuring terms", which places the responsibility and costs for all upkeep, decoration and repairs on the tenant. In addition, most leases over 3 years in length will have a provision to increase the rent in line with market conditions at pre-determined points throughout the lease. The standard clause allows for "upwards-only" rent reviews at 5 yearly intervals (this means that if the market rent rises, so too will the rent payable, but the rent payable will not come down if the market falls).

Businesses selecting the leasehold property option must also pay stamp duty land tax, which is calculated using the net present value of all rental payments due over the term of the lease.

Buying

Buying property in the UK is a straightforward process and, importantly, there are no restrictions on overseas companies buying real estate. In addition to the price of the property, purchasers must pay stamp duty land tax based on the size of the transaction and the location of the property as well as land registry fees payable on purchases, and in some circumstances on a letting.

Companies purchasing or leasing property should appoint an agent to represent them and are expected to pay legal fees, which incorporate conveyancing fees, as well as the costs for local authority searches and bank transfer fees. An experienced property solicitor is typically necessary to assist in the preparation of all the required legal documentation.

Location

London may be the obvious choice for most investors establishing their business in the UK, due to its position as an internationally accessible city, its international time zone, its proximity to the EU and its excellent telecommunications infrastructure.

However, running an office in London can be expensive, and some businesses may prefer to locate elsewhere in the UK. As the legal and tax regulations do not tend to vary between locations in the UK, the considerations when choosing a location are primarily practical: physical geography, labour, transport, etc.

DISPUTE RESOLUTION

Disputes in the UK are generally resolved through litigation in UK courts or by arbitration/mediation. Over 10,000 disputes a year take place in London, many with an international dimension, reflecting London's strong position as an international centre for legal services.[6]

The London Court of International Arbitration and the International Chamber of Commerce's International Court of Arbitration are leading international arbitration institutions. As a signatory to the 1958 Convention on the Recognition and Enforcement of Foreign Arbitral Awards (the New York Convention), the UK permits local enforcement on arbitration judgements decided in other signatory countries. The UK is also a member of the International Centre for Settlement of Investment Disputes and as such accepts binding international arbitration between foreign investors and the state.

Bilateral investment treaties (BITs) have been used as a means of protecting international investment and ensuring a more predictable and fair treatment of investors. The UK is party to 94 BITs that are currently in force.[7] A key feature of most of these BITs is investor-state dispute settlement arrangements that provide rights to those investing in the UK to seek redress for damages arising out of alleged breaches by the UK government of investment-related obligations. Key elements include provisions for equal and non-discriminatory treatment of investors and their investments, compensation for expropriation, transfer of capital and returns and access to independent settlement of disputes.

CONCLUSION

For the reasons discussed throughout this chapter, notwithstanding the challenging global economic conditions, the UK continues to be attractive to overseas businesses and inward investors.

---

6 Doing Business in the United Kingdom: A Country Commercial Guide for US Companies, US Commercial Service, 2010.
7 Ibid.

1.3 THE UNITED KINGDOM AND THE EUROPEAN UNION

Jonathan Reuvid
Legend Business

The EU remains the most important market for most UK exporters, accounting for around two-thirds of UK trade. The ratio represents a dramatic difference from the UK economy of the early 1970s. In 1972, the date of the UK's passing of the European Communities Act, most of its trade was with markets beyond Europe, mainly Commonwealth countries including Australia, New Zealand, Canada, the Caribbean, West and East Africa. This transformation in UK foreign trade was the direct result of EU membership and has been accompanied by far-reaching changes to the ways in which the UK does business and its regulation. Dependence on EU trade also means that the prosperity of the UK is inevitably linked that of fellow EU members.

OUTCOMES OF THE 2009 RECESSION
In its May 2010 forecast, the WTO predicted that world trade would recover by 9.5 per cent in 2009 against the increase of almost 28 per cent required to return to 2008 levels of trade. As noted in Chapter 1, the strongest economic growth is predicted for the four BRIC economies, particularly China and India where the UK

is focusing its trade and investment initiatives. Therefore the proportion of UK exports to these emerging markets is expected to increase over the medium term.

It is too early to forecast with any degree of certainty in what economic shape and when the constituent members of the EU will finally emerge from the 2009 recession, although the Economist Intelligence Unit (EIU) in its June 2010 forecast predicted resumed GDP growth for the Euro area of only 1.1% in 2010 and 1.2% in 2011.

The UK emergency budget of 22 June 2010 was framed against the forecast of a rather stronger recovery for the UK economy than for its main EU partners with the government forecasting GDP growth of more than 1% for 2010 and above 2% for 2011 for the Euro area but weaker performance in the EU would clearly affect the UK adversely.

THE UK CONTRIBUTION TO THE EU ECONOMY

One direct way of measuring the UK's contribution to the EU economy is in terms of GDP. Including the most recent members, the UK contributed 15.3% to overall EU GDP in 2009, against 19.8% by Germany, 15.4% by France, 12.6% by Italy and 8.8% by Spain. The 12 countries that joined the EU from 2004 onwards together contributed only 7.2 per cent to the total. Of these, Poland and the Czech Republic accounted for 3.5 per cent.

THE EVOLUTION OF EU GOVERNANCE

The competencies of EU institutions, fully recognised by the UK, are conferred upon them by the various treaties and according to the principle of subsidiarity. The basis of this principle is that action should only be taken by the EU where an objective cannot be achieved sufficiently by the member states alone. Law made by the EU institutions is passed in a variety of forms but primarily comes into direct force and must be passed in a refined form by national parliaments.

Legal acts of the EU come in four forms: treatise, regulations, directives and decisions.

● Treaties that are binding on member states and EU institutions requiring unanimous approval for enactment.
● Regulations become law in all member states as soon as they come into

force without implementing measures and override conflicting domestic provisions.

● Directives issued by the EC require member states to achieve a specified result allowing discretion to the member states as to how the result may be achieved.

● Decisions of the European Court of Justice of the Communities, which are binding in their entirety on the highest courts of member states (the House of Lords in the case of the UK).

The European Union was established by the Maastricht Treaty of 1992 which consolidated the three previous European Communities: the European Atomic Energy Community (EURATOM); The European Coal and Steel Community (ECSC); and the European Economic Community (EEC). The Maastricht Treaty introduced an enhanced political dimension and set in train the long process of discussion about an EU Constitution which was aborted but which culminated in the Lisbon Treaty of 2009 for which parliamentary approval was required by each government as an amendment to previous Treaties. Poland, the last country to endorse the Treaty, finally gave its approval at the end of 2009.

THE LISBON TREATY

The immediate consequences of the Treaty were the creation of a permanent Presidency of the European Council with a two-and-a-half year term to replace the previous six-monthly rotation by member state and the new office of EU High Representative in Foreign Policy to be held by a member of the European Commission. Under the Treaty the EU's bill of rights, the Charter of Fundamental Rights was made legally binding. Although the UK was granted a written guarantee that the Charter cannot be used by the European Court to alter British labour law or other laws that cover social rights, it is uncertain how effective this opt-out will be.

Other immediate changes brought about by the Treaty are:

● The EU is now able to sign international treaties in its own name. (e.g. the EU has now replaced the EC as a member of the World Trade Organisation).

● The European Council is now separated from the Council of Ministers, of which the legislative meetings are to be held in public).

● The European Parliament's powers are strengthened by extending co-decision with the Council of ministers to more areas of policy.

- National votes on a number of issues, including climate change measures, energy security and emergency aid are removed. Unanimity will still be required in the areas of tax, foreign policy, defence and social security.
- National parliaments are granted a longer time to scrutinise draft legislation enabling them to jointly compel the EC to review or withdraw legislation.
- Citizens initiatives must be considered by the EC if signed by more than 1 million citizens.
- Combating climate change is explicitly stated as an EU objective.
- There is a mutual solidarity obligation if a member state suffers a terrorist attack or is the victim of a natural or man-made disaster.
- A secession clause provides for member states to withdraw from the EU.

THE EUROZONE

The United Kingdom has not joined the European Monetary Union (EMU), which came into being from 1 January 1999. The negative impacts on sterling and the UK economy which was feared at the time have not been realised. UK importers and exporters adjusted quickly to trading routinely in the Euro and the City of London has retained its domination of European financial markets despite concerns that Frankfurt would become the centre of gravity.

Among the 15 countries that were EU members in 1999 only the UK together with Denmark and Sweden, which both rejected entry following national referenda, have held out from joining the EMU. The new government has affirmed that the UK will not consider eurozone entry during the life of the present Parliament.

MEDIUM-TERM OUTLOOK

The government has confirmed its intention to play an active role at the centre of the EU while rejecting any EU control over the taxation regime or submission of UK budgetary policies to the EC before their introduction.

However, in his early discussions with fellow heads of government, the Prime Minister has stated that the UK will not block any moves in that direction that EMU members may wish to introduce for the eurozone alone that may require Treaty ratification.

At the core of the longer-term debate among EU members are the contrasting visions for the EU as a more integrated political entity based on the original social model of its founding fathers or as primarily an outward-looking economic and trading entity.

1.4 GRANTS AND INCENTIVES WITHIN THE UK

Chris Wilshaw
PNO Consultants Ltd

Introduction

Thousands of different grant schemes, worth well in excess of £5 billion each year, are available for UK companies in an attempt to encourage, amongst others, innovation and economic development. Any enterprise looking to invest in the UK has the potential to access these financial incentives, which can be quite considerable and are certainly worth exploring further before deciding where to locate an investment. Although the UK has to compete with other locations in the world, especially Eastern Europe, the UK also has a lot to offer companies that are willing to invest. When obtaining grants, emphasis is placed on high value-added businesses and novel industries or manufacturing sites that will offer a nationwide service, regardless of where the head office is based. Different types of grants and incentives are there to persuade companies to favour an investment in the UK.

AVAILABLE grants and incentives

Besides grants, subsidies are also available in the form of tax relief and soft loan facilities. To find out what support is available in specific regions, companies can contact the UK's network of Regional Development Agencies (see:

www.ukti.gov.uk, www.scottish-enterprise.com, www.wales.gov.uk, www.investni.com).

Although on average there are over 1,500 funding programmes available in the UK, the most interesting ones for companies can be categorised into the following four different themes:

- capital investments in specific regions that create or safeguard jobs;
- innovation;
- energy/environment;
- training.

CAPITAL INVESTMENTS

While government funding schemes are often purpose and sector specific, depending on the areas that the government is particularly interested in supporting, location is the most important factor for companies looking to invest into the UK, as locating in certain areas will make them potentially eligible for the most lucrative and the greatest number of grants. In addition to the European Union (EU)'s designated 'Objective' areas referred to below, the UK government provides support through the discretionary Grant for Business Investment (GBI) in England and Regional Selective Assistance (RSA) to the Assisted Areas of Scotland and the Single Investment Fund (SIF) in Wales. Companies locating in Northern Ireland are eligible to apply for grants and incentives that are not available to companies in other parts of the UK. These areas, defined in the Assisted Areas Map (http://www.bis.gov.uk/assets/biscore/regional/images/assistyed-areas-in-greatbritain2007-20134.png), are designed for companies in the industries that supply national and international markets rather than a local area, and manufacturing sectors that are planning expansions, modernisations or rationalisations, or investing in the UK for the first time. For overseas companies investing in the UK where they qualify for GBI or RSA, the amount of funding that can be received ranges from tens of thousands to millions of pounds. These schemes cover the cost of new buildings, plant or machinery. The GBI scheme is delivered by the Regional Development Agencies, although in cases where the total requested grant exceeds £2 million, the grant will be administered by the Department of Business Innovation and Skills (BIS). The scheme is designed for projects that provide employment opportunities and increase regional competitiveness and prosperity, with the amount offered dependent on the needs of the project, the number of jobs safeguarded or created, and the impact the project will have on the economy. The amount provided and the terms of this assistance are generally negotiated as the minimum amount that would ensure the project can go ahead.

The UK's 'Objective' areas were considerably reassessed with new area boundaries laid out for the start of 2007, and these will remain in place until 2013. Therefore, potential investors should check carefully for up to date information on supported locations.

Certain local authorities in England, Scotland and Wales also offer financial assistance through grants or special loans and even venture capital, and all local authorities can be important sources of general support, for example for location searches. The EU also provides assistance in the form of low-interest rate loans from the European Investment Bank (EIB) that can cover up to 50 per cent of the cost of eligible projects.

Innovation

Many schemes within the UK focus on innovation, from 'blue sky' research to novel development on a product level. The key eligibility criteria for all schemes is that each innovation has to be new to the industry.

Although a lot of companies have made use of the R&D tax credit scheme since its launch in 2000 for SMEs and in 2002 for larger companies, a significant percentage is under spent and companies can improve their tax benefit by adopting a structural approach when making use of this scheme. The Technology Strategy Board's schemes for Collaborative Research have been very successful. Each year there will be numerous calls for proposals across a range of industry sectors (with multi-million pound budgets); each new call will focus on different themes. Grants for Collaborative Research projects are typically funded between 25 per cent to 75 per cent. Another source of funding for SMEs is the Grant for R&D scheme, which provides funds of up to £200,000 (£500,000 for exceptional projects) for new products and process development projects, as well as interest-free loans for environmental initiatives and projects that help reduce operating costs.

Funding is also available for businesses that collaborate with academia through programmes such as the CASE Studentship and Knowledge Transfer Partnerships.

Energy/environment

Sustainable development is another key target area of the UK government, in which first movers and innovators are incentivised. Both research into new technologies and investment in state-of-the-art technology could be eligible for different types of grants and incentives. There are also EU funded projects that can provide support towards the initial European demonstration of a novel technology that has significant environmental advantages to society. The total grant awarded is between 30–50 per cent of project costs.

The Waste Resource Action Programme (WRAP) helps businesses reduce waste by funding up to 30% of capital costs towards increasing processing capacity and hence diverting waste to landfill.

Training
Training or re-training of employees is of eminent importance to keep the workforce up to speed in rapidly changing environments. In some areas within the UK, these types of training courses may be eligible for public funding. Focus is on training for personnel below NVQ level 2 or minority groups such as asylum seekers.

The application process
Thorough preparation and a detailed project plan is the key to success in applying for grants. Conducting research and networking with specialists and/or grantor bodies before an application is submitted is a very important part of the application process. Application processing times differ significantly from scheme to scheme, with timescales ranging from three weeks to two years. For investment grants, it is more likely to be in the region of three to four months, so enterprises need to account for this in planning and provide for possible contingencies. One golden rule that is easily overlooked is that applications for funding need to be made in advance of making an investment, as applicants need to demonstrate that the project will not go ahead without this financial assistance. The amount of assistance rarely equates to more than 50 per cent (although 10 to 20 per cent is more common for investment projects) of the eligible project costs, and will be determined largely by negotiation, during which all companies are treated equally, irrespective of their home nation base. There is no guarantee that an application will succeed, regardless of its merits, as the majority of UK grants are discretionary, meaning that they are awarded on a case-by-case basis and, more commonly, on a competitive basis. It is therefore of vital importance to ensure that the application is of the highest quality so that it stands out against the competition. It is also prudent to maximise the chances of success by developing

a total grants strategy, rather than pinning everything on just one application. Sectors that currently attract the most funding include agriculture, food services, manufacturing, chemicals, waste management, bioscience, aerospace and ICT, while pet projects the government bodies are currently seeking to encourage are those involving energy, transport, the environment, education, research and development activities and training.

Assistance with applications

Very few companies possess the specialist knowledge or experience required to handle complicated grant applications successfully. The wiser operations choose to maximise the opportunities while minimizing the hassle, especially in applying for the larger schemes, by calling on external expertise. Support advice and providers can be found through the UK Government Business Link network. There is also a sprinkling of grant consultants, mainly one or two-man bands, but their reputation has been tarnished in the past by the actions of a few who have charged large upfront fees and ended up delivering little, if anything, in return. In continental Europe, where grants appear to be taken far more seriously than in the UK, many larger organizations, including Akzo Nobel, Inbev, Hewlett Packard, Nestlé and Nike, look to Europe's leading grants firm, PNO Consultants, to maximise the available grant opportunities. These clients are serviced by over 400 staff in 28 offices across Europe, including offices recently opened Eastern Europe. As significant sums of European money is now being directed towards Eastern Europe, PNO Consultants have been able to assist some of the major players in the market, realizing manufacturing sites in countries such as Poland and the Czech Republic. These high-level services are also available in the UK from PNO (www.pnoconsultants.co.uk), who have assisted many companies with their external funding strategies, including Procter & Gamble, Heinz and INEOS Chlor, with a success rate of over 80 per cent. PNO Consultants adopt an 'end to end' approach to funding, with a range of services that can be broken down into three main areas:

- identify (the identification and building of fundable projects);
- apply (proposal writing and submission);
- comply (support in financial project management).

Once an application has been approved, many companies find they are unable to claim the full amount approved, due to errors in the administration of the project, which is where PNO's 25+ years' of experience comes into play – maximizing the available grant funding.

Availability of funds from the EU

Structural Funds are one of the EU's key instruments for reducing disparities between regions, by supporting social and economic development and restructuring in regions that are lagging behind or in decline. Any type of organization can apply for funding, depending on the priority being addressed. Applications can be made by eligible bodies such as local authorities, business support agencies, universities, colleges of further education, voluntary sector bodies, non-profit-making organizations and others. The private sector can gain access to a range of support through grants made under the programme to intermediaries in the area. The type of projects funded varies from region to region. Projects supported are required to deliver a direct, measurable and positive impact on the economy of the region to which the application is being made. EU funding is also available to companies investing in an area that benefits from 'Community Initiatives', Including certain designated rural areas, urban areas, border regions and projects involving transnational cooperation, which are designed to promote equal opportunities in the labour market.

Conclusion

Grants can assist enterprises achieve their aims, and although they can potentially involve a lot of work, with the correct approach and some thorough planning, companies can minimise the inconvenience and maximise the possible returns. There are some very lucrative schemes around, but they generally require more complex applications, which is where many companies decide to employ the services of grant consultants. With the recent world economic decline, it has never been more important to review all forms of funding available but at the heart of the matter must be a great company and project, coupled with independent and professional external advice and support to deliver the opportunities.

Note:

At the time of printing, due to the new coalition government looking at all funding, the above information is subject to change at short notice.
More information on grants and incentives currently available in the UK may be found in UKTI factsheets on wwww.ukti.gov.uk

Part Two

2.1 COMPETITION LAW AND POLICY IN THE UK

Emanuela Lecchi and Jason Logendra
Watson, Farley & Williams LLB

INTRODUCTION – SUBSTANCE & ENFORCEMENT

Competition law has two levels of complexity. First, it is substantively complex. Second, it is complex when it comes to *enforcement* due to the interplay between the workings of various regulators and courts both at the national level (in each member State of the European Union) and at the European level.

In this very short chapter we aim to bring some clarity to the main concepts of competition law as it applies in the UK. Readers with an interest in competition law should consider a specialised text for an in-depth analysis.[1]

COMPETITION LAW – THE SUBSTANTIVE RULES

Competition law at the European level and in most member States of the European Union (including the UK) is designed to deal with three main substantive situations, namely:

(a) anticompetitive agreements (Art 81, EC Treaty; Chapter I Prohibition, UK Competition Act 1998);
(b) merger control (EC Merger Regulation; UK Enterprise Act 2002); and

---

1 This chapter is condensed from a longer chapter on competition law published in 2009 in the Law Society Commercial Law Handbook, edited and co-authored by David Berry.

(c) abuse of a dominant position (Art 82, EC Treaty; Chapter II Prohibition, UK Competition Act 1998).

In addition, both at the European level and in some member States (including in the UK) the competition authorities (and, in the UK, the sectoral regulators) can investigate sectors which may show features (often structural features) which impede competition in some way (so-called "sectoral investigations").

There are then two sets of rules often dealt with by lawyers specialising in competition law. These are, on the one hand, rules designed to deal with State Aids and rules designed to ensure a level playing field amongst companies bidding for public works and services; and, on the other hand, rules to ensure that parallel imports (usually of pharmaceuticals, or cars) are not impaired throughout Europe. The underlying rationale of these rules is based on competition economics. State Aids, public procurement and parallel import have a "common market" *raison d'être* and are assessed, amongst others, with reference to underlying concepts of distortion of competition. Space dictates that they cannot be considered further here.

THE THREE MAIN SUBSTANTIVE SITUATIONS

In the experience of the authors, the following Figure 2.1.1 helps to understand the three main situations with which competition law is mostly concerned, by visualising each situation by reference to a bar designed to represent market concentration.

Figure 2.1.1 The three main situations addressed by competition law

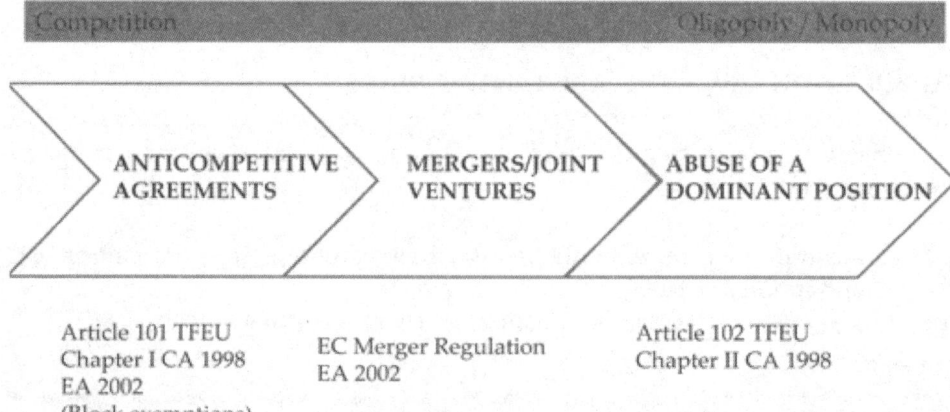

The left-hand side reflects a situation where the marketplace is close to a situation of perfect competition, progressively moving towards a situation of "dominance" and, on the extreme right, monopoly.

Anticompetitive agreements

The first situation, *"anticompetitive agreements"*, occurs in a relatively unconcentrated marketplace, where there would remain a sufficient number of "undertakings" to compete, provided that the market remained competitive. If these undertakings enter into anti-competitive agreements, and, for example, agree to fix prices, or partition marketplaces, then the fact that there may continue to exist a number of undertakings is irrelevant as those undertakings will effectively agree to act as one single independent undertaking (a monopolist).

The most pernicious form of anticompetitive agreements is, of course, the "cartel". In Europe, the focus is on tackling cartels: leniency and immunity applications are accepted by "whistleblowers" and the amount of fines has increased considerably. Jurisdictions in the European Union are for the first time introducing criminal sanctions for executives involved in cartels (cfr. Ireland, the UK, Hungary and Romania amongst others).

When practitioners talk about "block exemptions", they refer to a set of guidelines and rules that can offer a "safe harbour" for agreements which may otherwise, at their face value, be caught by the prohibition against anticompetitive agreements. Under no circumstances (at least under the law as it currently stands) can the block exemptions offer a "safe harbour" for conduct amounting to an abuse of a dominant position. The role of the block exemptions is often misunderstood. More information on the block exemptions is provided in Appendix 1.

Abuse of a dominant position

The third situation, *"abuse of a dominant position"* occurs in a relatively concentrated marketplace, where one undertaking or a small number of undertakings together can act in a manner that impedes competition, usually because of their market shares and the existence of reasons why these market shares cannot be eroded over time (for example, barriers to entry). The assessment of market dominance and of abuse is complex. Competition lawyers distinguish between *Exploitative Abuses*, those which affect companies and entities dependent on the dominant undertaking (customers and suppliers) and *Exclusionary Abuses*, which relate to actions which have as their object the elimination of competitors and/or competition. There are two principal types of exclusionary price abuse: excessive pricing and price discrimination. Exclusionary conduct can be categorised as either price related or non-price related. Price abuses include predatory pricing, margin squeezes and discounts. Non-price abuses include refusal to supply and tying and bundling.

Merger control

In the middle is *"merger control"*: markets become more concentrated as undertakings merge. Pre-screening of mergers is considered to be essential for the proper workings of the system. The European Commission has exclusive jurisdiction under the *EC Merger Regulation* ("ECMR") (Council Regulation (EC) No. 139/2004) to investigate mergers with a community dimension. Mergers should be notified to the European Commission if they meet each element of either of the tests set out in Appendix 2.

If a merger falls outside the scope of the ECMR, it is still necessary to determine whether clearance is required from any national merger authorities. (If the merger is notified to three or more countries within the EEA, the notifying party may request that the merger be referred to the European Commission (Art. 4(5) ECMR)).

When a merger in the UK does not have a community dimension, the UK system of merger control needs to be considered. The UK has a voluntary merger notification regime. Parties are not required to notify mergers to the Office of Fair Trading (OFT) but should be mindful of the OFT's ability to open own-initiative investigations into mergers after they have been completed. The OFT has jurisdiction to investigate mergers where either:

- the target has an annual UK turnover that exceeds £70 million; or
- the merging parties will together supply or acquire at least 25% of a particular description of goods or services in the UK, or in a substantial part of the UK, and the merger leads to an increment in share.

In each of the three situations outlined above, anticompetitive agreements, abuse of a dominant position and merger control, there are two main concepts to be considered at the outset. First, that the rules apply to "undertakings". Second, that "market definition" is the foundation of competition analysis.

The Concept of an "Undertaking"

"Undertaking" is not defined in either the EC Treaty or the Competition Act 1998, which applies in the UK. The ECJ has stated that the term "undertaking" *"encompasses every entity engaged in an **economic activity,** regardless of the legal status of the entity and the way in which it is financed"* (see *Höfner & Elser* v. *Macrotron* [1991] ECR I-1979).

Generally speaking, all companies, individuals and other entities (including charities) that engage in a commercial or economic activity will be undertakings for the purpose of competition law. There are two key difficulties with the definition of an "undertaking":

(a)   what are "economic activities"; and
(b)   whether two legally separate bodies (such as two companies) can be considered a single undertaking.

A group of companies can be a 'single economic entity' if they have unity of conduct on the market. For example, a subsidiary company and a parent company may be one undertaking if they act as a single unit on the market, e.g. if the parent company is the directing mind of the subsidiary. Therefore, coordinated conduct between a parent and subsidiary company that distorts competition is unlikely to be prohibited as there is only one undertaking (the test under Art. 81 is that there should be "two or more undertakings"). Similarly, commercial agents falling under the Commercial Agents Directive and their principals will usually be considered to be the same undertaking for the purposes of competition law as the agent typically provides a service on behalf of the principal.

The Concept of a "Market"

An agreement can only be anticompetitive when it has as its "object or effect" the "prevention, restriction or distortion of competition" in a "market". Every one of the block exemptions will only confer a "safe harbour" provided that the parties to an agreement have a market share in a "relevant market" below prescribed thresholds (parties whose market shares are above the thresholds do not necessarily fall foul of the competition rules). Merger control is designed to prevent those (and only those) mergers that lead to a significant impediment to effective competition in a market. Equally, an abuse can only occur when an undertaking is "dominant" (can exercise market power) in a market.

An undertaking is said to have market power if it can raise prices without suffering a significant decline in demand.

The definition of a product market involves consideration of demand-side substitutability and supply-side substitutability. Demand and supply-side substitutability are used to delineate the products concerned by and the geographic scope of relevant markets, which in some (limited) scenarios will also have a temporal dimension; for example, in the case of markets where it is not possible for customers to substitute between time periods, as in the case of, e.g., the supply of train tickets at certain times of day (see OFT Notice on Market Definition, Guidance Notice T403, point 5).

The exercise of market definition consists in identifying the effective alternative sources of supply for customers of the merging undertakings, both in terms of products or services and the geographic location of suppliers. Detailed rules on market definition apply.

ENFORCEMENT ISSUES

In the UK, competition law has been primarily enforced by the Office of Fair Trading. As the body of competition law becomes more developed, businesses and individuals are encouraged to bring actions directly in the courts.

If an undertaking is found to be in breach of the UK or EU competition rules, that undertaking can be fined up to 10% of its annual turnover. An "undertaking" means a single economic entity: a parent company can be fined up to 10% of the group's turnover if its subsidiary is in breach of competition law. Therefore, parent companies should take an active role in ensuring that all of their group companies are compliant with the competition rules.

Additionally, individuals that breach competition rules could be imprisoned, face personal fines and could be disqualified from being a director for fifteen years. In the UK, individuals may be extradited under the Enterprise Act 2002 s.191, if they breach competition rules in the USA or in any other country that has a criminal offence that corresponds to the cartel offence in the Enterprise Act.

SECTORAL REGULATORS

Utilities and communications services were historically provided by State-owned companies. With liberalisation, the sectors were opened up to competition. The UK regulators in the key sectors are listed below in Table 2.1.1.

Table 2.1.1 UK key regulators

Regulator	Responsibilities
Ofcom	Communications
Ofgem	Gas and electricity
ORR	Rail regulation
OFWAT	Water services
NIAER	Northern Ireland energy regulation
CAA	Aviation

COMPETITION ENFORCEMENT INSTITUTIONS

The key European and UK competition enforcement institutions, together with some of their responsibilities are set out in Table 2.1.2 below.

Table 2.1.2 Competition enforcement institutions

UK Institutions	
Office of Fair Trading (OFT)	The OFT has dual roles – as competition authority and and consumer authority
Competition Commission (CC)	The CC follows on from the OFT and other sector regulators in conducting in-depth investigations.
Competition Appeal Tribunal (CAT)	Hears: • appeals on the merits of decisions made under Competition Act 1998 – appeals against decisions of the OFT or other sector regulators; • hears actions for damages under Competition Act 1998; • reviews mergers and market references; • appeals against regulatory decisions of Ofcom.
High Court	Claimants can bring private actions for damages to the High Court. Claims can follow on from an adverse finding by the OFT, CC or CAT or can be brought directly to the High Court.

EU Institutions	
European Commission (DG Competition)	• enforces competition rules of the EC Treaty; • reviews mergers (phase I and phase II); • publishes guidelines on the application of competition rules for consumers, industry and national competition authorities.
General Court (was Court of First Instance (CFI))	Hears appeals against decisions of Community institutions, including DG Competition.
Court of Justice (was European Court of Justice (ECJ)	Hears: • references for preliminary rulings – the ECJ provides decisions or reasoned orders on specific points of law referred from national courts; • appeals against decisions of the General Court.

SUMMARY CHECKLIST

Activities in the contexts of:

- A. Negotiating with customers
- B. Cooperation with competitors
- C. Mergers/joint ventures
- D. Information gathering
- E. Unilateral action by "dominant" companies

which are likely to be permitted and those which are likely to be prohibited under EU Law are listed in Table 2.1.3 below.

The eight block exemptions at the time of writing are identified in Appendix I and threshold for European notification under merger control are listed in Appendix II.

Table 2.1.3 Activities likely to be permitted and prohibited

LIKELY TO BE PERMITTED	LIKELY TO BE PROHIBITED
A.NEGOTIATING WITH CUSTOMERS OR SUPPLIERS	
• Checking aggregated industry-wide statistical data. • Offering discounts to customers based on the suppliers' costs. • Setting recommended retail prices ("RRPs") for distributors, provided that there is no explicit or implicit pressure on the distributor to follow the RRPs and that you are not dominant.	• Agreeing minimum or fixed resale prices with a distributor or a supplier. • Preventing a distributor from exporting a product to another EU member state. • Charging a distributor prices that vary according to whether the goods are to be resold in a specific country or exported to another EU member state. • Preventing a distributor from selling a product to a customer because they intend to export the product to another EU member state. • Preventing manufacturers of components from selling these components as spare parts.
B. CO-OPERATION WITH COMPETITORS	
• Attending meetings of trade association. • Discussing health and safety. • Discussing proposed regulatory changes.	• Bid-rigging, i.e. allocating tenders between competitors. • Agreeing production quotas with competitors. • Agreements or arrangements with the effect of dividing product or geographic markets with competitors. • Warning a competitor to stay away from "our territory" or specialist field. • Discussing prices, profit margins, rebates or discounts with competitors.

LIKELY TO BE PERMITTED	LIKELY TO BE PROHIBITED
	• Discussing the cost of key raw materials with competitors that also source similar materials. • Agreeing to boycott particular suppliers or distributors. • Discussing prices or profit margins with competitors. • Agreeing current or future prices with competitors. • Discussing terms of sale or supplier/customer business relationships. • Discussing strategic plans, such as pricing strategy or product/territorial expansion. • Agreeing with a competitor to fix the timing for the introduction of a new technology that has been developed independently. • Delaying quoting a price until you know a competitor's price.
C.MERGERS / JOINT VENTURES	
• Entering into a research & development co-operation agreement with a competitor, where both parties are free to exploit the results independently.	• Agreeing with a competitor to fix the timing for the introduction of a new technology that has been developed independently.
D. INFORMATION GATHERING	
• Obtaining information on competitors' sales and prices from publicly available sources or from	• Contacting customers specifically to gather competitors' pricing information ("fishing trip").

LIKELY TO BE PERMITTED	LIKELY TO BE PROHIBITED
customers in the ordinary course of business. • Giving historical sales data to a third party which distributes aggregated, industry-wide sales figures to participants.	
E. UNILATERAL ACTION BY "DOMINANT" COMPANIES	
	• Excessively high pricing, i.e. where the price has no reasonable relation to the economic value of the product. • Selling goods below cost in order to foreclose competitors from the market. • Offering discounts to customers in a discriminatory manner, e.g. offering discounts to customers if they source all or most of their supplies from you. • Suggesting recommended retail prices to a distributor. • Refusing to sell a product to a purchaser with an existing business relationship. This will be permitted only if there are sound commercial reasons for refusing to sell, such as poor credit history. • Refusing to sell a particular product unless it is purchased with another non-essential product from your dominant market. • Insisting that a distributor must stock the whole range of your products.

APPENDIX 1
BLOCK EXEMPTIONS

The eight block exemptions in force at the time of writing are listed below:

Block exemption	Council Regulation
Vertical agreements – agreements between non-competitors	Regulation 2790/1999 Expires 1 June 2010
Specialisation/production agreements – unilateral specialisation; outsourcing; reciprocal specialisation; joint production agreements	Regulation 2658/2000 Expires 31 December 2010
Research and development – joint R&D and joint exploitation of findings	Regulation 2659/2000 Expires 31 December 2010
Motor vehicle distribution – purchase, sale and resale of motor vehicles or spare parts; repair and maintenance services	Regulation 1400/2002 Expires 31 May 2010
Technology transfer agreements – certain patents, know how and software copyright licensing agreements	Regulation 772/2004 Expires 30 April 2014
Insurance – joint establishment of calculations and tables; establishment of non-binding standard policy conditions for direct insurance	Regulation 358/2003 Expires 31 March 2010
Road and inland waterways groupings	Regulation 1017/68 Indefinite duration
Liner consortia – joint operation of liner shipping transport services	Regulation 823/2000 25 April 2010

The Commissions Notice on Agreements of minor importance (de minimis notice) 2001/C368/07 applies to agreements where the combined market share of competing/potentially competing undertakings ("horizontal agreements") is less that 10% and less than 15% for non-competitors ("vertical agreements"), provided they do not contain any hardcore restrictions.

APPENDIX 2
MERGER CONTROL:
THRESHOLDS FOR EUROPEAN NOTIFICATION

Issue	Primary test	Alternative test
Combined worldwide turnover	> EUR 5,000m	> EUR 2,500m
Individual EU-wide turnover	At least two parties > EUR 250m	At least two parties > EUR 100m
Presence in three Member States		Combined turnover of all parties in at least three Member States > EUR 100m AND Individual turnover of two or more of the parties in three of the Member States referred to above > EUR 25m
Exception	A merger will not have a Community dimension if each of the parties achieves more than two-thirds of its EC-wide turnover in one and the same Member State.	

The European Commission can refer the merger analysis to a national authority where the concentration would affect competition in a distinct market of a specific Member State (Art. 4(4) or Art. 9 ECMR).

2.2 REGULATION OF FINANCIAL SERVICES

Ravinder Sandhu
Watson, Farley & Williams LLP

INTRODUCTION

The existence of a legal and regulatory framework that provides investors and others with confidence in the market as a place to do business has never been more important than now. The system of financial services regulation in the UK has evolved over time to match developments in the international marketplace, taking account of the changing business environment, the increasing globalisation of investment business, new technologies, new products and new market participants.

The structure of the regulatory system in the UK comprises a single central regulator—the Financial Services Authority (FSA)—and an overriding framework statute governing all financial services businesses. This is intended to incorporate the flexibility to amend existing rules and issue new rules as circumstances require, but with common standards across all businesses. The intention has been to create an environment that is considered to be fair and transparent and one which does not discourage entrepreneurial activity. However, there are presently many challenges being faced by the FSA, and as London attempts to deal with the aftershocks of the financial crisis and depressed economic activity, the FSA (or its successor) will play an integral role in seeking to rehabilitate and restore confidence in the markets.

It is important to note that on 16 June 2010, the Chancellor of the Exchequer, George Osborne, announced that the current regulatory framework is due to be restructured with the regulatory functions of the FSA being transferred to the Bank of England and certain proposed new regulatory bodies by the end of 2012, effectively leading to the FSA ceasing to exist in its current form. Although only in their infancy, the proposals would see the most radical reformation of the regulation of financial services in over a decade.

The principal legislation governing businesses in the UK undertaking financial services—a term that encompasses a broad and diverse range of activities from banking and insurance to fund management, securities trading and even funeral contracts—is the Financial Services and Markets Act 2000 (the FSMA). The FSMA was enacted following an extensive consultation exercise in the UK, and replaced and consolidated legislation previously governing financial services, banking and insurance activities. It also enabled the movement away from self-regulation through various separate industry bodies by the establishment of the FSA.

THE FSA

The FSA is the UK's central regulatory body for the financial services industry. It has its main office in London, with another office in Edinburgh. The board of the FSA, which is appointed by Her Majesty's Treasury, sets overall policy, with day-to-day decisions and management being the responsibility of the executive. The FSA is directly accountable to treasury ministers, and through them to parliament.

The FSA regulates most financial services participants, exchanges and firms. It has wide ranging powers of rule making, investigation and discipline, which are derived from the FSMA. It also acts as the "competent authority" for the listing of shares on the London Stock Exchange (LSE) and maintains the "Official List". In its role as competent authority, it is referred to as the UK Listing Authority.

The FSMA currently imposes the following five statutory objectives upon the FSA:

1. market confidence – maintaining market confidence in the financial system;
2. public awareness – promoting public understanding of the financial system;
3. financial stability – contributing to the protection and enhancement of the stability of the UK financial system;

4. consumer protection – securing the appropriate degree of protection for consumers; and
5. the reduction of financial crime – limiting the extent to which financial businesses may be used for purposes connected with financial crime.

These statutory objectives are supported by a set of "principles of good regulation", to which the FSA is required to have regard when carrying out its functions. These include:

- using its resources in the most efficient and economic manner;
- recognising the international character of financial services and markets and the desirability of maintaining the competitive position of the UK;
- ensuring that the restrictions imposed on the industry are proportionate to the benefits; and
- recognising the need to minimise the adverse effects on competition that may arise from the FSA's activities and the desirability of facilitating competition between the firms it regulates.

THE FSMA

The FSMA is a framework statute. Its principal provisions form the basis of the UK's regulatory system, with secondary legislation, rules and regulations being made under and pursuant to those primary provisions. The two main provisions setting the overall parameters within which financial services businesses are required to operate are the general prohibition on the carrying on of regulated activities in Section 19 FSMA and the restriction on the making of financial promotions in Section 21 FSMA. These two sections effectively provide that, where regulatory protections are considered to be warranted, only those persons who have been licensed or authorised by the FSA are permitted to carry on or promote regulated business activities. These provisions are at the centre of the structure of the FSMA and form the basis for the regulatory system established beneath it.

General prohibition

As noted above, the FSA's regulation of financial services within the UK is based on a system of approval and licensing of market participants, whether they are commercial or investment banks, insurance companies, securities dealers, financial advisers or others. The system provides for minimum standards and criteria for persons to qualify for approval and licensing where the legislators consider that the persons with whom such businesses may interface require regulatory protection.

The activities requiring licensing are termed "regulated activities", and the FSMA provides a prohibition on the carrying on of any regulated activity in the UK other than by authorised or exempted persons. This prohibition is referred to as the "general prohibition" and is the central building block around which the FSMA and secondary legislation made thereunder is structured.

A person who undertakes a regulated activity without authorisation will be subject to criminal and civil sanctions. Furthermore, any agreement that results from a breach of the general prohibition will be unenforceable.

Although the FSMA provides examples of regulated activities, this term is not exhaustively defined in the FSMA itself. Instead, it is defined in secondary legislation—the FSMA (Regulated Activities) Order 2001 (RAO)—and includes the following activities:

- accepting deposits (ie. banking business);
- dealing in investments;
- arranging deals in investments;
- managing investments;
- safeguarding and administering investments;
- establishing or operating collective investment schemes; and
- advising on investments.

Investments are defined by the RAO and include deposits, contracts of insurance, shares, debt instruments, units in collective investment schemes and various derivative instruments.

As stated above, only authorised or exempt persons may carry out regulated activities. Such persons may include securities traders and advisers, firms of accountants or UK corporate finance firms that act as sponsors or brokers on a market listing. Exempt persons include recognised investment exchanges, such as the LSE.

Financial promotion

In addition to regulating the undertaking of certain activities described above, the FSMA also regulates communications made to third parties in relation to the undertaking of those activities. In particular, the FSMA prohibits a person from communicating, in the course of business, an invitation or inducement to engage in investment activity. This is more commonly known as "financial promotion".

The financial promotion regime is based on similar foundations to the general prohibition and does not apply if the person making the communication is an authorised person under the FSMA, or if an authorised person approves the contents of the communication.

Breach of the financial promotion restriction may give rise to civil liability, and also constitutes a criminal offence. Resulting agreements may be unenforceable, and recipients of the unlawful communication may be entitled to recover their investment and to claim compensation for any loss suffered.

Details of the financial promotion regime are also set out in secondary legislation: the Financial Services and Markets Act 2000 (Financial Promotion) Order 2005 (FPO). The term financial promotion is itself cast in extremely broad terms to encompass any communication in whatever medium, and includes face-to-face oral representations and representations made in telephone conversations (referred to as real time communications), as well as communications made in letters, emails or information available on a website (referred to as non-real time communications). Hence, communication with potential investors inviting them to purchase shares or other investment products will be caught, as will communications concerning insurance products, banking products and the provision of investment management and investment advisory services.

Although the financial promotion restriction is wide, the FPO contains a large number of exemptions from the restriction. Examples of exemptions include intra-group communications and communications made by a company to its members, creditors or employees. The application of certain other exemptions also depends on the type of communication being made and whether or not it is solicited by the recipient. Exemptions may also apply by virtue of the nature of the recipients of such communications, for example, where communications are made to investment professionals, or to certified high net worth individuals or companies, those communications will be exempt from the financial promotion prohibition as such investors are not regarded as requiring higher levels of investor protection.

The financial promotion regime applies to all communications originating in the UK (irrespective of whether the person being targeted is outside the UK) and all communications originating outside the UK that are capable of having an effect in the UK. Communications that originate outside the UK and that are not capable of having an effect in the UK are exempt.

The intention is to regulate the provision of business advice or the making of statements upon which a customer or client (other than more sophisticated investors) may seek to rely in making a financial or investment decision. The aim is to ensure that individuals and businesses establish the necessary credentials, legitimacy and expertise through a system of approvals and licensing before they engage with third parties and take a pecuniary reward as a result. This is supported by the requirement to treat customers fairly by recommending that when preparing and approving promotions, authorised firms consider whether:

- the material is clear, fair and not misleading;
- it provides a balanced picture of the product or service;
- the marketing matches what the product or service delivers; and
- the promotions will be easily understood by their customers.

SECONDARY LEGISLATION AND THE FSA HANDBOOK

Secondary legislation is issued, modified, replaced and supplemented as the marketplace develops, and is tailored for particular kinds of business, such as the carrying on of deposit-taking business by banks, dealing in securities and derivatives and the operation and promotion of investment funds and other collective investment schemes. Secondary legislation is further supplemented with rules and guidance issued by the FSA and contained in the FSA Handbook, which applies to all regulated firms.

The FSA Handbook includes overriding standards for all market participants, as well as detailed conduct of business rules and a code of market conduct. It also implements the requirements of the Markets in Financial Instruments Directive (MiFID), which came into force on 1 November 2007, with the aim of harmonising financial services regulation within the European Economic Area and increasing competition and consumer protection in investment services.

Conduct of Business Rules

The FSA's Conduct of Business rules are the requirements applying to firms with investment business customers in the UK. The extent to which the rules apply depends upon the nature of the products and services provided and the type of client to which they are offered. The rules are set out in the Conduct of Business Sourcebook (COBS), which came into force on 1 November 2007.

The COBS is designed to provide guidance on the regulatory requirements across the range of activities that may be carried on by regulated firms and covers, amongst other things:

- financial promotions;
- the provision of information and advice to clients; dealings in investments; and
- the management of investments.

The previous COBS was widely criticised by the financial services industry for imposing unnecessary burdens on the businesses regulated. The new COBS is intended to free companies from the prescriptive nature of the previous regulatory environment and enable them to design their business processes and promotional material to suit their particular circumstances and those of their customers. To this end, the COBS has been simplified and is based on general principles rather than detailed rules and processes. The COBS also implements the conduct of business requirements of the MiFID.

In March 2010, the FSA completed a post-implementation review of both the COBS and MiFID. This review aimed to assess the success of the new regime under the COBS against the FSA's intended outcome and in the context of its move to more principles-based regulation. The final statement on findings on the COBS review released by the FSA states that "COBS is now very much a part of our normal supervisory and policy activity and is itself the baseline for further changes", and that COBS "are now an integral element in our day to day regulation of firms' designated investment business". The FSA publication reviewing MiFID concludes that "most firms' MiFID implementation work had been well managed and that firms were compliant as at the visit date".

Market abuse

Although the FSMA primarily regulates financial services through a system of authorisation and licensing, it also sets out a framework for tackling wrongful behaviour on financial markets (better known as market abuse), which complements the criminal offence of insider dealing. These rules are designed to enhance market integrity and confidence for the benefit of market participants.

The FSA has made targeting market abuse a regulatory priority, and this is as strong as ever, particularly in an uncertain economic climate where market instability can increase the scope for market abuse. The FSA's market abuse strategy includes working in partnership with industry to tackle market abuse and focusing on bringing a greater number of criminal prosecutions.

The current market abuse provisions were introduced in the Market Abuse Directive, which was implemented in the UK on 1 July 2005, and harmonises the requirements relating to insider dealing and market manipulation across the European Union (EU).

Market abuse may arise in circumstances where market participants have been unreasonably disadvantaged (whether directly or indirectly) by others in the market who, inter alia, have:

● used to their own advantage information that is not generally available;
● created a false or misleading impression; or
● distorted the market.

Under the FSMA, the FSA has the power to impose financial penalties for market abuse. The FSA has also published a Code of Market Conduct (MAR) to supplement the provisions that deal with market abuse and provide guidance as to whether or not behaviour constitutes market abuse.

In order to combat volatility in shares and the perceived increased potential for market abuse in the market conditions during the worst of the global financial crisis, in 2008 the FSA saw fit to introduce new provisions to the MAR, aimed at restricting practices such as "short-selling", whereby a seller sells a financial instrument that he/she does not own at the time of the sale, with the intention of later purchasing the financial instrument at a lower price. These provisions expired in January 2009 but their possible reimplementation will be kept under review in light of market conditions and more onerous disclosure obligations have been imposed on persons holding a net short position.

Other provisions

In addition to the above, the FSMA also establishes the FSA's powers of intervention, which include broad powers of investigation and powers to penalise persons contravening the FSA's rules or the provisions of the FSMA, including the ability to fine contraveners or withdraw a firm's authorisation.

The FSMA is a comprehensive statute. This chapter provides a summary of the principal provisions upon which financial services regulation in the UK is based, but the FSMA also makes provisions in relation to other relevant matters, including provisions for:

● the official listing of securities derived from EU legislation;

- an investors' compensation scheme;
- the establishment and operation of an independent financial ombudsman to whom investors and market participants can complain;
- the establishment and operation of regulated and unregulated collective investment schemes;
- changes of control over authorised persons; and
- a prohibition on certain kinds of market behaviour, including a broad prohibition on making misleading statements or undertaking misleading practices, which are in addition to the provisions relating to "market abuse" referred to above.

FUTURE

As mentioned in the introduction, the FSA, which was recently referred to by George Osbourne, Chancellor of the Exchequer, as "a narrow regulator, almost entirely focused on rules-based regulation", is to be abolished and the Bank of the England given wide-ranging powers with the aim of preventing another financial crisis.

As set out in his speech on 16 June 2010 at the Mansion House, the Chancellor of the Exchequer stated that the intention is to create:

- **a new prudential regulator** – This as yet unnamed regulator will operate as a subsidiary of the Bank of England. It will carry out the prudential regulation of financial firms, including banks, investment banks, building societies and insurance companies;
- **an independent Financial Policy Committee at the Bank** – This committee will have the tools and the responsibility to look across the economy at the macro issues that may threaten economic and financial stability and take effective action in response;
- **a powerful new Consumer Protection and Markets Authority** – This authority will regulate the conduct of every authorised financial firm providing services to consumers. It will also be responsible for ensuring the good conduct of business in the UK's retail and wholesale financial services, in order to preserve the UK's reputation for transparency and efficiency as well as its position as one of the world's leading global financial centres; and
- **a new single agency to tackle serious economic crime** – The Government

would fulfil its commitment contained in the coalition agreement by creating a single agency to take on the work of tackling serious economic crime that is currently dispersed across a number of Government departments and agencies.

The next step is for a wide consultation to take place with the process being completed in 2012.

2.3 INTELLECTUAL PROPERTY

Mark Tooke
Watson, Farley & Williams LLP

INTRODUCTION

Intellectual property rights (IPRs) play an important and often essential role across business activities. There are many different types of IPRs that include the protection of intangible business assets, such as know-how, reputation and goodwill, and the products of creative effort. Most IPRs have a commercial value and can be bought, sold and licensed.

It makes good business sense to identify the IPRs you have (particularly where your business is investing in innovation and research, or sells goods or services on the basis of its reputation) and to ensure that they are properly protected. It is also important, where possible, to identify as early as possible areas of potential conflict with IPRs owned by third parties, so that infringements of their IPRs can be avoided.

Some IPRs attract protection automatically on their creation or commercialization; others require registration with an official body, usually the UK Intellectual Property Office (IPO), before they are recognised and afforded protection by the courts. This chapter gives a description of the main commercially significant IPRs that may be protected and exploited in the UK.

COPYRIGHT AND RELATED RIGHTS

Copyright is the collective name for the body of law that grants to makers of written, dramatic, musical and artistic works the ability to control how their creations are used. Both economic and moral rights are provided under the copyright law of the UK:

- Economic rights allow the creator to control the commercial exploitation of their work and to prevent it from being copied without permission.
- Moral rights protect works from being manipulated or distorted in a way that is detrimental to the interests or reputation of the creator.

In the most basic terms, copyright is a right to prevent unauthorised copying. Rights related to copyright include the ability for the owner of a work to prevent others from doing things that, although not strictly copying, are essential to the commercial exploitation of a work; for example, the public performance of music, the adaptation of a play or the broadcasting or public showing of a film or television programme.

Automatic protection

Copyright protection covers original literary, dramatic, musical and artistic works, published editions, sound recordings, films and broadcasts, where the creator has expended a sufficient level of "skill, judgement and labour" in creating the work.

Protection is automatic as soon as the work is recorded, in any form or medium. There is no official registration system in the UK and, therefore, there are no fees to pay or formal action required in order to obtain copyright protection. However, it is good practice to keep a detailed record of how and when the work was produced in case a creator is ever obliged to prove (e.g. in court) that they created the work and that it was not copied. Although not a legal requirement in the UK, owners can mark their work with the international copyright symbol ©, together with their name and the year of publication.

The UK is a member of several international copyright conventions, and works created by UK nationals or residents are automatically protected by the copyright law of other signatory countries; nationals or residents of these countries are automatically afforded reciprocal protection in the UK.

Ownership and duration

Copyright can be bought, sold, inherited, transferred or licensed (wholly or in part). As a result, the economic rights to a copyright work can belong to someone other than the creator. Moral rights can be waived, but cannot be transferred. The length of protection offered by copyright depends on the type of work and there are specific rules for each work, but in general, the length of protection is as follows:

- literary, dramatic, musical or artistic works and film: the life of the author, plus 70 years;
- sound recordings and broadcasts: 50 years; and
- published editions: 25 years.

Infringement

Copyright infringement occurs when a work is copied or used without permission. Matters of infringement are ultimately decided in court. Infringement will not occur if the work is used with the permission of the owner or in relation to certain very limited purposes, which include non-commercial research, private study, criticism, review and teaching in schools.

Database right

A database, for the purposes of protection, can be defined as a collection of independent works, dates or other materials that are, firstly, arranged in a systematic and methodical way and, secondly, are individually accessible by electronic or other means. Copyright protection will apply to a database if there is originality in the selection or arrangement of the contents. If there has been substantial investment in the creation of a database then, in addition to copyright protection, a separate, stand-alone database right may also apply. Copyright and the database right can both apply to the same database.

Database right gives automatic protection as soon as a database exists in recorded form and applies to both electronic and paper databases. It provides protection against the unauthorised appropriation and distribution to the public of the whole or a part of the contents of a database, and lasts for 15 years.

TRADEMARKS AND PASSING OFF

A trademark is a distinctive sign that identifies certain goods and/or services as those produced or provided by a particular person or enterprise. The owner of a registered trademark has the exclusive right to use or identify goods and/or services using that trademark. If a sign is being used by a business as a trademark but is not registered, it may be capable of protection using the law of passing off.

Trademarks can greatly assist the customers of a business by serving as a badge of origin for the business's goods and services. Registered trademarks also offer businesses the ability to protect the investment it makes in its brand identity and in the reputation of its goods and services. Additionally, without trademark protection the competitors of a business may try to take unfair advantage by using confusingly similar, distinctive signs to market their products and services.

Types of trademarks

Trademarks may be words, letters, numerals, symbols, drawings, fragrances, colours used as a distinguishing feature and/or three-dimensional signs (e.g. the shape and packaging of goods and sounds, as long as the trademark is capable of being represented graphically). Although the possibilities are many, and may seem almost limitless, a trademark must be distinctive and capable of distinguishing the goods or services of one undertaking from that of another.

Registration process

To be registered, a trademark must be distinctive, not similar to any earlier marks and not be deceptive, or contrary to law or morality. Both British trademarks and European Community (EC) trademarks have effect in the UK. There are two main ways to acquire such a trademark:

- apply to the IPO for a British trademark; or
- apply to the Office for Harmonization in the Internal Market for an EC trademark.

Official fees must be paid to obtain both types of registered trademarks. A British trademark offers protection in the UK only. An EC trademark has effect in every member state of the EC, as well as the UK, but the application process is generally more expensive and slower than for a British trademark.

A trademark application must specify the types of goods and services in respect of which protection is sought (the more types, the more expensive the application). Prior to registration, the application can be rejected by the relevant office on a number of grounds, or challenged and blocked by third parties. Once granted, registration lasts for 10 years but can be renewed indefinitely on payment of a renewal fee for successive ten year periods as long as the trademark is being used.

Benefits of registration

Registering a trademark confers on the owner the exclusive right to use the mark for the goods and services it covers in the UK. Once a trademark has been registered, the symbol ® can be put next to the trademark to warn others from using it. Care must be taken, however, as use of the symbol ® for unregistered trademarks is a criminal offence.

Other benefits conferred to the owners by registered trademarks include the following:

- the ability to sell or license the trademark;
- the ability to commence legal action against anyone who uses it without permission;
- the generation of value in an asset that may be used as collateral for financing; and
- the ability to involve the UK Trading Standards, the police and the other law enforcement agencies, who can bring criminal charges against counterfeiters and pirates.

Passing off

If an unregistered mark is used without the owner's permission, it may be possible to claim protection from the courts under the law of passing off. To be successful in a claim for passing off, a claimant must prove that:

- he/she is the owner of the unregistered trademark and has built goodwill or reputation attached to the goods and services he/she supplies to the public;
- the defendant has made a misrepresentation to the public (intention is irrelevant), leading or likely to lead the public to believe that goods or services offered by the defendant are the goods and services of the claimant; and
- he/she has suffered or is likely to suffer damage from the illegitimate use of the mark.

A legal action claiming passing off can be expensive, as proving the sufficient reputation or goodwill in an unregistered trademark is often difficult for the claimant, and usually involves showing an extensive and lengthy prior use of the trademark in the UK (five years or more).

PATENTS

If you have invented a product that is new or a new way of doing something, a patent may be granted. A patent having effect in the UK can be acquired in two ways:

1.   by application to the IPO for a British patent; or
2.   by application to the European Patent Office for a European patent (which is in fact a single-application process, leading to the grant of a "bundle" of separate national patents, including a UK patent).

Irrespective of which application process is used, a UK patent (once granted) has effect only in the UK, and lasts for 20 years from the date of filing of the application provided the prescribed annual renewal fees are paid following the expiry of the fifth year. A patent may not be the best or only way to protect an invention. It may be possible to protect aspects of the invention as registered or unregistered designs, registered trademarks or using the law of copyright.

Scope

In basic terms, a patent is designed to protect how things work, what they are made of or how they are made. To be granted a patent, the invention in question must be new, must involve an inventive step, must not be obvious to someone with knowledge and experience in the subject and must be capable of being applied on an industrial scale.

A patent will not be granted for certain types of innovations, including:

● scientific or mathematical discoveries;
● literary, dramatic, musical or artistic works;
● most computer programs;
● animal or plant varieties;
● methods of medical treatment or diagnosis; and
● inventions that are deemed against public policy or morality.

Application process

The process of applying for a patent can be complicated, and the assistance of a qualified patent attorney is recommended. It is also recommended that a search of published patents and existing public know-how (so-called "prior art") be conducted before an application is made to confirm that the invention is new and has not already been patented.

The registration process requires full disclosure to the IPO of information explaining how the invention works, and this information is made available to the public whether the application is successful or not. Once a patent is granted, yearly renewal fees must be paid for the rights to continue.

Protection
The owner of a patent can prevent anyone from using, distributing, selling or commercially making the invention without permission. If a patent is infringed, it is up to the owner to take appropriate action.

Designs
In the UK, a design may be legally protected in one of the three ways.

- *Registered designs*: the look of a product (including its surface decoration, colour and ornamentation) may be protected by seeking registered design protection, provided certain requirements are met, the main ones being that the design is new and has individual character (i.e. it is distinctively different from existing designs). To obtain a registered design, an application must be made to the IPO, with the required fee. Registration lasts for a maximum of 25 years.
- *Design right*: the shape or configuration of a product may be protected from illegal copying by use of the law of unregistered design right. Design right is free and, subject to certain qualifications, arises automatically where the shape of a new product is original. Design right lasts for the shorter of the 10-year period after the first marketing of products that use the design or the 15-year period after the creation of the design. Licences of right (meaning that anyone is entitled to a licence to make and sell products copying the design) may be available toward the end of the protection period. Design right does not protect two-dimensional designs (in respect of which registered designs or copyright may be relevant).
- *Copyright*: if an original design is artistic and is not intended to be mass-produced, it will be protected against illegal copying by the law of copyright.

PLANT VARIETY RIGHTS AND GEOGRAPHICAL INDICATIONS

There are a number of IPRs that, although less well known than those mentioned previously, can be valuable to those engaged in certain specialist areas of business. These include the following:

- plant variety rights (which offer protection to plant breeders); and
- geographical indications (which offer protection to producers of foodstuffs with a strong connection to a particular area, e.g. Stilton cheese).

CONFIDENTIAL INFORMATION AND TRADE SECRETS

Information that is not covered by one of the IPRs may nonetheless be protected by its owner if it is not public knowledge and the owner keeps it a secret. The law imposes or implies certain duties of confidentiality in particular situations, but these can be strengthened or widened by contract; for example, a new and distinctive business proposition may not meet the requirements for patent protection, but before disclosing it to potential new business partners the owner may require them to sign a confidentiality agreement that will prevent them from using the idea themselves or disclosing it to third parties.

REMEDIES FOR INFRINGEMENT

A range of remedies is available to the owner of an IPR depending on the IPR in question. These include the following:

- Account of profits: if the defendant has made profit out of infringing another's IPRs, the IPR holder can elect to have this awarded instead of damages.
- Damages: damages are usually calculated on a loss of profits or on a royalty basis. Generally, they are compensatory in nature and are to put the holder back in the position that they would have been in if the infringement had not occurred.
- Criminal penalties: serious infringement of certain IPRs, such as copyright, trademarks and patents, may amount to a criminal offence (.eg. piracy on a commercial scale), leading to criminal sanctions including imprisonment and fines.

Other remedies include delivery up and destruction of articles infringing IPRs.

Injunctions ordering a defendant not to carry on certain activities may be granted by the court; however, injunctions are discretionary remedies and may not always be awarded, and interim injunctions (awarded before the final decision of the court in an action for infringement) are granted only if it is a matter of urgency or in the interests of justice.

EMPLOYEES AND IPRS

In many cases, the IPRs created by an employee in the course of their employment will, according to UK law, belong automatically to their employer. However, the type and nature of the IPRs created and the scope of the employee's duties can sometimes result in the employee being considered the first owner of the IPRs; for example, a junior employee who invents something that is not directly connected with the main business of the employer may claim that they are the first owner of the invention, on the basis that it was not created in the course of their employment or as part of their normal duties.

To avoid such problems, it is strongly recommended that every UK employment contract contains clauses that expressly set out who will be the first owner of the IPR created while the employee is employed by the employer.

Where the creator of an IPR is not an employee of the business but is a contractor engaged by the business, the usual rule (that the business is the first owner of any IPRs created at its request) does not apply in the absence of an express agreement between the parties to the contrary. In this situation, the IPRs will usually belong to the consultant who created it, with an express or implied licence being granted to the business to use the IPRs. Although in some circumstances it may be inferred that a contractor is under an obligation to assign the IPRs to the business, a clear written agreement between all parties engaged in the work is highly recommended.

Useful websites

- www.wfw.com (Watson, Farley & Williams LLP)
- www.ipo.gov.uk (UK Intellectual Property Office)
- http://oami-europa-en (Office for Harmonization in the Internal Market—EC Trademark Office)
- www.epo.org (European Patent Office)
- www.lawsociety.org.uk (Law Society of England and Wales)
- www.lawscot.org.uk (Law Society of Scotland)
- www.cipa.org.uk (Chartered Institute of Patent Agents)
- www.itma.org.uk (Institute of Trademark Attorneys)

2.4 COMPANY FORMATION – METHODS AND LEGAL IMPLICATIONS

Ian Saunders
Artaius Ltd

REGISTRATION

There is no formal requirement in the UK to register with a local commercial registry or the tax authorities before commencing business.

A person wishing to start a business in the UK has a choice between the registration of an incorporated vehicle (a company) or trading through an unincorporated vehicle (a sole trader or partnership). If a corporation is already operating overseas, then the owners and managers of that business also have the option to consider registration of that corporation as a branch or having a place of business in the UK.

Unincorporated Vehicles

(i) Sole Trader

A person who carries on business as a sole trader is personally liable for all the debts and obligations incurred by his business; accordingly all of his business and personal assets can be called upon to meet payment of any liabilities incurred by his business.

(ii) Partnership

A partnership is usually governed by a written agreement, which binds the partners and is subject to the provisions of the Partnership Act 1890. With some exceptions, partnerships are limited to 20 partners.

The partnership has no separate legal entity and a trader who carries on business through this vehicle is jointly and severally liable with his other partners for all debts and obligations incurred by the partnership while he is a partner. Furthermore, he is jointly and severally liable with the other partners for loss or damage to third parties by the wrongful acts or omissions of any partner in the ordinary course of the partnership business.

(iii) Limited Partnership

These are governed by the Limited Partnerships Act 1907. As long as there is one or more partners liable for all the debts and obligations of the partnership, the Act allows a partner to limit his liability to the amount contributed by him by way of property or capital on joining the partnership. Such a partner is not entitled to take part in the management of the partnership.

Incorporated Vehicles

Corporations have distinct legal personality separate from that of their members.

(i)The Private Company Limited by Shares ("Private Company") is the most commonly used business vehicle in the UK. There is no statutory minimum capital requirement for a Private Company.

A private company is prohibited by law from offering any of its shares to members of the public, so no offer of shares of any kind can be made. It is the vehicle used mostly for owner/managed companies and new business start ups.

(ii) Public company limited by shares ("PLC"). The minimum capital requirement for a PLC is £50,000. If contributed in cash, one quarter of the value of each issued share is required to be paid up in the PLC (effectively £12,500) for it to obtain a certificate to commence trading.

A PLC can, under strict procedures, issue a prospectus and offer shares to members of the public. Under strict rules and regulations, larger PLCs can be admitted to the main index of the London Stock Exchange or one of the subsidiary markets.

(iii) Private company limited by guarantee and not having a share capital. This vehicle is used chiefly by trade associations, clubs, charitable companies and management companies for apartment blocks. There is no share capital. Instead each member "guarantees" that in the event of the company being wound up it will pay a specified sum towards the funds. The articles of association govern the terms of membership of the companies.

(iv) Unlimited companies, with or without a share capital. The members' liability is unlimited with this type of company. The chief advantage of this organisation is that accounts are not required to be submitted to Companies House and are thus not available for public inspection.

(v) Limited Liability Partnership (LLP). Introduced 6 April 2001, an LLP comprises a corporate entity distinct from companies incorporated under the Companies Act, but sharing many characteristics.

An LLP is a legal person quite separate from its members, with capacity to contract in its own name. Members of an LLP enjoy limited liability; they do not have to be employees of the LLP.

LLP Incorporation

A minimum of two people is required when the LLP is incorporated; they subscribe their names to an incorporation document. The LLP must carry on a lawful business with a view to profit.

An LLP must prepare and publish Accounts similar to those regarding a company and file an Annual Return accordingly. An LLP may change its name and registered office. Members may change.

Unless members agree otherwise, they share profits and losses equally and may all participate in managing the LLP. Members may enter into an Agreement that, among other things, deals with profit shares, involvement in management and remuneration.

As with incorporating a company and settling its Memorandum & Articles of Association, those intending to incorporate an LLP and drafting a Members Agreement should seek expert advice at an early stage.

Members of an LLP are taxed as if the business was carried on by a partnership, rather than by a company.

(v) Community interest company. Community Interest Companies (CICS) are limited companies, with special additional features, created for the use of people who want to conduct a business or other activity for community benefit, and not purely for private advantage. This is achieved by a "community interest test" and "asset lock", which ensure that the CIC is established for community purposes and the assets and profits are dedicated to these purposes. Registration of a company as a CIC has to be approved by the Regulator who also has a continuing monitoring and enforcement role.

Registration of a UK Establishment

A UK Establishment is effectively an extension of the Overseas Company operating in the UK, and as such, the UK office is subject to UK Law. A UK Establishment is not a separate legal entity from the Overseas Company and any such contractual arrangements or liabilities entered into are binding to the Overseas Company.

A UK Establishment must have a trading address in the UK and present evidence of this for formation purposes.

The information needed on formation of a UK Establishment is as follows:

- the corporate name of the Overseas Company;
- its legal form, i.e. whether it is a private or publicly-quoted company, and its manner of limitation, i.e. by shares;
- the law under which the Company is incorporated;
- the identity (name and address) of the authority in the home state responsible for keeping the records of the Company;
- its registration number in the country of incorporation (if applicable);
- the objects of the Company;
- the share capital of the Company;
- a list of its Directors (and if applicable, Company Secretary) and the home addresses, dates of birth and business occupation of such persons;
- the extent to which Directors can represent the company, i.e. whether they can act alone or must act jointly;
- whether the company is a credit or financial institution;
- the address of the Branch in the UK, the date on which it was opened and the business carried on by the Branch;
- a list of the names and addresses of persons in the UK authorised to accept service on behalf of the Company in respect of business at the Branch;

● a list of those persons resident in the UK and entitled to represent the Company and whether any powers of representation are limited in any way; the address of its principal place of business in its country of incorporation.

The Overseas Company must, for registration, also submit a copy of its last filed accounts and a copy of its constitution document. These must be certified by a notary and translated into English if necessary.

Although the accounts of the UK Establishment will not be required to be filed on public record at Companies House, the accounts of the Overseas Company will need to be so filed if there is requirement to publicly file the accounts of the Overseas Company in its home state. If accounts are not required to be publicly filed, a special set of accounts will need to be prepared and filed under the Companies Act 2006.

THE PROCESS OF FORMING A COMPANY

Private Company Limited by Shares
The great majority of companies formed in the UK are private companies limited by shares and the process of the formation of these companies will be examined first.

(i) Company Name
The proposed company name should be checked to ensure that it is not identical to an existing registered name or does not contain a word restricted or prohibited. The UK authority dealing with the registration of companies ("Companies House") maintain a list of already registered names and restricted words. This is available at their website www.companieshouse.gov.uk/info

The Companies Act 2006 imposes new rules on the identification of names as identical to existing names. Certain words (including "UK" and "Services") are ignored when comparing names and the new name will not be allowed if a name is different from an existing company only by words or characters that are disregarded. For further information please see Companies House website.

Care should also be taken to avoid clashes with companies of similar names. Although this will not prevent the registration of the name, a new incorporator may find a subsequent objection to the new name has been made and in such cases Companies House have power to direct a new company to change its name.

In addition the new company could face a case of "passing off" if an existing company considers that their trade has been infringed.

New companies should also be advised to ensure their proposed name does not conflict with any registered trade or service marks. Further information can be obtained from the UK patent office at www.patent.gov.uk/tm

In addition, with effect from 1 October 2008, the Companies Act 2006 introduced new provisions allowing any person or company to object to a company name for "opportunistic registration" if the company's name is:

a)   the same as a name associated with the complainant in which he has good-will; or

b)   so similar that its use in the United Kingdom would be likely to mislead by suggesting a connection between the company and the complainant.

For further information refer to: www.ipo.gov.uk/cna

The company name chosen must end with the word "Limited" or "Ltd" and these words must not appear anywhere other than as the last word in the name.

(ii) Shareholders

A private company limited by shares can have one or more shareholders. The first shareholder(s) of the new company will be those person who subscribe for shares in the Memorandum of Association of the Company, which is a document required to be submitted for the incorporation and which is detailed below.

Subsequent to the incorporation, the Directors of the company may allot further shares if so authorised by its Articles of Association.

The liability of any shareholder is limited to any amounts unpaid on the shares agreed to be taken.

(iii) Directors

The Directors of a company will be those persons who consent to act as such on Form IN01 submitted with the incorporation papers. The directors are required to provide their full name and residential address, date of birth, nationality and business occupation.

There is no restriction on non-UK residents acting as directors, but there may be restrictions on what work some nationals who are not based in the European Economic Area can do in the UK. For further information refer to the UK Home

Office website at www.ind.homeoffice.gov.uk

A private limited company requires a minimum of one director. A UK or foreign registered corporation may be a director, but the Companies Act 2006 requires that at least one director must be an actual person. This section of the Companies Act 2006 was effected from 1 October 2008.

The directors will be responsible for managing the business and affairs of the company. As such, they are required to act at all times in the best interests of the company and are regarded as the equivalent of trustees of the company's monies.

(iv) Secretary

A Secretary, if appointed, will be responsible with the directors for ensuring that the company meets its obligations with filing accounts and returns etc in good time. The new companies act removes the compulsion for a private company to have a secretary, effective 6 April 2008.

(v) Registered Office

A company incorporated in England and Wales must have a registered office in either England or Wales, a company incorporated in Scotland must have a registered office in Scotland and a Company incorporated in Northern Ireland must have a Registered Office there. A company is required by UK law to keep at its registered office registers of directors, shareholders, legal charges, debentures and minutes of directors and shareholders meetings. Certain of the registers must be made available for inspection by any member of the public presenting himself or herself to the registered office. The registered office should therefore be a place that such inspection can take place and which any legal notice should be served on the company.

(vi) Documents required by Companies House to form the company

a)   Memorandum of Association
     This sets out the name of the company and lists the first shareholders of the Company (the Subscribers). It must be signed by these subscribers.

b)   Articles of Association
     These set out the rules for the running of a Company's internal affairs i.e. the rules for meetings of directors and shareholders and the relationship between the owners (shareholders) and managers (directors), transferring

of shares etc.. There is a default set of Articles, which will be implied if no articles are submitted (called "The Model Articles"). These Articles are available to view from Companies House.

Company registration agents will be prepared to supply tailored versions of the Articles of Association for a proposed company for a small fee.

c) Form IN01

This sets out the details of the Directors and Secretary of the company, its registered office address and lists the first shareholders, the amounts paid for each share and the rights attached to the shares issued. It must be signed by these officers and also contains within a Statement of Compliance under the Companies Act 2006 which must be signed by the subscribers to the Memorandum of Association or an agent for the subscribers.

d) Cheque for Companies House fees

Companies House require a cheque in the sum of £20 to complete the incorporation.

If the documents submitted are in order, Companies House usually issues a Certificate of Incorporation within four to five working days.

UK company registration agents can assist with the whole process of forming a company and can arrange for the relevant declaration to be carried out very simply. In addition, it is possible for agents with the necessary software to file private limited company incorporations electronically at Companies House. This speeds up the process still further and companies can now be formed usually within 24 hours. The fee for an electronic formation is reduced to £15.

Public company limited by shares

The process for forming a public company is very similar to that of forming a private company; the differences being:-

1. *Company Name*

The name must end with the words "Public Limited Company" or "PLC"

2. *Shareholders*

A public limited company must have a minimum of two shareholders and must have an issued capital of £50,000 minimum.

3. *Directors*
    There must be a minimum of two directors.

4. *Secretary*
    There must be a Secretary appointed and such person must be qualified i.e. be a barrister, solicitor or advocate admitted in the UK, or be a qualified Chartered Accountant, Certified Accountant, Certified Management Accountant or Chartered Secretary.

The documents required to be submitted to Companies House for the formation of the Company are the same as for a private company, but the Memorandum and Articles of Association must be suitable for the management of a public company.

In addition, following incorporation, a public company must undertake a further declaration that it has met the minimum capital requirements and that it has paid up its capital as necessary (one quarter of the nominal value of each share). It will then be issued with a further certificate allowing it to borrow money and trade.

STATUTORY REQUIREMENTS FOLLOWING INCORPORATION

1. *Registration with the UK Tax Authorities*
    Within three months of the date of commencement of trading, the Company is required to register for Corporation Tax by the completion and submission to HM Revenue and Customs of a New Company Details Form (CT41g). This form is available from HMRC.
    If the Company has any paid employees registration with HMRC is also required under the Pay As You Earn regulations.
    The Company may also require registration under VAT (Value Added Tax) rules if its turnover reaches pre-set limits in any one year/month.

2. *Accounts*
    Companies are required to submit accounts prepared in accordance with the Companies Act 2006. Companies House and the UK tax authorities (HM Revenue and Customs) must receive these not later than 9 months following the company's year-end date. (6 months for public limited companies).

A company's year-end will be set automatically by Companies House as the anniversary of the end of the month of incorporation. i.e. a company incorporated at any time during, for example, June 2010 will have a year-end of 30 June 2011. A company's year-end can be changed by the submission of a form to Companies House and can be extended to a period of up to 18 months. However, directors of new companies should note that if this extension is made, the first set of accounts will still be due 21 months from the original incorporation date (18 months for plc's).

Civil Penalties are imposed by Companies House for the failure to file accounts on time. HMRC will also apply penalties if the Corporation Tax return and any tax due are not filed on time.

3. *Annual Return*

Companies are required to submit an annual return to Companies House within 28 days of the anniversary of the date of incorporation. This return sets out the current business activities, details of directors and secretary and shareholders of the company. A fee of £30 is payable to Companies House for this return. The fee can be reduced to £15 if the annual return is submitted electronically via Companies House web-filing service or via an agent with the necessary software. Failure to file the annual return can ultimately lead to the Company being struck-off the index of companies.

4. *Other documents*

The Companies Act 2006 specifies that returns shall be made to Companies House in the event that the company undertakes certain actions. For example the issuing of shares, changing the rights attached to shares, changes being made to the Articles of Association, the granting of a charge over the company's assets, changes to the details of any director or secretary or the resignation or new appointment of these officers. There are various time limits imposed for the submission of these returns and the officers of a company are advised to familiarise themselves with these requirements or to employ a local agent who will have the required compliance knowledge.

The management of a company's statutory affairs (such as the submission of annual returns and changes to shareholders and directors) is often carried out by specialist company formation agents, company secretarial service providers, solicitors or accountants.

NEW COMPANIES ACT 2006

The Companies Act 2006 received Royal Assent on 8 November 2006 with the aim of cutting costs and red tape for businesses and in particular smaller companies. The idea was to make the law in this area more accessible and to allow easier changes to it where it no longer corresponds to modern business.

The act was brought into effect in stages ending on 1 October 2009. It is therefore fully in operation. Those familiar with older legislation may need guidance in respect of the new rules.

Note: The information in this chapter is current at May 2010

2.5 UK IMMIGRATION

Angharad Harris and Devan Khagram
Watson, Farley & Williams LLP

INTRODUCTION

The UK government is keen to promote economic opportunities by encouraging overseas investment and the immigration of skilled individuals. The government has implemented a new points-based system (PBS) to replace the various immigration options that were previously available to individuals wishing to enter the UK to seek employment or to explore business and investment opportunities. The aim of the PBS is to enable the UK to:

- control migration more effectively;
- tackle abuse; and
- attract the most talented workers into the economy.

This chapter sets out an outline of the main business immigration options and key requirements under each category.

CAN I VISIT THE UK ON BUSINESS?

It is possible to enter the UK as a business visitor, although there are restrictions on the type of activities that can be undertaken. Permitted activities include:

- attending meetings, including interviews that have been arranged before coming to the UK, or conferences;
- arranging deals or negotiating or signing trade agreements or contracts;
- acting as an adviser or consultant to a UK firm;
- speaking at a conference where this is not run as a commercial concern and the conference is a "one off";
- undertaking fact-finding missions; and
- undertaking specific, one-off training in techniques and work practices used in the UK, provided this is not on-the-job training.

Advisers, consultants, trainers or troubleshooters entering the UK as business visitors must be employed abroad, either directly or under contract, by the same company (or group of companies) to which the UK company belongs. In addition, they must not get involved in actual project management or provide direct consultancy services to clients of the UK company. A business visitor must:

- only intend to transact business directly linked to his/her employment abroad;
- normally live and work abroad and have no intention of transferring his/her base to the UK (even on a temporary basis); and
- receive a salary from abroad (although reasonable expenses may be paid for travel and subsistence during the visit).

Recent changes also mean that in restricted circumstances, secondees from overseas companies that are not linked to the UK company may also qualify as business visitors.

HOW DO I KNOW IF I NEED TO OBTAIN A VISA BEFORE TRAVELLING TO THE UK?

Not all individuals travelling to the UK require a visa. The Foreign and Commonwealth Office website[1] has a list of all countries from which nationals will require a visa before travelling to the UK.

1 www.ukvisas.gov.uk

Entry clearance

If an individual is already legally in the UK but is changing their immigration status from one category to another, they can sometimes "switch" their immigration status without leaving the UK. This requires the applicant to make an application to the UK Border Agency before their current leave to remain ends, although they will need to check whether they are eligible to "switch" in-country.

Most visa applications under the PBS will require an application for prior entry clearance before the individual can travel to the UK. If an application for entry clearance is required, the applicant must make their application to a British Diplomatic Post in their country of nationality or legal residence before travelling to the UK.

IF I HAVE A SCHENGEN VISA, DOES THIS ALLOW ME TO TRAVEL TO THE UK?

A Schengen visa allows an individual to travel freely among its European member countries. The UK is not part of the Schengen Treaty and therefore having a Schengen visa will not permit someone who would otherwise need a visa and/or other immigration permission to enter the UK. As of May 2010, the Schengen Treaty countries are:

Austria	Hungary	Poland
Belgium	Iceland	Portugal
Czech Republic	Italy	Slovakia
Denmark	Latvia	Slovenia
Estonia	Lithuania	Spain
Finland	Luxembourg	Sweden
France	Malta	
Germany		
Switzerland	The Netherlands	
Greece	Norway	

Schengen visas are issued for varying amounts of time, but an individual will be allowed a maximum stay of 90 days within any six-month period. The scheme is intended for individuals who wish to move around Schengen member states for the purposes of business and tourism. A Schengen visa does not provide a right to work in a Schengen participating country, and in order to do so, an individual will generally need to obtain permission to work from the relevant country.

WHAT RIGHTS DO I HAVE AS A EUROPEAN UNION NATIONAL?

Nationals of certain countries have the right to live and work in the UK. This is known as a right of residence. Nationals with a right of residence include:

● nationals of the European Union (EU);
● nationals of Iceland, Liechtenstein and Norway; and
● Swiss nationals.

Iceland, Liechtenstein and Norway are not EU countries but are part of the European Economic Area (EEA) Agreement, which provides nationals of these countries with the same rights to enter, live and work in the UK as EU citizens. Swiss nationals are also included in the definition of "EEA nationals". Although not essential, people from the EEA can apply for a UK residence permit.

Nationals of those EU member states that have joined since 2004 (except Cyprus and Malta), namely Czech Republic, Estonia, Hungary, Latvia, Lithuania, Poland, Slovakia or Slovenia, who wish to work for more than one month for an employer in the UK need to register under the Worker Registration Scheme (WRS) (unless they are going to be self-employed). Once they have been working legally in the UK for 12 months without a break, they will acquire full rights of free movement and will no longer need to register under the WRS; they can then apply for a residence permit confirming their right to live and work in the UK. Nationals of Bulgaria and Romania, despite being EU citizens, will still need to obtain authorization to work before starting any employment.

Where an individual has a right of residence, their spouse/partner, children under 21 and other dependant relatives may generally join them in the UK. However, if their family members are non-EEA nationals, they should get an EEA family permit, which is a form of entry clearance (like a visa) prior to travelling to the UK. The spouse/partner of an EEA national is permitted to work in the UK without requiring his/her own permission to do so.

If an individual is not an EEA national or the family member of an EEA national, they will generally require permission to undertake employment in the UK. Permission will be required even if they are going to undertake work-based training for a professional or specialist qualification, or a period of work experience.

TIER 1 OF THE PBS

The Tier 1 (General) category is designed to allow highly skilled workers to come to the UK to look for work or self-employment opportunities. Points are scored for qualifications, previous earnings, UK experience, age, English language skills and available maintenance (funds). Tier 1 (General) is an attractive option for applicants as it is a permission to work that is granted to them personally, and is not attached to any particular employer. This category was adapted in April 2010 to open it up to more highly skilled and high earning individuals.

An applicant needs to score a minimum of 75 points for attributes. An additional 10 points are required for English language and 10 points for available maintenance (funds) to qualify as a highly skilled worker. Points for attributes are scored in three main areas:

1. educational qualifications;
2. previous earnings; and
3. UK experience.

In relation to educational qualifications, an applicant will score points according to the highest level of educational qualifications that they hold; this can be a PhD, a Master's degree or a Bachelor's degree. It should be noted that since April 2010, individuals who do not have any qualifications can also qualify if their previous earnings are sufficiently high.

Points for previous earnings are based on gross earnings before tax, over a total period of up to 12 months in the 15-month period prior to the application being made. This can include total earnings from several jobs or from self-employment. The points scored depend on the amount earned in accordance with bandings for various countries. Points can also be earned for previous experience of living in the UK through either earnings under the scheme or the completion of qualifying studies in the UK. In recognition of the difficulties experienced by younger applicants in meeting the earnings categories, there are points available on a graded scale for those under 40 years of age at the time of applying. Applicants must have received a salary of £25,000 or above (after converting the currency and applying the uplift ratio where appropriate, depending on the country where the money was earned) during their previous employment in order to claim points under the "previous earnings" attribute. An applicant must have a minimum level of understanding of the English language and score 10 points in this section. This may require an applicant to pass an English language test, although this may be avoided if an applicant is a national of a majority English-speaking country, or holds a Bachelor's degree (or above) that was taught in English.

Applicants who obtain their Bachelor's or Master's degree and certain other post graduate qualifications in the UK can apply for a Tier 1 (Post-Study Work) visa within 12 months of obtaining the relevant qualification. This is a two year visa that allows the individual to work in the UK and accumulate enough earnings to qualify under Tier 1 (General) or meet the requirements of another visa category, such as Tier 2. It should be noted that, as with student visas, time in the UK under Tier 1 (Post-Study Work) cannot be taken into account when calculating the length of UK residence required for Indefinite Leave to Remain (see below). In addition, students who have obtained a postgraduate diploma or certificate will no longer be able to apply under the Post-Study Work category, unless they have a UK Postgraduate Certificate in Education (awarded to trainee teachers).

CAN I ESTABLISH A BUSINESS IN THE UK?

Under Tier 1 (Entrepreneur) of the PBS, an individual may apply for entry into the UK in order to set up, take over and be actively involved in the running of one or more businesses. To apply under the PBS and be accepted into the Tier 1 (Entrepreneur) category, an applicant must pass a points-based assessment, and must score a minimum of 75 points for attributes, 10 points for English language and 10 points for available maintenance (funds). They will need to have access to £200,000, which must be in a regulated financial institution and disposable in the UK. They must also provide the UK Border Agency with a letter from each financial institution holding the money, confirming the amount of money available, as well as additional evidence of third-party funding. This £200,000 fund should be invested into a new or existing UK business within three months of the visa being granted.

ARE THERE SPECIAL RULES FOR INVESTORS IN THE UK?

An application under Tier 1 (Investor) is suitable for individuals who have substantial capital assets available to invest in the UK, and who wish to make the UK their main home. In order to be granted leave to enter the UK under this category, an applicant needs to show that they have at least £1 million to bring to the UK (this can either be their own money over which they have full control, i.e. not held in a trust or similar restriction, or be money borrowed from a Financial Services Authority regulated institution if they have a personal net worth of at least £2 million).

Where the loan method is chosen, the calculation of net worth may include not only financial assets, but also property. Assets held through an offshore company or trust, where the applicant is the beneficiary, can be taken into account when assessing personal net worth.

These funds need to be held by the applicant for the three months prior to the application or they need to show the source of the funds. Within three months of the visa being granted or the date they first enter the UK under this visa, the applicant must bring £1million into the UK (if it is not here already) and invest at least £750,000 of their capital in UK government bonds, or in share capital or loan capital in active and trading UK registered companies (other than property investment companies). There is more flexibility regarding the remaining £250,000, however it must be held or invested in the UK.

Applicants are now permitted to seek employment or can be self-employed or non-executive directors/consultants.

In addition, it is possible for a potential investor currently in the UK under certain other immigration categories to "switch" into the Tier 1 (Investor) category. Furthermore, once established in the UK, the investor can extend their stay in the UK, provided that they can show sufficient evidence that they have invested at least £750,000 within three months of arriving in the UK and still have a net worth of over £1 million in the UK.

Unlike most of the other categories, there is no English language requirement to qualify for this visa.

TIER 2 OF THE PBS

Tier 2 of the PBS incorporates and adapts the old work permit regime. The main change to the system is that employers require a sponsorship licence and are required to issue certificates of sponsorship to employees they wish to employ. The employee will then apply to their local entry clearance officer (embassy/visa application centre) for entry into the UK to work, at which stage the UK Border Agency will assess the application to ensure the applicant scores sufficient points to qualify. Points will be awarded based on aptitude, experience and age, as well as the level of need in any given sector.

Tier 2 (Skilled Migrant) is available in two categories:

1. Tier 2 (General); and
2. Tier 2 (Intra-Company Transfer).

Tier 2 (Intra-Company Transfer) applications involve a simplified procedure where the employee of a global company is transferring to a skilled post in a UK-based branch of the same company. Since April 2010 this category has been split into 3 subcategories:

3. Established Staff – for those who have worked for the company outside the UK for 12 months or more;
4. Graduate Trainees – to allow multi-national organisations to transfer recent graduate recruits to the UK business for up to 12 months of training; or
5. Skills Transfer – for migrants to transfer to an organisation or UK business to learn or transfer skills and knowledge to/from the UK offices for a period of 6 months.

Before an application is made under this category, the applicant must have:

● a sponsor; and
● a valid certificate of sponsorship.

When an application is made, the applicant is awarded points based on their:

● qualifications;
● future expected earnings;
● sponsorship;
● English language skills; and
● available maintenance (funds).

When applying for permission to come to the UK under this category, or extending their permission to stay, the applicant does not have to meet the English language requirement if their extension does not take the time of their stay to more than three years.

Other applications may fall within the Tier 2 (General) category and, in addition to requiring numerous supporting documents to show that the applicant has the skills, qualifications and experience purported, require the employer to show that it cannot fill the post with a "resident worker" (including EEA nationals). This usually involves advertising the post in Jobcentre Plus and other methods, which depend on the relevant industry sector that the job is in.

CAN I COME TO THE UK AS A SOLE REPRESENTATIVE OF AN OVERSEAS FIRM?

A sole representative application is only suitable where an overseas company that does not have a presence in the UK wishes to send one of its existing employees to set up a wholly owned subsidiary or register a branch. The company must be in genuine operation; where it has been established for less than one year, it is unlikely to be deemed an eligible sponsor for these purposes.

In order for an application to be considered, the individual must:

● be authorised to take operational decisions on behalf of the overseas firm without reference to the parent company;
● have been recruited to the parent company from outside of the UK;
● be directly employed by the company; and
● have been employed by the parent company for some time and hold a senior post.

The employee must not, however, be a major shareholder in the overseas company and should not intend to carry out any other work while in the UK. In addition, the individual must be able to support themselves (and any dependants) in the UK, without recourse to public funds.

A sole representative application is normally made by the individual employee at a British Diplomatic Post in their country of nationality or legal residence. Applicants are expected to spend a minimum of nine months a year in the UK; those who spend less time than this are not considered to be making genuine efforts to establish a commercial presence here.

Once an application has been successful, the sponsor company must continue to conduct the majority of its business overseas. It will not be permitted to gradually move its operation to the UK by exploitation of this category.

INDEFINITE LEAVE TO REMAIN (SETTLEMENT)

Generally speaking, an individual will become eligible to apply for indefinite leave to remain after they have spent a requisite period of time in the UK; for most people, this is five years continuous and lawful residence in a qualifying category. Adult applicants (aged 18-65) are required to demonstrate knowledge of language and life in the UK, in addition to meeting the usual requirements for settlement. Certain applicants will need to pass a "Life in the UK" test or will otherwise be required to pass an approved English for speakers of other languages (ESOL) qualification.

Once settlement is granted, there will no longer be any immigration related restrictions on the work or business the individual may do in the UK, and no time limits on their stay here, provided that in general they do not spend longer than two years outside of the UK, maintain ties here and consider the UK to be their home.

From July 2010 this category is to be closed to new applicants and will be replaced by probationary citizenship (see below).

BRITISH NATIONALITY

An individual can normally apply for naturalization as a British citizen one year after being granted indefinite leave to remain and as long as they meet the residence requirements. There are two ways to naturalise as a British citizen:

1. naturalization based on five years' residence in the UK; and
2. naturalization based on marriage/civil partnership and residence in the UK.

There are various requirements that will need to be satisfied, such as age, capacity, residence requirements, good character, language skills and intention. The applicant will also need to pass an ESOL course or "Life in the UK" test. If the application is approved, the applicant will be required to attend a citizenship ceremony after which a certificate of naturalization is issued. Once naturalised, they are eligible to apply for a British passport.

The Borders, Citizenship and Immigration Act 2009 will introduce several changes to the naturalisation and permanent residence process in the UK. The Act introduces an initial stage of probationary citizenship, following which an applicant progresses to either full (earned) citizenship or permanent residence. The process to citizenship will be faster for those who carry out government recognised voluntary work and longer for those who do not.

An important change to note is that, in order to obtain probationary citizenship, an applicant cannot have spent more than 90 days per year outside the UK over the previous 5 years (subject to potential UKBA discretion), whereas previously absences were averaged over that period (except the final year).

Note: The information contained in this chapter is correct at the time of writing, but the authors would recommend that readers check the current position.

2.6 MONEY LAUNDERING REGULATIONS

Mark Saunders
Wilder Coe LLP

INTRODUCTION

In accordance with the requirements of the Second European Community Money Laundering Directive of 2001, the United Kingdom government introduced the Proceeds of Crime Act 2002 and the Money Laundering Regulations 2003 which came into force largely with effect from 1st March 2003. The legislation has since been updated and the latest rules are contained within The Money Laundering Regulations 2007.

The purpose of the Money Laundering Regulations is to implement a regime whereby those businesses and individuals operating within the "regulated sector" will report any knowledge or suspicions of money laundering they might have to the Serious Organised Crime Agency (SOCA)

WHAT IS MONEY LAUNDERING?

Originally, Money Laundering legislation concerned itself primarily with identifying funds which are the result of terrorist activities or illegal drug trafficking.

However the scope of the legislation was widened to encompass the possession, dealing with, or concealing the proceeds of any crime. This obviously still includes terrorist funds, funds that may be used for terrorist purposes or the proceeds of terrorism or illegal drug trafficking.

Money laundering involves the hiding, converting, transferring or taking out of the country of any criminal proceeds. It covers anyone who agrees to or is involved in helping, or suspects that are involved in helping another person to acquire, keep or use criminal property. It also includes anyone who themself acquires, uses or possesses any criminal property.

Criminal property in this case includes anything, whether it is money or property, by which a person or company gains, either directly or indirectly, as a result of criminal activity. It is worth clarifying that this definition of criminal property also covers the proceeds of tax evasion, bribery or corruption.

WHICH BUSINESSES HAVE TO COMPLY WITH MONEY LAUNDERING REGULATIONS?

The regulations define relevant businesses– being those businesses that have to comply with the money laundering regulations – as including: -

- banking generally;
- any business that accepts deposits;
- the effecting or carrying out of long term insurance;
- dealing in investments either as principal or as an agent;
- arranging deals and investments;
- managing, safeguarding or administering investments;
- advising on investments;
- the operation of a Bureau de Change;
- transmitting money by any means or cashing cheques which are made payable to customers.
- estate agency;
- casino operation;
- insolvency practitioners;
- those who offer tax advice;
- those who offer accountancy services;
- those who offer auditing services;
- those who offer legal services;
- those who offer services in relation to the formation, operation or management of a company or trust;
- those dealing in goods of any description where a transaction will involve

the acceptance of a cash payment of 15,000 euros or more – this includes acting as an auctioneer.

It can be seen that the above list largely involves those individuals and businesses that are involved in financial transactions. Significantly, it includes banks, accountants, solicitors and estate agents, at least one of whom is likely to be involved in assisting any proposed new business within the United Kingdom.

REQUIREMENTS FOR BUSINESSES IN THE REGULATED SECTORS
Businesses and individuals within these regulated sectors need to do the following

1. Appoint a representative who will be the money laundering reporting officer.
2. Train all employees in relevant positions in recognising and reporting money laundering. Those employees will be responsible for reporting to the money laundering reporting officer.
3. The money laundering reporting officer has a responsibility to report any knowledge or suspicion that a money laundering offence has been committed to the SOCA. This report has to be made no matter how small the amounts involved or how serious the offence appears to be.
4. In a situation where a report has been made the persons making the report must do nothing to help the suspected money launderer for a period of 7 days unless told to do so by the SOCA. This may result in any work on a particular transaction being suspended during this period. If nothing is heard from the SOCA at the conclusion of that period of 7 days, then the reporting business can continue to deal with the respective transaction. If the reporting business is in itself not involved in the transaction but has become aware of its suspicious nature and has reported it then they do not need to await any consent from the SOCA to continue working.
5. Maintain Identification Procedures in respect of every business and individual with whom they do business (see below).

"TIPPING OFF" AND FAILURE TO MAKE A REPORT
The law makes it an offence to "tip off" a suspected money launderer that a report has been made or is contemplated to the SOCA. It is also an offence to fail

to make a suspicious transaction report.

Further, it is an offence for any person who receives information in the course of their business within the regulated sector to fail to inform SOCA or their businesses money laundering reporting officer of that knowledge or suspicion that another person is engaged in money laundering.

The penalties for failure to report or tipping off can lead to prison sentences of up to 5 years and monetary fines.

IDENTIFICATION PROCEDURES

Every business within the regulated sector will be required to maintain identification procedures with regard to every person and business with which they do business. This means that, as soon as is reasonably practicable after contact is first made with a business or individual, that this business or individual must produce satisfactory evidence of their identity and their residential or business address. This would usually require the provision of at least 2 documents.

For an individual the documents would include:

- In order to confirm identity – a current signed passport, a UK photo card driving license or a home office residency permit.
- In order to confirm address – a recent utility bill, local authority tax bill or bank or building society or mortgage statement. In some cases a visit to the persons home may establish proof of address.
- With regard to a corporation, a copy of the deed of incorporation would confirm identity and, if the entity is within the United Kingdom, this can be checked with details held at Companies House. In other nationalities if there are similar public registers then this information can be checked independently.

In order to obtain proof of address of a company then similar evidence to that above including utility bills or rent statements would suffice, or once again a visit to the company's premises.

In the case of unincorporated organisations such as trusts or partnerships, then a copy of the trust or partnership deed would be obtained and similar identification procedures to those relating to individuals carried out in respect of each trustee or partner.

Businesses within the regulated sector are required to maintain evidence of the identity checks they have made.

Checks should also be made against the databases of Politically Exposed Persons, Specially Designated Nationals and those on the Bank of England Sanctions Register. There are now a number of commercial agencies who carry out such checks electronically on behalf of Businesses in the Regulated Sectors.

PRACTICAL CONSIDERATIONS FOR THOSE CONSIDERING DOING BUSINESS WITHIN THE UNITED KINGDOM

For anyone considering doing business within the United Kingdom it is almost inevitable that they will have contact and carry out business with one or more organisation within the regulated sectors. The most basic business functions such as opening a bank account or appointing an accountant or lawyer will require compliance with identification procedures.

Under such circumstances, therefore, each such business should be prepared to provide the identification evidence indicated above. Having such evidence readily available and having anticipated a need to provide it will greatly facilitate commencing business within the United Kingdom.

Secondly, in order not to arouse suspicion that any transaction taking place could conceivably be construed as money laundering it would be wise to be as frank and open as possible in relation to any business carried out. Details of the source of all funds being used should be freely shared and at no point in time should any doubt be allowed to enter into the details of any transaction. Most business and trading activities will be of a relatively routine and repetitive nature and should never cause a problem. It is likely to be the unusual or large transactions that might arouse doubt or suspicion.

A ready compliance with all United Kingdom taxation requirements would also be recommended, particularly those relating to employment tax – Pay As You Earn (PAYE) – which should be administered by all employers, and VAT.

TRADING IN THE REGULATED SECTORS

If you are considering commencing a business within the United Kingdom that falls within one of the regulated sectors, then you will clearly need to comply with the requirements of the money laundering regulations.

Many of the regulated sectors have their own professional bodies or trade associations who will be able to advise on the specific requirements of the business sector in which the operations are planned to take place. In the case of any doubt advice should be sought at the earliest possible opportunity. In such cases professional advisors such as accountants or solicitors, who should all be well versed in the obligations of the money laundering regulations as they relate to their own activities, should be able to advise on how to proceed.

CONCLUSION

Similar regulations to those being applied in the United Kingdom have been enacted throughout the world. The legislation continues to be developed and it is important to keep abreast of these changes.

The international fight against terrorism and drug trafficking, which has provided the impetus for this kind of legislation, has caused it to be expanded to include all areas of crime in particular the areas of tax evasion and the 'cash' economy. However, compliance with these regulations should hold no fears for those involved in honest business activity and, although the cost of compliance in terms of time and money may initially seem great, the eradication of crime from business should result in a level playing field for all and greater integrity within the business environment worldwide.

Part Three

3.1 THE AUTOMOTIVE INDUSTRY

Mark Norcliffe
TheSourcingSolutions Ltd

AT THE CROSSROADS

At the end of the 20th century – a century once dubbed "the age of the motor car" – the global automotive industry appeared to have entered a period of stability and continuity. The mature markets of the USA, Europe and Japan accounted for the lion's share of both sales and production. Vehicle development was evolutionary rather than revolutionary, and the internal combustion engine was the almost universally accepted form of propulsion.

After a period of rationalisation, a dozen multinational car manufacturers – each building more than one million units per annum – dominated global sales. A second group of regional manufacturers principally served their own domestic markets. A similar process of consolidation had also taken place in the components sector, with major tier 1 suppliers acquiring smaller companies, as they positioned themselves to produce whole vehicle systems for the car makers in whatever region of the world their customer chose to assemble vehicles.

But, less than a decade into the new century, new challenges have arisen to disrupt the established order. Whilst sales in mature territories have slumped against a background of economic uncertainty, developing markets are surging ahead. China leapt past the USA in 2009 to become the world's largest car market, and India and Brazil have also shown impressive growth. The epicentre of the world auto industry is shifting. At the same time, new competitors are emerging from these countries to challenge the established automakers on the global stage. Faced with declining sales and production over-capacity, even the global industry giants have struggled. General Motors briefly entered bankruptcy and Ford has sold off non-core brands. Many of the component conglomerates, assembled only a few years ago, have unravelled.

At the same time, auto companies are under intense pressure to develop a new generation of low carbon vehicles, which will simultaneously reduce dependency on fossil fuels and cut emissions. The best technologies, market potential and likely costs for such new-energy vehicles are still far from clear. In 2010, the future direction and development of the global auto industry appears much more fragmented and uncertain that it did a decade earlier.

This shifting landscape has major implications for countries and/or regions seeking to bolster their economies by attracting inward automotive investment. Potential new investors are appearing, but the scope and style of their projects, and the products, skills and infrastructure that they require are all changing. Meanwhile, existing investors are seeking to re-structure their existing operations to match the trends within the industry.

A BRIEF HISTORY OF AUTOMOTIVE INVESTMENT IN THE UNITED KINGDOM

The UK has a long tradition of attracting automotive inward investment. Ford Motor Co started building cars in the UK as long ago as 1911, and General Motors, naming the Vauxhall brand after its first production site in South London, was not far behind. Component suppliers from both Europe and America also arrived to support both these foreign VM's and the fragmented domestic manufacturers.

The pace quickened in the 1980's with the arrival of the Japanese. Nissan, Toyota and Honda all chose the UK as their manufacturing base within the European Community. In each case – Nissan in Sunderland, Toyota in Burnaston, and Honda in Swindon – they elected to construct new, modern plants in areas with a strong tradition of engineering skills, but high levels of unemployment. They also brought their lean manufacturing philosophy and their major component suppliers, who either established their own facilities or amalgamated with existing British companies.

Throughout this period of expansion, the UK government and industry pursued an "open door" policy to inward investors, in marked contrast to some EU countries where there were dark mutterings about "a Japanese aircraft carrier, moored off the European coast." Their reward was a rejuvenation of the British motor industry. Productivity and quality standards soared. In 1982, the UK turned out only 888,000 vehicles – by 2005, production peaked at over 1.8 million units.

A further wave of investors took over existing production facilities during the 1990's, though with mixed fortunes. Despite achieving record production levels at the former Rootes/Chrysler plant at Ryton, PSA concluded that it did not match their global plans and withdrew in 2007; BMW divested itself of the old Rover Group in 2000 (although retaining and greatly expanding the Mini brand) and Ford acquired but subsequently re-sold Jaguar and Land Rover – to India's rapidly expanding Tata Group. By this time the pattern of automotive investment in Europe was irrevocably changing, with the new EU member states in Central Europe offering cheaper land and labour for mass production plants.

The UK was, however, already promoting new investment trends, which are likely to take on increasing significance in the changing automotive landscape of the 21st century. Encouraged by the availability of local engineering expertise, government support and a discerning customer base, a number of global automakers have established major design and development centres in the UK.

Again, Ford was one of the first on the scene. Its R&D centre at Dunton, Essex opened in the 1960's and has grown to become the global base for small and medium-sized passenger car projects. Ford expects to invest £1.5 billion, over a five year period from 2010, in new engine and other research programmes. Nissan's European R&D facility, inaugurated at Cranfield, Bedfordshire in 1991, was responsible for re-engineering the Primera, Micra and Terrano models for the European market, and was heavily involved in the development of the best-selling Qashqai model, which is now built in Sunderland and other plants around the world. More recently, India's Tata group has underpinned its acquisition of Jaguar Land Rover by entrusting much of its luxury model development work to its UK subsidiary, whilst China's SAIC Motor Corporation and ChangAn Motors have both opened R&D operations in the Midlands.

The UK has also nurtured a reputation as a good place to build premium and specialist models, for which British heritage and craftsmanship are strong selling points. The BMW-owned Mini is perhaps the most striking example of this trend. Annual production at the Cowley, Oxford plant now tops 200,000 – more than double the volume originally predicted. Both VW and BMW have found it advantageous to keep the assembly of their respective Bentley and Rolls Royce luxury brands within the UK. Tata Group is now hoping to achieve similar success with the Jaguar and Land Rover brands. The UK is the second largest producer of premium cars in the world.

THE UK MOTOR INDUSTRY TODAY

The combination of native engineering and production skills with the capital and best practice injected by foreign investors – all supported by the "open door" policy of successive governments – has created a strong, modern industry that contributes substantially to the UK's overall economic performance.

Today, seven global car manufacturers and eight commercial vehicle builders have production facilities in the UK. They are complemented by more than 30 niche vehicle makers, to create the most diverse automotive mix in Europe. To support this range of production, 19 of the world's top 20 component suppliers also have a presence in the UK. British-based assembly plants are regularly rated the most productive in Europe.

Total automotive turnover is estimated at £51 billion, and the sector provides employment – directly or indirectly – for around 800,000 workers. Annual automotive exports, worth in excess of £26 billion, account for more than 10% of the UK's total export earnings.

AREAS OF SPECIAL EXPERTISE

The UK has gained a global reputation for excellence in some of the motor industry's most dynamic, competitive and technically innovative sectors.

Motorsport

In the high-octane world of motorsport, the UK is a clear world leader. At the pinnacle of the sport, it provides the home base for eight of the twelve Formula One teams, who need a unique blend of engineering skills and rapid development capability. In rallying and other racing disciplines, top competitors also rely on British experts to build, tune and maintain their cars. New technologies first developed for use in motorsport often migrate into mainstream vehicle engineering – KERS (Kinetic Energy Recovery Systems) is one recent example.

Engine development and production

The UK is also a recognised centre for the development and production of modern, efficient engines. British companies that have been behind some of the world's most famous propulsion units – names like Lotus, Ricardo and Cosworth – continue to offer their design and engineering expertise to international customers for both conventional internal combustion engines and alternative energy electrical and hybrid systems. To utilise the advantages offered by the combination of these development skills and a sophisticated component supply base, global manufacturers – such as BMW, Ford, Honda, Nissan and Toyota – have designated the UK as a key location for engine manufacturing. In 2008, over 3 million units were produced in UK plants.

University research

Many British universities have an international reputation for conducting advanced automotive research, usually in collaboration with industrial partners. At a time when automotive companies are faced with the additional challenge of exploring and developing new technologies (e g battery composition) alongside their "traditional" products, it is especially valuable to have access to such academic research resources.

UK SUCCESSES IN MEETING THE NEW CHALLENGES

The pattern of 21st century automotive investment in Europe will be very different from model followed during the industry's first 100 years. Rapid expansion during that time has left a legacy of production over-capacity, and, for the immediate future, it is unlikely that any new vehicle assembly plants will be built within the European Union.

Against this background, the primary challenge is to maintain production in existing facilities, and to ensure that both the plants themselves and the supply chain that support them have the capability to build the latest generation of vehicles, including the low carbon, new-energy products that are now moving into volume production. On this front, the UK has already received a substantial vote of confidence from existing automotive investors. Nissan has announced that the Leaf electric vehicle will be built at their Sunderland plant from 2013, and work has already commenced work on an adjacent site to produce the battery packs. Meanwhile, Toyota has launched the hybrid version of the Auris, driven by an engine wholly produced at their Deeside factory – the first time that the company has built hybrid power units outside Japan.

The UK has also been successful in winning automotive investment from new sources – particularly the emerging economies of China and India.

When Indian industrial giant Tata Group bought Jaguar Cars and Land Rover from Ford there were initial fears that the purchase could lead to the transfer of production out of the UK and consequent job losses. However, in reality the change of ownership has lead to considerable investment in JLR's engineering capability to support a range of new vehicle programmes.

The take-over of MG Rover's assets by two Chinese automakers – Shanghai Automobile Industry Corp (SAIC) and Nanjing Automobile Corp (NAC) – also made an unpromising start. But once the Chinese government had pressured the rival suitors into a merger, a clearer, and more positive, business strategy has emerged. Following a period of co-operation with Ricardo, SAIC has now inaugurated its own European Engineering Technical Centre on the old Longbridge site, with a multi-million pound investment and a brief to develop the company's future models and power units. Another Chinese vehicle manufacturer – ChangAn Automobile Group – has also announced that it will locate its European R&D Centre at Nottingham, where it eventually expects to employ 200 engineers. As a result, the UK will become home to the European operations for two of the top three automakers in China, and British engineering DNA will be in many of the new models appearing in the world's largest auto market.

It is not just vehicle manufacturers who have been making new investments. Producers of the new components and systems that will be required by the low carbon and electric cars of the future also see the UK as an attractive location. Contour Energy Systems from the USA are just one example of the new breed of component suppliers who have established a British base.

WHAT THE UK OFFERS : AN INTEGRATED APPROACH AND A CLEAR ROADMAP

For the last 20 years automotive investors have been attracted to the UK by, and have benefited from, such factors as :

- a stable, low-inflation economy;
- a generally strong domestic market;
- good labour relations and flexible working practices, which allow UK plants to achieve high levels of productivity;

- an open business environment, with a welcoming approach to inward investors from both government and industry;
- a skilled and professional workforce, with a strong tradition in engineering and production skills. (The decline in sectors such as shipbuilding and railways has given inward investors the opportunity to establish greenfield operations close to existing pools of engineering talent);
- a network of research and development centres, embracing world-class testing facilities, independent design engineering companies and academic institutions.

The Automotive Council

Both industry and government recognise the need to build on these strengths with a clear vision and plan for the future. They have, therefore, set up the high-level Automotive Council to ensure that the UK takes a leading role in the transition to new-energy vehicles, that the local supply chain is capable of meeting the new technological challenges, and that the brands, skills and opportunities with the British motor industry are properly promoted.

The Council has drawn up a technology roadmap, charting the expected course of vehicle development over the next 20-30 years. It demonstrates that, over this period, there will be a number of different technologies in the market, some of which will be more dominant and sustained than others. The roadmap now forms the basis for a prioritised research agenda, covering short, medium and long-term projects. It also forms the background to a matrix of the UK's advanced technology capabilities.

A broad package of support measures has been unveiled to encourage the development, production and sale of new-energy vehicles in the UK. In addition to £150 million for specific R&D projects these include :

- £30 million to support pilot charging infrastructure schemes;
- £25 million for vehicle trial programmes;
- Buyer incentives, including a grant of up to £5,000 on the purchase price, and tax exemptions.

The Technology Strategy Board and Knowledge Transfer Networks

Complementing the Automotive Council, the Technology Strategy Board channels, and funds, research into the most promising innovative technologies whilst specialist Knowledge Transfer Networks (KTN's) are tasked with encouraging information exchange and best practice. Particularly relevant to the automotive sector are:

- Cenex, which takes the lead on low carbon and fuel cell technologies in transportation; and
- InnovITS, which focuses on transport telematics and technology for sustainable mobility.

A practical demonstration of the latter's work is the construction – on the MIRA site near Nuneaton – of a world-leading facility specifically designed for the testing and development of Intelligent Transport Systems in a controlled, but realistic, operating environment.

Industry Forum & SEMTA

Work on continuously raising standards within the UK-based supply chain rests with Industry Forum – a joint government/industry initiative originally started in 1996 to provide practical training to automotive component producers, but so successful that its role has been expanded into other manufacturing sectors – and with the Sector Skills Council for Science, Engineering and Manufacturing Technologies (SEMTA), which has been promoting improved levels of skills and competitiveness since 2003.

THE ROAD AHEAD

The first quarter of the 21st century promises to be a challenging time for the automotive industry, with new markets, new players and new technologies coming to the fore. There will be many twists and turns – and a few dead-ends – on the road ahead.

To navigate this route successfully, automotive companies will need to be nimble and flexible, and able to operate in an environment that offers them both economic stability and a wide rage of skills and technologies. The UK, with an established reputation for offering a world-class development and production base and a clear blueprint for the future, is well placed to meet those needs.

Further information and key websites

Further information on patterns of automotive investment in the UK, and the support available, can be obtained from a variety of sources. These include:

The Department for Business, Innovation and Skills:	**www.bis.gov.uk**
UK Trade & Investment:	**www.ukti.gov.uk**
The Society of Motor Manufacturers and Traders:	**www.smmt.co.uk**
The Motorsport Industry Association:	**www.the-mia.com**
Industry Forum:	**www.industryforum.co.uk**
Technology Strategy Board:	**www.innovateuk.org**
Cenex:	**www.cenex.co.uk**
InnovITS:	**www.innovits.com**
Sector Skills Council:	**www.semta.org.uk**

3.2 AVIATION MANUFACTURING

Jonathan Reuvid
Legend Business

INDUSTRY STRUCTURE

Representation of the UK aviation manufacturing sector came under the umbrella of A|D|S from 1 October 2009 when the Association of Police and Public Security Suppliers (APPSS), the Defence Manufacturers Association (DMA) and the Society of British Aerospace Companies (SBAC) were merged, incorporating the British Aviation Group (BAG) and Farnborough International Ltd (FIL). As a single stream-lined organisation A|D|S is an effective trade body providing improved services and representation to promote the interests of UK companies operating in the civil aerospace, defence, security and space sectors.

Within A|D|S, BAG operates under its separate brand, representing the aviation and airport sector and running a separate programme of events and activities including overseas events that help UK companies to explore emerging markets and meet potential partners and customers. The Farnborough International Airshow managed by FIL is the internationally famous showcase for the technical development and new products of the British aerospace industry, attracting more than 1,500 companies from around the world and 180,000 trade visitors.

THE CIVIL AVIATION SECTOR

A key component of the UK's high value added engineering and manufacturing base, the civil aviation sector provides 100,000 direct and 225,000 indirect jobs and maintains its world market share through high levels of research and technical investment. Mitigating the effects of the recession and the downturn of the economic cycle has set a major challenge for members of the industry, particularly SME suppliers, over the next few years. Since the late 1990s, the UK's space sector has enjoyed annual growth around 9% and is possibly one of the UK's most underrated manufacturing sectors. The industry generates more than £20 billion annually in added value and contributes around £2.8 billion to the UK balance of trade.

A prime characteristic of the industry is its large scale need for a broad range of high value skills and disciplines, ranging from engineering and science to production and service, training and financial skills at every level. The industry has shown resilience through many economic cycles and is confident of doing so again in current difficult times.

Product offerings

Over the last 20 years, the sector has invested predominantly in wide-bodied aircraft enabling it to position itself as a worldwide leader within the aerospace industry. The investments have created sustainable intellectual property (IP) from the associated research, technology and development programmes. In addition to the significant high value-added manufacturing work which has been gained, the industry has developed, over the last 10 years, a service capability to support its product offering which has created additional jobs and captured more of the whole life value chain.

The civil aviation market

Global civil aviation may be defined as predominantly aircraft development, design, manufacture and support, including dual use civil/defence capabilities and products. Over the past 25 years it has grown by about 5% per annum, equivalent to about 1.7 times the growth rate of global GDP over the same period. In 2008, the global civil aerospace industry generated revenues of about US$130 billion of which 60% was for new deliveries in regional business, narrow body and wide body aircraft and civil helicopters, the areas of prime interest for the UK.

Looking ahead, in spite of the continuing impacts of the global recession over the next two or three years, the industry has been forecast to continue growing at an average rate of 5% over the next 20 years. Growth will be particularly strong in the Middle East, India and the Far East. Although growth is expected to fall short of this average over the next three years, the longer term forecast predicts a requirement for between 23,400 new fixed wing aircraft worth US$2.6 billion (Airbus New Aircraft Demand 2007-2026) and 29,400 aircraft worth US$3.2 billion (Boeing Current Market Outlook 2008-2027). In addition Augusta/Westland forecasts delivery of 30,000 rotorcraft up to 2027 worth about $300 billion. The strong growth forecasts take into account the expectation of likely new environmental regulations and considerations within the same timescale.

Although the barriers to entry are higher for civil aerospace than for many other manufacturing industries, the UK's current share of the global civil aerospace market is 17% with strong positions in the segments of:

● propulsion (engines);
● airframe (including wings);
● aircraft power and control systems.

Manufacturing timescales

A large scale civil aviation platform or engines programme involves very long timescales: a relatively steady engineering effort over the lifetime of the product; manufacturing workload peaking during the initial production phase; and a lengthy extended support 'tail'. As a consequence of this profile, the successful manufacturer needs to maintain a 'conveyor' belt of programmes to ensure that the various skills and employment populations are secured in the long term.

The entire global aviation sector is focused on achieving greater airspace efficiency while reducing overall costs and enhancing safety. With these objectives at the forefront of overall business strategy and having regard to the heavy up-front investment and exceptionally long programme lives, both airframe and engine original equipment manufacturers (OEMs) have increasingly shared development and programme risks with their supply chains, both domestic and international. As a result, the risk-sharing load of today's aviation industry is spread across a wide range of companies which, in turn, drives changes to investment funding demands.

Changes in market focus

As a result of the global recession, carriers have cur seat capacity across many market sectors; lower demand has exerted extreme pressures on many low cost carriers and the significant fall in premium traffic has caused disproportionate damage to the profitability of legacy airlines. Many aviation development and airport projects have been shelved with an even greater focus on cost reduction and value improvement. The formation of relationships with international partners and concentration on opportunities in emerging markets are paramount to future prosperity.

The focus on key emerging markets such as the BRIC countries (Brazil, Russia, India and China) is in response to the modernisation and expansion of their aircraft fleets and facilities to meet the rapid growth in demand of both domestic and international passengers. Major investment also continues to be made in Middle East states such as Saudi Arabia, Abu Dhabi, Oman, Kuwait, Bahrain and Qatar where BAG is active in helping its members to capture business.

THE AEROSPACE INDUSTRY IN THE UK
A strategic overview

The strategic aim of the UK aerospace industry is to secure the high value sector through:

- large scale, high value manufacturing;
- environmental acceptability;
- high value employment;
- capturing emerging growth opportunities.

The key enablers that the UK industry offers investors within an innovative business environment are a combination of:

- sector skill;
- strength and scale of supply chain;
- IP and knowhow;
- ATM policy and operation;
- Satellites and operations.

and these enablers are applied across the UK's range of competitive manufacturing capabilities in:

- Wing design and manufacture.
- Propulsion and support.
- Advanced structures.
- Control and power systems.
- System integration.
- Autonomous operation (UAS).
- Rotorcraft design and manufacture.

The key enablers are the essential foundation blocks for a successful outcome given an economic climate conducive to encouraging long term high value investment, development of the critical skills in high technology engineering and the maintenance of a robust supply chain. Of the competitive capabilities listed, wing, engine and systems integration are prominent features. Government support for the generation of large scale programmes with high value employment and the development of new capabilities within the sector is an essential ingredient.

Employment in the sector has been more stable than for other UK manufacturing sectors and average salaries for high skilled jobs are higher than the UK manufacturing average. Manufacturing is located in all UK regions. Research and Technology (R&T) investment is consistently high and is second only to the pharmaceutical industry in terms of R&T intensity, although it has lagged behind R&T investment in France, Germany, Italy, Spain and Sweden for several years. However, UK aerospace companies rank prominently in the Business Innovation and Skill (BIS) R&D scoreboard of top 10 investors. The "spillover" effects of R&T investment in aerospace have also been highlighted as being significantly larger than the manufacturing average.

Recognition that the aerospace industry is one of the highest in terms of gross value added and net capital investment per employee within manufacturing have contributed to conspicuous success in attracting investment into all areas of the sector.

New opportunities
There are substantial new opportunities for the UK aviation industry to exploit within the twenty year timescale of current industry planning. At the same time, there are growing challenges for the UK manufacturing base that aviation manufacturers need to address. The following are some of the identified opportunities:

- New short range (NSR) airframe, engines and advanced materials: the most important programme for sustaining and developing the existing UK indus-trial base; crucial as the technology driver for next generation aircraft.

- Unmanned aerial systems (UAS): an important emerging source of future growth in the civil sector where UAS experience in defence is a catalyst for development to achieve greater efficiency through autonomous systems, cost effectively and with enhanced safety.
- Next generation rotorcraft: focus on operational safety in all operating environments and lower cost of acquisition and ownership rather than higher levels of performance; driven by requirement for lower environmental footprint (particularly noise).
- Future air traffic Management (ATM): a crucial enabler in civil sector traffic growth for optimizing routes and flight paths; ATM improvements expected to contribute 10% towards European target for 2020 of reducing carbon dioxide emissions by 50%.

Challenges to the UK industrial base

Capturing the opportunities will be contingent upon addressing the following challenges to the UK industrial base:

- Technology driven by environmental legislation and regulations: require-ment for innovative technology solutions (particularly in propulsion) with higher degrees of innovation at both platform and total system's levels.
- Growth of strategic offset/outsourcing in low cost/emerging markets: tem-pered by need of certain OEMs to convert more of their cost base into US dollars.
- Determination of a number of governments to develop domestic competi-tion: challenges to established OEMS, such as Airbus and Boeing, and the top "Tier 1" suppliers.
- The switch from 'metal' manufacturing sites to composite facilities: will diminish the advantage of previously invested capital in the UK sector and, potentially, offer an advantage to overseas start-ups.
- The need to maintain sufficient scale and scope of activity within the UK: need for a firm industrial base able to invest substantial funds in R&T, pro-gramme participation and a high level of system integration.
- Air Traffic Management (ATM): with Single European Sky ATM Research Programme (SESAR) underway, a critical need for other ATM developments to ensure seamless operations within a coherent global environment.

Both industry and the Government will have to work effectively together to maintain UK participation in the face of new technology demands, growth in overseas competitors and market shifts. However, some of the pressures play to the UK's strong points, such as the environmental considerations driving technology development.

Supply chain manufacturing capability

A major capability of the UK aviation industry that distinguishes it from many of its overseas competitors is the strength and depth of its supply chain which will face a number of serious challenges ahead from the emergence of low cost and strategically positioned competitors (often with their own government's support) to the disadvantage of operating from a sterling cost base. However, the long term technical and risk management profile of the UK aerospace sector means that the current UK sector's scale and scope of activities are major advantages in positioning it for future industry demands.

The supply chain has evolved over the past 10 years, with significant consolidation resulting in stronger, more competitive companies and the outsourcing of responsibility and activity down the supply chain. For example, Airbus and BAE Systems have sold their Filton and Prestwick manufacturing operations to GKN and Spirit Aerospace respectively.

Organised and operated through A|D|S, 21st Century Supply Chain (SC21) is a major industry programme aimed at improving the operations of all levels of the supply chain. The SC21 mission is to embed best practice and a commitment to continuing improvement throughout the industry sector. To date awards have been made to 10 companies that have achieved world-class performance.

Major new investment in production facilities and equipment is underway as a result of the new aircraft entering service over the next five years, including the Airbus A350XWB, Bombardier CSeries and the Boeing 787. In many cases, the programmes involve the wholesale replacement of conventional plant and machinery with radically new, often composite, production capabilities. The SC21programme recognises that new levels of technical and responsibilities within the supply chain are emerging which are increasing the risk profile to the lower tiers of the supply chain.

Skills

The UK aerospace industry generates a high proportion of highly skilled jobs, with proportionally more graduates (34% in 2007) than any other manufacturing sector and an average annually salary across the sector estimated at £33,650 in respect of about 100,000 direct employees (nearly one third of the sector total), broken down (with some overlap explaining double-counting) between:

- R&D   - 26,000
- Production   - 75,000
- Maintenance, repair and overall (MRO)   - 12,000

In the aerospace industry, 2.5% of all 350,000 employees are apprentices and there is a high training completion rate of about 95%. The industry is committed to work with the Science, Engineering and Manufacturing Technologies Alliance (SEMTA) and the National Skills Academy for Manufacturing (NSAM) in support of the government objective of increasing the number of apprenticeships.

SUMMARY

The UK aviation industry will have to prove itself robust against a range of uncertain and changing macro-economic factors and the following are among the prerequisites for future success over the next 10 years and beyond:

The UK sector must retain scale

 The requirements for environmentally-driven R&T, the UK's pole position in key capabilities such as large wings, and propulsion systems and the urge of OEMs to team with a smaller number of highly capable partners are all drivers for scale.

Effective response to aerospace growth

There is a strong link between global GDP and passenger travel which will continue to drive the need for significant new aircraft, as well as greater airspace and airport capacity in spite of likely reductions in short haul operations in areas where viable alternative modes of transport become available. Capture of the follow-on in-service revenues is dependent on taking original equipment design and manufacture responsibilities (e.g. Rolls Royce).

Following shifts in the market

Over the next cycle the main driver for civil aerospace growth is expected to be the growth of Middle East, China and India passenger traffic rather than the US and Europe.

Drive to lower costs
The UK aviation industry must respond to the recent experience of both Airbus and Boeing in overcoming difficulties in putting their programmes into service on time and within budget by accepting increased risk management responsibility and addressing pressures for significant reductions in the in-service costs for the next generation of platforms.

Adapting to fixed infrastructures
Ground navigational aids necessary to achieve greater traffic capacity through reducing aircraft separations at airports while maintaining safety levels requires complementary technologies in aircraft systems design (e.g. satellite navigation).

Development of unconventional platforms and engines
Numerous unconventional concepts are under serious consideration for the NSR programmes, Such as open rotor engine architectures. (It is not yet clear whether any of these concepts will mature and be adopted).

Absorbing the impact of environmental legislation
The number and speed of measures introduced could have a major impact on the growth of the civil aerospace sector with serious distortion if the measures are not introduced globally. Addressing likely legislation will drive a number of key platform and operating system decisions involving high investment in R&T.
With continuing collaboration between all sub-sectors of the aerospace industry, industry bodies under A|D|S and the government, the UK aviation manufacturing sector is well placed to accept all these challenges and exploit the new business opportunities which each challenge presents.

Note: The content for this chapter is a distillation of the various current reports of A|D|S. Further information for potential investors about the aerospace industry and relevant contacts may be found by visiting the A|D|S website at: www.adsgroup.org.uk.

3.3 LIFE SCIENCES

Jonathan Reuvid
Legend Business
and Belinda Clarke
One Nucleus

A GLOBAL OVERVIEW

The UK is a global centre for life sciences creativity and delivery, enabling businesses to drive innovation through to market success.

As such, it is one of the high-tech industries that underpins and will further strengthen the UK economy. Already, the UK medical biotechnology sector is the European leader in the number of drugs in all stages of clinical development and, globally, is second only to the US in the number of bio-therapies in clinical trials.

Inward investors look for opportunities to reduce cost and achieve excellence. The UK is not the cheapest location for development of medical biotechnology but participants in the industry understand and are responsive to the cost drivers for companies; the UK industry offers the best value for money.

The sub-sectors of the life sciences industry discussed here are medical technology, medical biotechnology; and industrial biotechnology. As well as focusing on the management and therapies of disease, increasingly there is a strong interest in the "wellbeing" and assistive living market opportunities, in addition to bioscience underpinning the low carbon economy. Commercially, companies in each sector generate higher value products and services for their niche markets; many have potential global scale and require continuous innovation to be successful.

Medical technology market

The medical technology market worldwide is estimated at £150-170 billion with an annual growth rate of 10% predicted for the next 5-6 years. The drivers for this growth are the ageing of the world's population and increased per capita healthcare expenditure across developed markets. In these terms the value of the market is forecast to approach £300 billion by 2015.

Europe

In Europe medical technology expenditure represents 6% of overall healthcare expenditure and is on the increase as the capability of the technology is expanded by innovation. The European market worth £57 billion ranks second to the US with a supplier base employing 435,000 people.

USA

The US market is worth just over £70 billion and has a strong supply base of its own with most of the world's largest medical technology companies having domestic origins.

Medical biotechnology market

As a result of the rapid evolution of knowledge in genetics, medicinal chemistry, biochemistry and physiology, new small molecule drugs for diseases such as cancer and diabetes are being discovered and developed by innovative companies. The pressure to develop new drugs for unmet clinical needs continues; identifying at an early stage those molecules most likely to succeed or fail is an area in which the UK's capabilities can help reduce attrition rates, through its *in vitro* diagnostics capabilities and strengths in in silico molecule design.

Large molecules and biologics are the fastest growing group, accounting for 17% of global pharmaceutical sales with approximately 145 products on the market and 11% of all clinical tests involving a large molecule or biotechnology based product. The largest proportion of sales in global market therapies, however, is derived from therapies based on small molecules.

The global medical biotechnology market grew by more than 20% per annum over the period 2002-2007 which is more than twice the growth rate for the pharmaceutical market. The major product classes which account for over 45% of sales are erythropoeitins, anti-cancers and anti diabetic treatments.

As for medical technology, the US is the largest single market accounting for 65% of global sales.

Industrial biotechnology market

The strong growth potential of industrial biotechnology is driven by its ability to provide alternative production processes traditionally derived from fossil-based fuels. Using biological processes for the production of liquid fuels or renewable feedstocks for industrial processes are established technologies being used across the world. The UK is a leading player in this sector, ranging from a strong academic research base to demonstrator commercial fermentation facilities.

LIFE SCIENCES IN THE UK

The three life sciences sub-sectors discussed here (medical technology, medical biotechnology and industrial biotechnology) collectively employ 78,000 people in nearly 3,600 companies with combined sales of £15 billion. Many of these companies are developing innovative technologies, products and processes in diverse areas such as anti-cancer drugs, imaging and biopolymers. Importantly, the UK supply chain is well placed to serve all these sectors – all within a few hundred kilometres of each other. While other, lower cost markets are offering similar services, the high quality, robust and trustworthy foundations of the UK's sector provide an attractive return on investment.

Medical Technology Sector

The largest of the three sectors, medical technology serves a complex UK market ranging from systems that enable body scanning during minimally invasive surgery to consumables such as disposable surgical gloves. There are 2,771 companies in the sector employing 52,000 with annual sales estimated at £10.6 billion.

Product definition

The four largest sectors each with a turnover in excess of £1 billion collectively comprise 40% of total UK turnover and account for 41% of employees in the sub-sector. These are:

- wound care management;
- in-vitro diagnostics;
- orthopaedic devices; and
- single use technologies

Company size and activity profile

The composition of medical technology companies by number of employees shows that the sector consists primarily of small but active SMEs.

Almost 50% of companies employ less than 5 people, and around one third have 5-20 staff. Around 6% have a workforce of more than 100.

Geographicl dispersion

While medical technology companies are spread across the UK, there are some areas of concentration, the West Midlands, East Midlands and the East of England, together account for 42% of the total. The largest employer is Yorkshire and Humberside with 12% of the total UK medical technology workforce. London, the North East and Northern Ireland each have less than 100 companies.

Sector investment

There is recognition that the medical technology and biotechnology sectors share many of the same attractive features, such as strong growth rates and high barriers to entry; however, there is a shorter and less complex product approval process for medical technology products. In addition there is increasing convergence of technologies from both the medical technology and biotechnology sectors, such as in the development of drug-device combinations, which the UK is proactively pursuing.

All types of investment in the sector across the US and Europe decreased by 37% from 2007 to 2008. In Europe, total investment would have been down by 44% but for two large deals that contributed 73% of the total, thereby skewing the sector result.

Even in 2008, however, the UK attracted the highest level of venture capital (VC) financing after France and was second after Germany for all types of investment. The largest single deal in 2008 involved the UK company ApaTechTM, a developer of bone graft technologies.

Medical Biotechnology Sector

As the second largest sector in the life sciences industry with annual sales of £4.2 billion, UK medical biotechnology represents an estimated 30% of European and

9% of the global sector turnover. Again, the 777 companies in the field are dominated by SMEs. The sector collectively employs an impressive workforce of 24,000 (which represents 25% of the European medical biotechnology sector); of these, over half are engaged in working as R&D or fee-for-service companies in a network of specialist suppliers. The sector is driven by innovation and 86% of companies are engaged in R & D with a balance between established and young businesses. Some 26% of companies are invested in the manufacturing infrastructure.

[Note: Divisions of large pharmaceutical companies that develop or manufacture medical biotechnology products are included in the sector. Activities of large phar - maceutical companies in the development and manufacture of small molecules are excluded.]

Company size and activity profile
As in the case of medical technology the sector is dominated by SMEs with 42% of companies employing less than 5 and nearly half employ 10-49 people. This profile is similar to the rest of Europe and the USA where companies with 20 or fewer employees predominate.

The predominance of small companies is a characteristic of this industry, with many start-ups and spin-out from the academic research base. While some operate on a "virtual" model, this is still relatively uncommon and most are housed within their host university or the numerous science parks and incubators located across the UK to provide support for early stage companies. Crucially, these sites also provide an environment suitable for open innovation, enabling partnerships and risk-sharing models with between large and small companies.

Sector definition
Further features of the biotechnology sector are:

- 109 medical biotechnology companies with a turnover of more than £5 million are located in the UK. The highly skilled 24,000-strong workforce represents 25% of European employment in the sector.
- There is a pipeline of 447 drugs in development, of which the majority are small molecules.

Geographic dispersion
The regions with the highest concentration of medical biotechnology enterprises

in respect of sales turnover, employment and the number of companies are the South East, the East of England, the North West and Scotland. Together with London these regions account for 87% of turnover, and almost three quarters of the UK's employment and companies in the sector.

Analysis of the turnover profiles of companies in these regions suggests that their pre-eminence is not due to a preponderance of larger companies, but the heavier concentration of medical biotechnology companies located there.

Further examination of the concentration of companies in these five regions reveals the primacy of the East of England, which is home to a quarter of all UK-based medical biotechnology companies by the following seven final product types:

- blood and tissue products;
- small molecules;
- vaccines;
- advanced therapy medicinal products;
- therapeutic proteins;
- antibodies;
- specialist services

All seven product segments are represented by companies based in the majority of the regions. There also appears to be a similar ratio of specialist suppliers to final product companies, averaging 1.67.

The South and East of England are the two strongest regions in medical biotechnology accounting for 60% of the total sector, 67% in the small molecule segment (excluding large pharmaceutical company activity) and 93% in the advanced therapies segment (gene and cellular therapies).

Sector investment

Total investment in the European biotechnology sectors (of which medical is the largest) reached £4.5 billion in 2007. The UK was the largest recipient of all types of funds and second only to Germany for VC funding. VC investment in Europe declined over the period 2004-2007.

Industrial biotechnology sector

The nascent UK industrial biotechnology sector is underpinned by the Companies based in the UK use chemical based products for a range of uses such as fineand bulk chemicals, pharmaceuticals, bio-colorants, solvents, bio-plastics, vitamins, food additives, biopesticides and liquid bio-fuels such as bio-ethanol and bio-diesel.

The UK companies whose primary business is in industrial biotechnology ranging from biofuels through to pharmaceutical intermediaries together generate annual sales of £230 million with a combined workforce of 1,600.

[Note: These statistics exclude industrial biotechnology activities carried out in large chemical or energy companies. Companies that provide specialist services to the sector, such as enzymes development or fermentation, are included.]

Product definition

The sector includes enterprises employing biological substances, systems and processes to produce materials, chemicals and energy but excludes the production of primary pharmaceutical products. The sector includes enterprises that support industrial biotechnology manufacturers with contract R & D or other sector specific services including the associated supply chain.

Sector size and activity profile

Excluding final products that are derived from industrial biotechnology, the sector has a turnover of £230 million. Fine and specialty chemicals, biofuels and pharmaceutical intermediaries account for 77% of total sector turnover. The long-established production of chemicals by fermentation or the application of enzymes to make pharmaceutical intermediaries has grown into a significant activity. The distribution of employment in the sector shows a similar pattern with 77% of the sector workforce employed in the same three segments.

Of the 64 companies in the sector, around one third is engaged in the production of pharmaceutical intermediaries and of food or drink products. Nearly one fifth provide specialist services, another fifth are engaged in environmental work and yet another fifth in biofuels. Two-thirds of all the UK industrial biotechnology companies carry out R & D while half have a manufacturing capability and infrastructure.

Only one UK company employs more than 250 people and has a turnover of more than £5 million; the remainder are SMEs. Unlike the two other sectors of the life sciences industry, only 10 per cent were formed in the last three years and 44% have been in business for more than 10 years. The incentives to establish new companies in the sector have increased as the market for low carbon products and processes has become important and the segment has grown, with more public funding opportunities (both domestic and European) to develop and implement the technologies

Geographical dispersion

The North East, Wales, Yorkshire and Humberside and Scotland are currently home to around two thirds of all UK industrial biotechnology companies. Only one or two companies are located in the West Midlands and South West.

CHOOSING THE UK FOR LIFE SCIENCES INVESTMENT

There are a number of compelling reasons for channelling Life Sciences investment into the UK: a research base known for its creativity, quality and talent, built on a history of internationally recognised excellence;

● a proven strong reputation based on achievement (15 of the world's top-selling medicines were discovered in the UK)
● the National Health Service is the largest publically funded unified health care system in the world with 60 million residents and a robust patient record system
● a close and supportive collaborative relationship between industry, government, academia, and the regulatory and patent bodies
● open and trustworthy, with internationally respected regulatory bodies and highly effective and enforced IP laws
● a pro-science investment climate with sophisticated venture capital markets and a wide spectrum of targeted, accessible public and charitable funding sources
● value for money

Collaboration

Supported by the Government, industry and the public sector have driven forward translational research in critical areas of high disease burden.

Three examples of such collaboration are:

● The Translational Medical Research Collaboration (TMRC) – £50 million partnership between: the Universities of Aberdeen, Dundee, Edinburgh and Glasgow; the four associated NHS Boards; Scottish Enterprise; and

Wyeth, part of Pfizer Inc.

- A £37 million Bioscience Campus on the Stevenage site of GlaxoSmithKline (GSK), funded by a partnership of the Government, GSK, The Wellcome Trust,Technology Strategy Board and the East of England Development Agency.
- Development of a new Translational Medicine Unit at a purpose-built hospital in Manchester under a collaborative agreement between ICON plc and Central Manchester University Hospitals NHS Foundation Trust (CMFT).

Together, these positive elements in the landscape of UK life science development form a compelling argument for the UK as a global centre for life sciences creativity and delivery, enabling businesses to drive innovation through to market success

Note: The content for this chapter was sourced from the various publications of UK Life Sciences available from its marketing portal at www.uklifescience.co.uk. For more information and how UK Trade & Investment can support investment in the UK readers should call +44 (0) 207 215 8000, e-mail: lifescience@ukti.gsi.gov.uk or visit www.uktradeinvest.gov.uk.

3.4 CHEMICAL AND RELATED INDUSTRIES

Neil Harvey and Alan Eastwood
Chemical Industries Association

MEETING NEEDS AND EXPECTATIONS

The UK chemical industry lies at the heart of the European industrial economy, serving every branch of manufacturing industry, providing a source of innovation, intermediate products and process enabling technologies. It employs directly around 170,000 highly skilled people nationwide, and accounts for 1.5% of Gross Domestic Product and 12.9% of manufacturing industry's gross value-added. It invests about £3 billion annually, typically representing about 19% of total manufacturing investment, with a further £5 billion being spent on R&D (the majority in pharmaceuticals.) It is the UK's top positive contributor to the balance of trade among manufacturing sectors, with an annual trade surplus averaging £6 billion in recent years on turnover exceeding £50 billion. Other countries in the European Union account for around 60% of exports and 70% of imports.

The UK's chemical sector is a powerhouse among the country's manufacturing sectors. It is made up of approximately 4000 "local units", grouped under 3,300 separately tax registered companies.[1] The UK has long been, and remains, one of Europe's most attractive locations for international chemical investment.

A commitment to free enterprise, low taxation, deregulated utilities, absence of restrictive labour practices and regulations, freedom to manage, English

---

1 45% of local units and 48% of enterprises are "micro" organisations employing fewer than 5 people.

language and business practices similar to those in the United States, all combine to make the UK a logical location for global investors. Over 200 international chemical companies with manufacturing facilities in the UK clearly agree.

GEOGRAPHICAL DISPERSION WITHIN THE UK

Chemical production is distributed throughout the UK. Historical, geographic, economic and logistical factors have led to the development of clusters based around Grangemouth (Scotland); on Teesside in north east England; in a much larger and more dispersed area centred on Merseyside in the north west of England; and along the M62 motorway corridor to West Yorkshire and Humberside in the east. A national ethylene pipeline network links Grangemouth, Teesside, Hull and Runcorn in NW England. All four regions are within 200 miles of each other and each has access to major port facilities that are interconnected by an extensive road and rail network. The Teesside group is extending north to Tyneside and beyond, where there is a strong focus on pharmaceuticals, biotech and service providers.

While the north of the country is the base for most of the bulk commodity chemicals producers – with other speciality chemical producers also located near them – there are many more speciality, consumer and pharmaceutical chemical company operations spread across the rest of the UK. There are smaller clusters in the Midlands (Nottingham, Loughborough, Birmingham), the south and south west of England (Southampton, Bristol/Severnside) and South Wales. There are many research based science companies close to Oxford and Cambridge, while London and the south east of England host many major pharmaceutical companies' research establishments and corporate headquarters. Cornwall is also developing a new cluster of small, highly-specialised research chemical producers.

The geographical distribution of chemical companies is shown below in Table 3.4.1. The share of activity in London and the South East is larger than casual observation of the landscape might suggest. The reasons are that many sites undertake both high value manufacturing and formulation activities as well as serving as offices, storage and warehousing.

Table 3.4.1 Distribution of UK chemical companies by UK region, by% of companies and by% of staff

Region	Coverage	% companies	Est % of staff
North West	Manchester, Liverpool, Cumbria, Lancashire, Cheshire	16	21
Yorkshire & Humberside	Leeds, Wakefield, Halifax, Bradford, Huddersfield, Hull, York, Grimsby, Immingham	9	10
North East	Teesside, Tyneside, Wearside, Durham, Northumberland	4	8
East	Norfolk, Suffolk, Essex Cambridgeshire, Bedfordshire, Hertfordshire	10	8
East Midlands	Derbyshire, Nottinghamshire, Lincolnshire, Leicestershire, Northamptonshire	9	9
West Midlands	Birmingham, Wolverhampton, Coventry, Shropshire, Staffordshire, Warwickshire, Worcestershire	9	5
South West	Bristol, Avon, Somerset, Devon, Cornwall	7	5
London and South East	Berks, Bucks, Oxfordshire, Hampshire, Sussex, Kent	23	21
Scotland		6	7
Wales		5	5
Northern Ireland		2	1

PRODUCT DIVERSITY OF THE UK CHEMICAL SECTOR

The UK's chemical sector is very diverse, not just geographically but in product coverage too. Petrochemicals and basic organics use North Sea oil and, in particular, gas reserves. With a substantial inorganic sector too, the UK has a solid foundation upon which further speciality chemical production is based. Further down the supply chain, the UK is a major European manufacturing and distribution centre for pharmaceuticals, paints and coatings, detergents and personal care products, as well as specialised products and process enablers for other manufacturing industries such as the automotive and electronics sectors. Plastics processors in the UK generate annual turnover of some £22 billion.

Table 3.3.2 provides a range of statistics explaining the size of the UK speciality chemicals industry sector versus the other industry sectors. They were derived from government surveys of the industry and reported according to Standard Industrial Classification (SIC) codes.

Table 3.4.2 UK statistics for the UK chemical commodity, speciality, pharmaceutical and consumer products sector, 2008

Sector[2]	Number of companies	Employment '000	Turnover £ billion	Sales from local mfr £ billion	GVA £ billion	GPD % Total	Trade balance £ billion	Capital expenditure £ billion
Commodity	875	44	23.0	13.1	5.4	0.42	-1.2	0.92
Speciality	1230	52	11.6	8.1	3.8	0.29	1.3	0.35
Pharmaceutical	375	45	15.2	12.1	8.6	0.66	6.1	0.66
Consumer	565	30	4.2	3.5	1.4	0.11	0.1	0.21
Total	**3040**	**171**	**54.0**	**36.9**	**19.3**	**1.48**	**6.3**	**2.15**

UK CHEMICAL TECHNOLOGY AND THE BUSINESS ENVIRONMENT

Many of the world's greatest inventions emanate from the UK, which has some of the best university chemistry departments to be found anywhere in the world. This knowledge base serves several multinational companies with global or European R&D centres in the UK. They recognise that the UK provides a business

2 "Commodity" is defined as industrial gases, inorganics, organics, fertilisers, plastics, synthetic rubber and man-made fibres; "Speciality" includes dyestuffs, agrochemicals, paints, explosives, adhesives, flavours and fragrances, photographic chemicals, unrecorded media and miscellaneous industrial specialities; "Consumer" includes soaps, detergents, cosmetics and personal care products.

and regulatory environment to help push technological changes to meet:

- increasing demand for 'lifestyle' products;
- quality and cost improvements, especially in life science products;
- public health and environmental challenges;
- expectations for cleaner chemical processes and products with less environmental impact;
- requirements for protecting intellectual property and profit repatriation.

To respond to these future business drivers, the UK has an evolving and flexible industrial, regulatory and academic infrastructure to accommodate and welcome new investments that, for example, seek:

- the ability to perform a range of complex chemistries and formulations at scales from kilos to tonnes using flexible technology platforms;
- provision of special customer services such as research and screening, the supply of research and laboratory chemicals, contract synthesis, contract and/or toll manufacture of reaction and/or formulation chemistry;
- well-supported, multi-functional assets on sites capable of operating to current good manufacturing practice (cGMP) standards, typical of the pharmaceuticals sector;
- a robust regulatory and analytical infrastructure;
- fast-track development and manufacture;
- strategic commitment to custom synthesis and formulation Manufacture in order to support a complex web of alliances and joint ventures between major players, especially in pharmaceuticals;
- secure technology licensing arrangements.

OUTLOOK FOR THE UK CHEMICAL INDUSTRY IN EUROPE

The UK government is a staunch supporter of international free trade and a free enterprise culture. One aspect of this is the comparatively low level of personal taxation. The basic rate is 20%, the higher rate 40% and the maximum rate applying to taxable income over £150,000 is 50%. UK corporate tax is also competitive: the new coalition government has indicated its intention to reduce the current 28% rate to 24% by 2014/5. Small companies pay an even lower rate, currently 21%; this will be reduced to 20%.

There is also a big gulf in employers' social contributions. For the UK chemical industry these amount to 28% of wages and salaries; for other European countries they range from 31% to 49%, with an average of 39%.[3]

Flexible labour laws are particularly appealing to cyclical businesses and the UK chemical industry's strike-free record in recent years is testimony to the cooperative culture that has developed between management and labour.

The UK leads other European countries in its approach to privatisation. Telecommunications, electricity, water and gas are all in the private sector and domestic and industrial consumers have the freedom to purchase from competing suppliers.

While safety and environmental regulations are similar to those in many other leading industrial countries, UK regulators understand that high standards can be achieved without excessive bureaucracy. Statutory consents and permits for new facilities can be obtained rapidly, usually in a matter of weeks.

Europe is the world's biggest chemicals market and the UK is an integral part of that market. This is why the UK is first choice for so much chemical investment. The East Coast ports of Felixstowe, Humber, Teesside and Grangemouth are major chemical and container ports with large export and import flows. They also offer frequent delivery services to Continental Europe and deep-sea access to the rest of the world. Likewise, the Port of Liverpool is the deep-sea gateway for the chemical industry hub in North West England. The UK also has more transatlantic and global air connections than any other European country.

A wide variety of brownfield and greenfield sites are available in the UK, many of which are eligible for investment grants. Grangemouth and Teesside are obvious locations for the petrochemical and polymers sector. Both have the advantage of pipeline links with the North Sea oil and gas fields. Both are well-established major petrochemical locations with a wide range of utilities, services and engineering support for new investors.

Teesside has spare land and a utilities supply infrastructure already supporting one of Europe's largest chemical complexes. It is home to established large companies such as Ineos, Huntsman and Sabic as well as newer ventures such as the Ensus world scale bioethanol from wheat plant. With the support of the local Regional Development Agency and the Department for Energy and Climate Change, Ineos is about to construct Europe's first advanced bioethanol from household waste plant using proprietary technology. There are also many smaller, speciality chemical producers. All can draw on the R&D, pilot plant and scale-up facilities of the Wilton Centre, which has 90 serviced laboratories of varying sizes

---

3 Source: Eurostat, Labour cost structure, data for latest available year: Austria (2007), Belgium (2008), France (2008), Germany (2007), Italy (2002), Netherlands (2005), Spain (2007), UK (2007).

occupying a total of 86,000 sq ft.

Further south, the Humber offers opportunities for methane-based investments as well as a range of intermediates and specialities and has access to the UK ethylene pipeline system. The site's location on the Humber deep-water estuary further increases the range of manufacturing options. Products can reach markets serving 170m people within 24 hours. Greenfield sites are available with access to 300 storage tanks alongside deep-sea port facilities. Emphasising its commitment to the future, a local training facility which includes a full scale chemical plant has recently been established.

North West England is already linked into the ethylene pipeline and has a large, well-established primary plastics sector. It is also home to much of the UK's flourishing speciality chemical sector, with sites available for further growth, and is the principal base in the UK for chloralkali production. Continental Europe is easily accessible via excellent road connections to the Humber and other East Coast ports.

Indeed, there are a host of options. Whatever an investor needs by way of project capital, raw materials, utilities, effluent treatment, well-located sites or partners, the solution lies somewhere in the UK.

3.5 CLEAN TECHNOLOGY AND THE LOW CARBON ECONOMY

Neil Budd
Watson Farley & Williams LLP

The UK government has in recent years focused on trying to make the UK a low carbon economy and to encourage the development of clean technology (often abbreviated to "cleantech"). To some degree this has been based on political initiatives in the UK itself but also has been driven in large part by legislation coming from the EU.

The Climate Change Act 2008 imposed a legally binding requirement on the government to reduce greenhouse gas emissions in the UK by 80% (compared to the level for 1990) by 2050. It also created the carbon reduction commitment which imposed emissions limits and introduced emissions trading for businesses in the UK which are not heavy pollutants and are thus not covered by the existing emissions trading scheme for power plants and other heavy industry which came into effect in 2005. The carbon reduction commitment is discussed further below.

In 2009 the Department of Energy and Climate Change (DECC) brought out a White Paper entitled *The UK Low Carbon Transition Plan* which set out a number of policy proposals designed to make the UK a low carbon economy and to "lead the clean industries of the future". In the electricity sector, this meant increasing the drive for renewable energy, encouraging nuclear energy, development of a "smart grid" and encouraging carbon capture and storage (CCS) by providing a support mechanism for demonstration CCS installations and by requiring new coal-fired power plants to incorporate a CCS facility. For homes and businesses, it meant encouraging energy efficiency and reduction of carbon emissions through various schemes. With regard to transport, the proposals included encouraging low carbon cars and buses and the development of electric cars and the infrastructure for charging them. In relation to agriculture, the plan to 2020 is intended to cut emissions from farming and waste through more efficient use of fertiliser and better management of livestock and manure, support for anaerobic digestion (a technology that turns waste and manure into renewable energy), reducing the amount of waste sent to landfill and better capture of landfill emissions.

Alongside the White Paper, the Department for Business, Innovation and Skills (BIS) and DECC produced *The UK Low Carbon Industrial Strategy*. This strategy document addressed business opportunities in clean technology. It states, based on an industry analysis[1], that the global market for low carbon and environmental goods and services was worth £3 trillion in 2007/8 and could grow to £4.3 trillion by 2015. Further, the UK low carbon and environmental goods and services market "is worth £106 billion and employs 880,000 people directly or through the supply chain". Key policies would include trying to develop a UK offshore wind industry and wave and tidal industry, investing in nuclear power, developing low carbon vehicles and vehicle-charging infrastructure and developing renewable construction materials, chemical and low carbon manufacturing.

Although the White Paper and accompanying strategy document mentioned above were promulgated during the period of the Labour Government which lost power in May 2010, the Coalition Government which replaced it has demonstrated its intention to continue with the green agenda. In the Queen's Speech given on 25 May 2010, it was confirmed that there will be a new Energy Bill which will contain measures which would, amongst other things, deliver energy efficiency in homes and business, regulate carbon emissions from coal-fired power stations and put in place a framework to guide the development of a smart grid for supply and demand for electricity. It is also intended to create a "green investment bank" to support investment in low carbon projects.

It can therefore be seen that clean technology embraces a number of elements, in various sectors, which have common themes of benefitting the environment and being energy efficient. Thus clean technology covers sectors as diffuse as energy, water, waste, transportation, manufacturing, agriculture and

1 Innovas (2009) Low Carbon and Environmental Goods and Services: an industry analysis

homes and businesses generally. We have reviewed renewable energy in chapter 3.10. In this chapter we will review some of these sectors and examine current developments in them. These sectors are:

- reduction of waste going to landfill and development of recycling and waste-to-energy facilities;
- schemes to encourage energy efficiency in homes and businesses (including carbon reduction schemes and development of smart grids);
- carbon capture and storage;
- development of technology in the water sector;
- development of low carbon transport and transport infrastructure.

THE WASTE SECTOR

The drive to reduce waste going to landfill and encourage waste-recycling and waste-to-energy schemes has been driven largely by EU legislation. The general framework on waste in the EU was established by Directive 75/442/EEC on Waste [1975] and revised in 2008 by Directive 2008/98/EC. This is a framework directive setting out general requirements of member states to implement an EU-wide policy on waste. Member states must apply a hierarchy of steps when dealing with waste management. The preferred option is waste prevention; failing that re-use, recycling, recovery and (as a last resort) safe disposal of waste. The Directive also requires member states to implement waste prevention programmes by 2013. The Directive has to be implemented by member states by 12 December 2010.

The EU also has policies on specific types of waste. These cover waste types such as biodegradable waste, batteries, waste oils, waste electrical and electronic equipment, polychlorinated biphenyls (PCBs),[2] packaging and packaging waste and end-of-life vehicles. The common thread running through these polices are re-use and recycling of waste where possible and, if not possible, the treatment and disposal of waste in ways that are least-environmentally harmful. For example, in the case of biodegradable waste, current EU policies[3] are to move away from disposal of biodegradable waste (as landfill sites produce methane is which a greenhouse gas) to biological treatment of waste, e.g. by using compost in agriculture or horticulture and production of green energy with the residue used for soil improvement in the case of biodegradable waste that is suitable for anaerobic digestion.

2 PCBs are man-made chemicals with an extraordinary chemical stability and heat resistance. They were therefore extensively employed as components in electrical and hydraulic equipment and lubricants up to the 1980s. In 1985, the use of PCBs in the EC was very heavily restricted as they are classified as probable human carcinogens and produce a wide spectrum of adverse effects in animals and humans.
3 Relevant legislation includes the Landfill Directive 99/31/EEC and the Sewage Sludge Directive 86/278/EEC.

Policy drivers already exist in the UK for dealing with waste.[4] These include the granting of Renewable Obligation Certificates (ROCs) for energy-from-waste power plants in respect of the biomass content of waste which is used as a fuel to produce electricity. The power plant developer will sell the ROCs to the purchaser of the electricity (normally a licensed electricity supplier), thus providing the power plant developer with an additional source of revenue. Energy-from-waste plants using an advanced conversion technology such as gasification, pyrolysis or anaerobic digestion will be eligible for a higher level of ROCs under ROC banding arrangements introduced in 2009 under the Renewable Obligation Order of that year.[5]

Local authorities, which are responsible for collection and disposal of municipal waste, are under pressure to reduce the amount if waste that they send to landfill. The Landfill Allowance Trading Scheme, which was introduced in 2005, sets an allowance of biodegradable municipal waste (BMW) that local authorities are allowed to send to landfill: if they send more, they have to pay a penalty of £150 per tonne of BMW over the limit. There is also a landfill tax which increases by £8 per tonne each year. The intention of these measures it encourages local authorities to look for other methods of disposing of BMW in accordance with the waste hierarchy mentioned above.

ENERGY EFFICIENCY

The Climate Change Act 2008 and the White Paper *The UK Low Carbon Transition Plan* have outlined a number of projects aimed at making UK homes and businesses more energy efficient. These schemes range from the development of new technologies to the creation of a domestic emissions trading market. It remains to be seen whether these initiatives will be supported in their current form by the Coalition Government although early indications are that there will not be radical policy reversals in regards to the schemes referred to below.

Smart grid and smart metering

One aspect of energy efficiency policy to which the Coalition Government remains firmly committed is that of developing a smart grid to manage the UK's energy supply. Essentially, a smart grid would replace the existing national grid that supplies UK homes with gas and electricity. A smart grid would allow for greater energy efficiency by taking advantages of advances in digital technology; for example domestic appliances such as washing machines could be turned on remotely during times of low energy demand and off in times of peak demand.

4 See UKTI guidance note "Energy from Waste: A guide to opportunities in the UK" http://www.ukinvest.gov.uk/UKTI-publications/103412/en-GB.html
5 Further details of the ROC mechanism can be found in chapter 3.10.

This could provide the consumer with significant financial savings over the long term as energy providers would charge less for off-peak consumption.

Furthermore, a smart grid would expand the capacity of the national grid and increase connections to renewable energy sources such as wind farms and tidal generators. The *UK Low Carbon Transition Plan* provided for £30 million[6] of direct funding for network related research in order to accelerate the development of smart grid technology within the UK.

A further technical development outlined in the *UK Low Carbon Transition Plan* is that of smart meters. Smart meters would replace traditional gas and electricity meters and provide users with more detailed and accurate information as to how much electricity and gas is used by their household. Subsequently, smart meters will allow suppliers to produce more flexible price plans based on the times when most electricity and gas are used – rewarding customers for consumption in off-peak times. The aim set out in the White Paper was to have smart meters installed in every UK home by the end of 2020.[7]

Carbon reduction commitment

In addition to technological advances designed to improve energy efficiency, the Climate Change Act 2008 introduced a programme designed to create an emissions trading market within the UK for organisations which are not heavy pollutants (including banks, hotels, supermarkets, large retailers and public bodies such as local authorities).[8] The scheme is known as the Carbon Reduction Commitment (the "CRC"). The CRC came into operation in April 2010. The scheme is estimated to apply to 4,000 – 5,000 businesses in the UK.

Under the CRC, businesses participating in the scheme will register to buy allowances for their energy use. Initially these allowances are set at a fixed price of £12 per tonne of CO2. From April 2013, following a three year introductory phase the CRC will operate on a cap and trade basis, with the Government auctioning a limited number of allowances via closed bids, which can then be traded on a secondary market.

Performance throughout the scheme will be monitored and the Government will publish annual league tables showing each organisation's commitment to reducing emissions. Not only will this league table confer a reputational boost, potentially attracting customers and investors who are enthusiastic about environmental issues, but it will also confer a potentially significant financial boost. The scheme is intended to be revenue neutral with all money spent on allowances each year paid back to participants via a recycling payment.

---

6 p.10, The UK Low Carbon Transition Plan (DECC, 2009)

7 The represents an £8 billion private sector investment. p.71 The UK Low Carbon Transition Plan (DECC, 2009)

8 Heavy polluting industries are regulated, in terms of their emissions, by an emissions trading scheme which was introduced in 2005.

Community Energy Saving Programme

The *UK Low Carbon Emission Plan* also outlines a programme to encourage greater energy efficiency in low income UK households with the launch a new Community Energy Saving Programme ("CESP"). This scheme is to be run by local partnerships of energy suppliers, generators and local authorities who will have access to £350 million of Government funding. The aim of CESP is to improve energy efficiency and lower household fuel bills in disadvantaged areas by providing the funding needed to install modern insulation, wood pellet boilers and solar water heaters in households that would not be able to afford such measures privately. CESP includes initiatives such as the Decent Homes Programme that aim to implement similar fuel efficiency changes for social housing.

CARBON CAPTURE AND STORAGE

There are carbon abatement technologies (CATs) which reduce CO2 emissions from fossil fuel usage, the most prominent of which is carbon capture and storage (CCS) from power plants which burn fossil fuels. The EU passed a CCS Directive in 2009[9] which laid down a framework for CCS technologies to be implemented. The Energy Act 2008 had already established provisions for licensing of storage activities.

CCS was one of the CATs reviewed by the Government in a strategy document published in 2005, *A Strategy for Developing Carbon Abatement Technologies for Fossil Fuel Use*. It was recognised that CCS was the most radical of the CAT options reviewed and required an ambitious development of a chain of technologies. The first stage of the CCS process involves capturing the CO2. This can be done before combustion at the power plant or afterwards. Once the CO2. has been captured, it is then transported by pipeline to a designated storage area. It is then stored at the storage area.

The strategy document recognised the potential for business offered by CCS to a wide range of sectors including power engineering, electricity generation, process engineering, petroleum engineering and project development. It was also pointed out that the UK is well-endowed with the natural resources for storage of CO2 in its offshore oil and gas fields and deep saline aquifers.

In 2010, the Government pressed forward with development of a programme for implementation of CCS. Within DECC an Office of Carbon Capture and Storage (OCCS) was created tasked with facilitating the delivery of CCS in the UK and helping to promote its rapid deployment globally. The Labour Government which lost

9 Directive 2009/31/EC

office in May 2010 passed, as one of its final pieces of legislation, the Energy Act 2010 which gave enabling powers to DECC to provide financial assistance for development of CCS demonstration projects. In March 2010, a new strategy document was published by DECC and the Department for Business, Innovation and Skills: *Clean coal: an industrial strategy for the development of carbon capture and storage across the UK*. This set out the aims of the two Departments to develop these demonstration projects and to take measures to develop a sustained CCS capability in the UK through development of supply chain and skills needed to manufacture and service CCS projects. It is likely that these measures will be built on by the Coalition Government.

THE WATER SECTOR

In response to the Water Framework Directive [2000][10] the Environment Agency published the *River Basin Management Plans* (RBMPs) which received ministerial approval in late 2009. The RBMPs launched a number of initiatives to improve water quality throughout the UK. One of the key themes of the RBMPs was the desire to tackle pollution at source rather than treating water at a later stage.

Linking into the RBMPs and forming part of the Environmental Agency's wider water policy the *Code of Good Agricultural Practice* provides advice for farmers on how they can minimise water usage and the steps they should take to record how much water they are require on a daily basis. Moreover, new homes in the UK must now adhere to the 2009 minimum water efficiency regulations and local authorities can impose yet stricter standards in areas of low water reserves.

The *Water Resources Strategy for England and Wales (2009)* targets water leakage throughout the distribution network, setting strict yearly targets for the amount of water considered acceptable to be lost in this manner. It also affirms the Environment Agency's commitment to the development of smart meters and increased water metering in general. Smart meters would provide households with more detailed and integrated information regarding their water, gas and electricity usage – removing the need for traditional meters for each utility. The intention is for water meters (smart or traditional) to be installed in every home by 2020 in order to encourage a more responsible use of water (as consumers will have to pay for how much they use rather than according to estimates).

10 2000/60/EC.

LOW CARBON VEHICLES

The *UK Low Carbon Transition Plan* set out the former Government's plans to encourage production of lower carbon and electric vehicles as part of a broader strategy to reduce carbon emissions in the transport sector and it is likely that the Coalition Government will continue this.

A key aspect to the development of electric vehicles is to have an infrastructure in place to charge them. The Department of Transport launched Plugged-In-Places in November 2009 to provide seed funding of up to £30 million to support installation of charging infrastructure in various urban locations. However, the charging infrastructure will to a large extent be determined by how people decide to use and charge their electric cars. For example, if there is strong demand for fast charging, that may require a particular type of charging infrastructure whereas other types of infrastructure may be possible for people who are willing to leave their vehicles for long periods to be charged. The type of journeys that people make may determine whether all-electric cars or hybrid cars become more prevalent: all-electric cars would be suitable for people who only drive short distances and can then charge their cars whereas hybrid cars are going to be more suitable for drivers who want to drive long distances and do not want to have to charge their cars during the journey.

3.6 CREATIVE DESIGN: OPEN INNOVATION

Maxine Horn
British Design Innovation

WHERE IPR PROTECTION FAILS

Current IPR protection is incapable of drawing a distinction between ill-defined early-stage ideas on the one hand, and fully-articulated knowledge- and solution-based business propositions on the other. A new intellectual property right that properly protects pre-patent concepts and propositions created by professional originators would stimulate open innovation on a truly massive scale.

Open Innovation is widely considered to be the ideal business growth model going forward. Unfortunately, many people also appear to believe that it denotes a completely open free-for-all, where ideas can be purloined at will. For that reason, professional originators – those industrial designers, inventors, scientists, technologists, design engineers and others whose living depends upon creating new-to-market products, processes and propositions – have always felt threatened by open innovation's poorly-regulated remuneration structure. Until now.

It is already accepted that knowledge transfer has a tradable value: universities consistently trade and transfer knowledge commercially with industry – an activity encouraged, promoted and funded by the government. (In some regards knowledge-based professional originators are little different from universities, apart from the fact that they have the know-how to take the knowledge further and translate it into market applications in the form of user-led products, services and propositions. To commercialise it to its maximum, in other words.)

But amid rising confusion about what the differences between 'open innovation' and 'open source' actually are, misconceptions abound – with major implications for the intellectual property (IP) sector, innovation and industry if things are not ironed out.

Professional originators utilise their know-how and expertise to progress unrefined ideas to a state of applied knowledge, yet current IP protection is incapable of drawing a distinction between ill-defined early-stage ideas on the one hand, and fully-rationalised knowledge- and solution-based business propositions on the other. A new intellectual property right (IPR) that protects pre-patent concepts created by professional originators would stimulate open innovation on a truly massive scale; so, it is a hotly-debated topic.

Put simply, open innovation is where industry seeks external sources of innovation. In a world of widely-distributed knowledge, companies cannot afford to rely entirely on their own research, but should instead buy or license processes or inventions (e.g. patents) from other companies and individuals. In addition, internal inventions not being used in a firm's business should be taken outside the company through licensing, joint ventures, spin-offs etc.

OPEN INNOVATION

In fact, open innovation can be broken down into five distinct areas: open source, consumer- or user-led crowdsourcing, expert knowledge-led crowdsourcing, proposition sourcing (involving entrepreneurs), and concept sourcing (involving professional originators). All are outlined in more detail below.

Open Source
New and shared knowledge, enabling reputation and status-building
Open source is a practice most common in software development and digital productions, where enthusiasts (of music, for instance) share knowledge, code and digital files to build reputations or contribute to end products.

Software companies use open source to encourage web developers to build on their platforms in order to make money from upgrades and end-user licenses for support products, and thus have a vested interest in free shareware. In this sense, 'free' does not mean valueless.

Shared ideas can become valuable if those ideas make a contribution to a greater end product that is worth money. In a structured framework focused on a common goal and with profit-share agreements in place, this is considered co-creation. In an unstructured open source environment, enthusiasts or new practioners are often more interested in enabling and reputation-building than making money

The results of publicly-funded university research discoveries are made freely available through journals publication, allowing open source access to all who purchase or download them. However, although universities are strongly encouraged to commercialise results using traditional IPR and knowledge transfer methodologies, small discoveries and new technologies are chasing problems to address but lack any real market application. So this is a form of open source, though not necessarily an immediately practical one.

IP structure
A Creative Commons license was introduced some years ago to denote materials that are free to use without seeking permission. Open source can build new knowledge; spawn innovation, new products and businesses. It serves a purpose to those who make a personal decision to work in such a way.

Consumer- or user-led crowdsourcing
User insights, ideas-based competitions, PR, no defined problem, no safety or quality control
User-led crowdsourcing is a modern form of consumer insight research that has replaced the small focus groups used by traditional market research firms. Large corporate brand owners launch competitions, often through PR firms, to source new product ideas and improvements from a consumer or user base; an expert panel sifts the ideas and declares a winner. Although the ideas submitted are of variable quality the PR value can be beneficial. Occasionally a good submission can lead to a commercial payback.

IP structure
 In general these types of competitions do not attract professional originators due to the negligible IP terms, where all commercial advantage is often assigned to the brand owner running the competition as a condition of entry. Rewards rarely exceed a small cash prize, free product samples or a little PR.

Expert knowledge-led crowdsourcing
Intellectual knowledge, web-based, proprietary data and defined problem, solution-driven, quality and safety-based
This type of crowdsourcing, often promoted via a web portal, seeks to attract professionals, academics and subject enthusiasts. It relies upon proprietary knowledge and a defined problem being placed in the public domain for problem-solvers to find and resolve. Speculative knowledge sourcing of this kind is less successful than that which offers significant monetary reward to the problem-solvers.

One of the more successful examples of expert knowledge crowdsourcing is offered by Gold Corporation, a Canadian gold-mining company then in financial difficulties. The company knew they had more gold on their 20,000-hectare property, but didn't know where. The cost of searching for gold was going up, while successful finds were going down. The CEO decided the only way out of the crisis was to admit the problem and mount a competition, with a major financial incentive to attract as many external parties as possible.

The Gold Corporation Challenge was launched with prize fund of $500,000 to be awarded to those who provided the methodology for finding gold, and required the company to publish 45 years of proprietary geological data online. Responses from 1,400 interested parties in 50 countries were received, the majority of whom understood geological data. Gold Corporation's 14 geologists reviewed the online proposals, filtered the submissions to 25 semi-finalists, then sifted down to three finalists who were asked to submit sophisticated proposals.

110 sites were identified by the solvers, 50 per cent of which were new and 80 per cent of which produced gold. 8 million ounces of gold were found. Gold Corporation's value before the competition was $100 million and after the competition rose to $9 billion, and the company now owns the world's richest mine.

Open crowdsourcing of this nature was unprecedented in a sector as commercially secretive as mining, but was a risk the CEO was willing to take to enable expert problem-solvers to identify gold deposits and save the company. Although Gold Corporation risked open access to its proprietary mining data for the Challenge, the expert-led problem-solving it attracted literally paid dividends.

Proposition sourcing (involving entrepreneurs)
Businesses need ideas and entrepreneurs need businesses to sell ideas to. Propositions need to be bought and sold across all sectors
Every year, thousands of entrepreneurs spot a gap in the market and develop new

business propositions. But while the digital age, the internet, social networking and so forth have arguably made reaching the customer easier and more cost-efficient, business start-up costs are now at a minimum of £5,000 for an individual operating on cheapest options and £40,000 to £100,000 for start-ups seeking to launch a professional brand. Costs include website creation and, for online transactions, a bank account, a payment system, telephone lines, brand and supporting infrastructure, while some require a terrestrial retail space as well.

Those who lack the financial resources, creativity or know-how to bring their propositions to market unaided are reliant upon partnering with other businesses, so need to be assured of confidentiality when seeking to negotiate deals at pre-commercialisation stage. However, although open innovation is a good way to harness the knowledge, know-how, skills and ideas of large numbers of people, if ideas are considered to be free to be commercialised by those with the wealth and resources to grab them themselves, what motivation exists for entrepreneurs to participate?

A proper IP right with a regulated rewards mechanism needs to be in place if open innovation is to attract entrepreneurs in this situation.

Concept sourcing (involving professional originators)

Professional marketplace, user-centered, creatively-articulated concepts to proof-of-concept stage

Here we arrive at arguably the most mutually rewarding of open innovation partnerships – but also the most contentious on the IP front.

When professional originators (who predominantly work in the creative industries) are commissioned by brand owners on a fees-for-services basis, they are paid for their knowledge, know-how and skill in creatively executing a brief. In this model, brand owners generally own or buy out any IP arising. In open innovation calls, however, or where professional originators generate their own concepts without a formal brief, brand owners do not pay fees. Instead the originators seek to trade fully-articulated propositions based on their customer- and sector-led knowledge and know-how with brand owners on a shared risk-and-reward basis.

In order for originators to communicate the value of such propositions, it is often necessary to also communicate a good deal of the knowledge supporting them. And quite often the propositions are not subject to patents, but might instead be proposed brand extensions, a new business model, the evolution of an existing product or service, or a new product, packaging or service proposition.

The problem confronting professional originators in these situations is that their knowledge-based propositions are often treated in the same way as ill-defined early-stage ideas proposed by those without the know-how, creativity or resources to take an idea to proof-of-concept stage. In situations where brand owners refuse to sign non-disclosure agreements (in case they impinge upon concepts the owner could potentially already be working on), originators are totally unprotected from misappropriation of their propositions by those who believe that ALL pre-commercialised or pre-patent ideas are free to use as they choose, regardless of the stage they are at or the expertise put into formulating them.

Pre-patent concepts, including unprotected designs, 3D applications, service design, business models, propositions and processes, are consistently purloined by others on the basis that "ideas cannot be protected". It is as if some companies believe business meetings are held under a Creative Commons license, which denotes that a piece of work, code, image or file is open source and may be utilised by anyone for any purpose without requiring permission.

But professional originators' propositions are tradable knowledge-based solutions developed by industry experts with requisite know-how – in effect, proprietary but unprotected information. And these originators do not in the main set up competitive brands and companies, but more often seek to transfer knowledge and license concepts to brand owners.

I have personal experience of presenting propositions to organisations under non-confidential terms in order to enable negotiation to take place under normal conditions of business confidentiality – only for the same organisations to later assert that such exposure is in the public domain. But public domain is exactly that – ideas that have been fully exposed on public platforms such as a journal, conference or website.

It is disingenuous to assert that a one-to-one business meeting is in the public domain. All businesses are subject to a duty of confidentiality and most modern businesses have a Corporate Social Responsibility policy in place. They are duty-bound, if not legally constrained, from acting in an unethical manner through the misappropriation of innovative works brought to them by the owners with the express intent of negotiating a mutually-agreeable purchase of such works.

SO WHERE DO WE GO FROM HERE?
A new trading model is required that respects proposition ownership and value

If Open Innovation is ever to reach its full potential, a new trading model is required that respects the ownership and value of pre-patent concepts and propositions devised by professional originators and described in commercial negotiations with route-to-market businesses. Such a trading model needs to be based on unimpeachable business ethics, best professional practice and permission-based commercialisation. And it needs to hand some semblance of pre-patent IP protection back to the professional originator.

As noted above, the bad news is that the market cannot rely upon ethics alone. The good news is that a new digital barcode system that could prevent the misappropriation of confidential new ideas and proprietary information is to be rolled out. Creative Barcode™ denotes ownership of propositions and concepts that require the owner's permission to exploit them, and offers prospective buyers the route to collaboration, purchase or licensing of any given proposition idea. And no element of the proposition, however relayed to the interested party, may be commercialised without the written permission of the originator.

This innovative business model bridges the gap between walking naked into a business negotiation and a non-disclosure agreement. It removes any doubt about whether and when route-to-market businesses are free to utilise an originator's idea, and also comprises a beneficial co-creation and innovation management tool for brand owners, protecting them from litigation.

The misappropriation of originators' previously-unprotectable work has been the biggest single issue affecting industry and the IP sector, and has become an enormous barrier to open innovation and knowledge exchange.

Luckily, the new rules of engagement in the trading model outlined above are not complex: "Do not commercialise the work of others without their permission and an agreed commercial remuneration on mutually agreed terms."

Clear enough? I think so. Now let's get to work trading propositions and generating wealth.

3.7 HOTEL & LEISURE INDUSTRIES

Felicity Jones
Watson, Farley & Williams LLP

INTRODUCTION

The Hotel and Leisure industry is a very important part of the UK economy. Britain had 28 million international visitors in 2009, of which at least half stayed in London. Whilst the impact of the global recession is taking its toll, there is a slow growth in inbound visitor numbers and some positive signs. We have focused on the Hotel market rather than leisure facilities, bars and restaurants although some of the principles apply to all sectors of the Hotel and Leisure market.

Just as any potential hotel guest has a wide range of products from which to choose, the hotel investor has to consider the type of hotel and market they wish to invest in (ranging from budget to five star), the location (City Centre or Provinces), the nature of the project (new development or established site – possibly trading below expectations) and the degree of involvement they require (from owner/operator to a purely financial investor with a management contract with a major brand). All these matters will be relevant to the value of the project, the attitude of funders and the degree of risk.

The experienced Hotel investor will know the importance of taking advice at an early stage to understand the industry in the relevant location, the feasibility and/or trading history and issues that go to value and funding as well as the legal issues relating to any project. Whether new to the sector or not, it is vital to get advice at an early stage in relation to valuation, financing, structuring a transaction, the prospects (whether by way of a feasibility study or a review of existing trading) through to brand selection and asset management going forward. An experienced owner may not need the full range of advice and they will benefit from knowing the industry generally but an understanding of the specific sector of the industry in the relevant location will be crucial.

For example, there are currently several UK Cities which are extremely sought after where occupancy rates remain good (although room rates have suffered) whilst provincial Hotels, save for those with very good management, have felt the effects of the downturn more acutely. There are some good propositions in prime cities; there are limited schemes intended to regenerate areas and fill empty office blocks but any purchaser will need to fully understand the market place if they are to be sure their Hotel will trade successfully.

Whatever the industry sector in which you operate, the law is the same and elsewhere in this publication experts have addressed intellectual property, real estate and employment law. The Hotel sector is no different from other specialised areas in this respect. However, having an understanding of the industry is important when looking to structure arrangements, particularly given the nature of the asset and that an owner of a hotel investment ("Owner") may well be entering into a contract that may be in place for thirty years.

Assuming that the potential investor has decided upon the segment of the Hotel market in which they wish to invest or where they see the greatest opportunity, any investor in the Hotel market needs to decide what degree of participation they want in the management of their property and the degree to which their investment may benefit from introducing or removing a brand.

OPERATING STRUCTURES
Where an Owner (or lender) requires a brand under which to operate or market the hotel and the benefit of the reservations, marketing and support that may bring, one of the following structures will usually apply:

Leases
In recent years a combination of factors has seen the profile and use of the hotel management contract grow at the expense of the lease. This trend has been due to stamp duty issues, the preferences of some brands and the investment

community for the "Opco/Propco" division, and the growth of investors and lenders with experienced asset managers who are comfortable with management contracts. Whilst many experienced property investors prefer the comfort of a lease structure where the employees, maintenance obligations and business risk are primarily the tenant's responsibility, there is much debate as to whether the lease (or a hybrid version thereof) will become more common once again but this is by no means certain.

Some budget brands have shown a willingness to continue to lease in contrast to few mid market and upscale brands (save in a small number of circumstances). The 'budget' leases are typically focused on a limited service for longer terms of 15-35 years and, in some cases, the tenants have been offering minimum guarantees to appeal to the investors. Where the tenant is a budget brand with an investor following which is understood by the market, they are likely to be perceived to be a sound investment risk. This is unlikely to be the case where the tenant is less experienced or well supported.

Management contracts

A management contract is entered into where an operator (who is frequently also the brand owner) enters into a contract to "manage" or "direct and supervise" the operation of a Hotel under one of their brands. It is also possible that the management company could be a third party management company operating under the hotel owner's own brand or a franchise; i.e. the Owner enters into a franchise agreement to brand its hotel and also uses a small experienced management company rather than operating the business itself. All management companies ("Operators") should understand the need to present flexible terms that do not adversely impact the bottom line in the early years of operation and some of the up market brands are offering creative solutions to mitigate Owners' risks.

However, this will rarely happen unless it is in a site which they are particularly keen to operate. During recent months Operators have become more realistic and more prepared to consider break options, incentive structures and soft loans to achieve a financial position that attracts debt funding. Given the unusual nature of a management contract, in the next section, we have outlined some typical terms. These primarily relate to where a brand owner is the operator but some of the provisions will be relevant where the hotel is operated by a third party under a franchise.

Franchise agreements

A franchise agreement is one under which the brand owner will licence the owner of the hotel to operate directly (or through a third party manager) under its brand. The main difference is that the headline fees payable under a management contract are significantly larger than those under a franchise agreement (broadly 8% of gross operating profit) but an Owner will still need to check carefully the additional costs and expenses that the brand owner may require to make a direct comparison.

In recent years a number of property developers have used the franchise model to grow significant portfolios. As a result of the significant reduction in bank lending, those developers are now having to look at different ownership structures and are taking more equity involvement to maintain their interest but are tending to maintain the franchise model.

COMPARATIVE BENEFITS AND MANAGEMENT CONTRACT ISSUES

The current economic climate has encouraged a "flight to brand" but whether this is a flight to quality (or a more profitable option) will depend very much on the property and the proposed brand. The broader network of online options and the development of alternative platforms has led some Owners to develop their own brands or use smaller brands who are often more flexible (or more suitable to an independent owner of a single or limited number of assets). Funders used to assessing the operations are likely to be influenced by the perceived size and resources of particular brands although this may not necessarily benefit the Owner in the longer term. Those Owners who want a recognised brand but more control and lower fees should consider a franchise. A lease will only be considered by an operator in limited circumstances. This leaves the management contract option. Before entering into a long term commitment the Owner needs to understand the nature of the management contract.

The following is intended to provide the traditional property owner more accustomed to acting as a landlord with a guide to some of the terms they can expect to see in a management contract and to see how very different it is from a lease (although some will be relevant considerations irrespective of lease or management contract). There can be no doubt that under UK law it will be easier (for both Owner and Operator) to terminate an unsatisfactory relationship under a management contract than an underperforming turnover lease. It is therefore important for a potential Owner to understand the nature of the agreement, the liabilities it will be taking on and the relatively limited liability of the Operator.

Whilst some provisions will be key to the Operator, the Owner should seek to find a balance which gives it approval rights in relation to key liabilities; it will be a long relationship during which the Operator will be managing the Owner's business and it is important to establish a clear working relationship from the outset. This chapter does not address whether a brand is actually essential to the success of the hotel or the contribution the brand makes in terms of valuation but certain rights and restrictions in the management contract will undoubtedly affect value.

The principle behind a management contract is that the Owner remains responsible for funding the operation of the hotel, the maintenance of the building and all other aspects of the operation and the Operator is paid a fee. The relationship may be one of principal and agent or the Operator may insist that it is no more than a service provider. The Operator will endeavour to ensure that it has control over all matters necessary to ensure that the hotel is maintained and operated to the relevant brand standard (i.e. to protect and enhance the value of its brand). Whereas an Owner would produce a lease, the starting point with a management contract is often a standard form management contract produced by the Operator. Whilst there is a general view in the industry that these agreements are becoming more Owner friendly it is highly unlikely that the starting point will be favourable to the Owner, and there is a tendency for the Operator to behave as if it is their asset (albeit funding entirely by the Owner).

Key points the Owner will need to consider fall principally into the following categories:

Fees

The fee structure is generally divided into a base fee based on a percentage of turnover, an incentive fee based on profit and various other licence fees and charges for reservations, sales and marketing, accounting and other central services provided by the Operator throughout its brand hotels. Broadly speaking the average base fee in Europe is around 2-3% of revenue and the incentive fee is in the region of 10% of adjusted gross operating profit ("AGOP"), generally adjusted by the deduction of the management fee and some other specified items e.g. possibly non-property related insurances. A franchise fee is significantly lower.

It should be noted that the adjustments are a matter of negotiation and the costs of property insurance, taxes and other costs generally payable by Owners are often not deducted in the AGOP calculation. Sliding scale incentives are also becoming more common on the basis that higher fees based on profits are a strong form of incentive.

Term and Termination

The most common pattern in Europe still seems to be a term of approximately 20 years with up to two 5 year renewals. Depending on when they expect to achieve profit an Operator may agree a shorter term for a management contract than a lease. The renewal is a double-edged matter; if one side is not happy then it may wish to walk away. The Operator will often seek rights which make it unattractive to terminate on a change of Ownership (its aim being to achieve the security of a lease without the risk).

Operating Standard

Whilst most contracts will provide that the hotel will be operated to the operating standard contained in the Operator's manuals, it should be made clear that it will also be operated to the standard of an experienced prudent Operator with a view to maximising revenue and gross operating profit. Clearly, the final negotiated position will be some variation of this but, as the operating standard as set out in the Operator's manuals must necessarily be slightly fluid to ensure that the brand can remain current, an overall objective standard should also be imposed.

Other payments

Licences and development services agreements all include other fees and charges which need to be carefully watched. In addition to these and reservations fees, an Operator is likely to be looking for a contribution towards its head and/or regional office expenses for sales and marketing based on a percentage of rooms revenue. Whilst the Operator needs to be allowed flexibility to maintain the brand in the market it is important that the Owner has a clear idea of the central services (e.g. accounting, IT purchasing, trade shows etc) it will be required to pay for and the likely level of those fees.

Performance Guarantees/Non Disturbance

Whilst some Operators will give parent company guarantees or key money, the price of these may often be reflected in the remainder of the commercial terms. Similarly, it may be better for an Owner to share the risk by contractual methods such as performance clauses or guarantees and/or subordination of incentive fee rather than seek an equity investment from the Operator.

The Owner should also be wary of agreeing to produce a non-disturbance agreement in relation to borrowings without ensuring the form is reasonable, allows the Lender to terminate for poor performance or otherwise will not increase costs of borrowing or prevent the Owner from selling the asset.

Budgets/Capital Expenditure

The management contract will contain a process for the Operator to produce an operating and capital expenditure budget each year. The contract will usually provide that if the Owner makes no objection within a specified time then the budget is deemed to be accepted. We recommend that budget items in dispute are referred to an independent expert as opposed to an arbitration provision which will inevitably prove more costly.

Many Operators seek to force the Owner to comply with its requests for capital expenditure for structural changes as well as standard repairs and works necessary to maintain the operating standards of the relevant brand. The Owner would be well advised to seek a position whereby the Operator can use the funds in the case of an emergency or to comply with legislation but, unless agreed in the budget, consent must otherwise be obtained from the Owner

CONCLUSION

In this section we have endeavoured to give a potential hotel investor some guidance as to the key areas they need to consider at an early stage if they have an interest in investing in the Hotel sector in the United Kingdom. At the time of writing this there is uncertainty with regard to when more stock will become available in the market place and when the Banks will start to assist purchasers and developers. What is clear is that when they do they will be valuing the investment as a business and looking hard to ensure that the prospective borrower understands the market place, has a realistic and achievable business plan and the necessary experience (or experienced team) to achieve its goals.

3.8 ICT INFRASTRUCTURE
Jonathan Reuvid
Legend Business

OVERVIEW

A critical location factor for investors across all business sectors is the quality and reliability of a host country's ICT infrastructure. In the UK, privatisation of the major ICT service providers has led to greater competition and lower prices, giving the UK one of the strongest ICT infrastructures in the world as Figure 3.8.1 confirms:

Figure 3.8.1 Network readiness index*

Country	Ranking 2009-2010
Sweden	1
Singapore	2
Denmark	3
Switzerland	4
US	5
Finland	6
Canada	7
Hong Kong	8
Netherlands	9
Norway	10

UK	13
Germany	14
France	18
Japan	21
Belgium	22
Ireland	24
Spain	34
Czech Republic	36
China	37
India	43
Hungary	46
Italy	48

*Global index benchmarking key ICT infrastructure factors
Source: World Economic Forum, "Global Information Technology Report", 2010*

With a global ranking of 13, the UK is one place ahead of Germany, five places before France and well ahead of Spain and Italy, its main Western European competitors. Within Europe, London is rated by businesses as the best location for telecommunications ("European Cities Monitor" Cushman & Wakefield, 2009).

THE UK ICT INFRASTRUCTURE
The key requirements of international companies are:

● a strong e-business environment;
● the wide availability of broadband;
● the wide availability of Wi-Fi, and
● the provision of secure servers.

The UK ICT infrastructure meets all these requirements fully.

A strong e-business environment
In the "e-readiness" rankings produced by the Economist Intelligence Unit (EIU) the UK is again ranked 13 with a score of 8.14 out of 10 compared to 8.87 for Denmark, the top scorer, and 8.60 for the US. The rankings for all the UK's major global competitors are listed in Figure 3.8.2.

Figure 3.8.2 E-readiness rankings

Country	Global rank	Score (out of 10)
Denmark	1	8.87
Sweden	2	8.67
Netherlands	3	8.64
Norway	4	8.62
US	5	8.60
UK	13	8.14
France	15	7.89
Germany	17	7.85
Ireland	18	7.84
Japan	22	7.69
Spain	25	7.24
Italy	26	7.09
Czech Republic	31	6.46
Hungary	35	6.04
China	56	4.33
India	58	4.17

Source: EIU, 2009

Wide availability of broadband

The total number of broadband subscribers in the UK reached 18.2 million in the third quarter of 2009, bringing the penetration rate of broadband technology up to 30.2 %, well ahead of the EU average of 24.7 % (source: European Competitive Telecommunications Association [ECTA]) and above that of its main European competitors except France.

Wide availability of Wi-Fi

As Figure 3.8.3 shows, the UK has the third highest number of verified public Wi-Fi hotspots after the US and China and the highest number in Europe:

Figure 3.8.3 Leading Wi-Fi locations, 2009

Rank	Country	Wi-Fi Hotspots, March 2010
1	US	72,419
2	China	36,592
3	UK	28,187
4	France	26,603
5	Germany	14,841
6	Russian Federation	14,707
7	South Korea	12,817
8	Japan	12,101
9	Sweden	7,226
10	Switzerland	5,542

Source: Wi-Fi Alliance, 2010

At city level with over 4,000 Wi-Fi hotspots, London has one of the highest numbers globally; several UK cities are currently implementing Wi-Max technologies to enhance their wireless connectivity further.

Provision of secure servers and choice of ICT service providers

After the US and Japan, the UK has the third highest number of secure servers globally and the highest number in Europe.

Further information and details of specific providers among the wide range of registered telecommunications and internet service providers can be found by visiting the following websites:

● Fixed line telephone services:
www.telecomsadvice.org.uk/infosheets/buyers_guide_to_fixed_telecom+
telephone_services.htm or www.ofcom.org.uk/consumeradvice/landline/
● Mobile telephone services:
www.telecomsadvice.org.uk/infosheets_buyers_guide_to_mobile_phone_
services.htm
● Broadband / ADSL services:
www.thinkbroadband.com

INTERNATIONAL ICT COSTS

Companies are able to choose from a range of providers and tariffs offering highly competitive ICT prices to suit their specific requirements. Figure 3.8.4 indicates relative costs in Europe with the average of ten minute calls in key European locations:

Figure 3.8.4 Average cost of 10 minute national telephone calls

Country	Cost (Euro)*
UK	0.51
Germany	0.51
Belgium	0.60
EU average	0.67
France	0.77
Ireland	0.86
Spain	0.90
Italy	1.15

* Excluding taxes
Source: OECD, 2009

UK broadband costs are also highly competitive and amongst the lowest in the European Union, as detailed in Figure 3.8.5:

Figure 3.8.5 Average monthly broadband cost (per advertised Mbits/s)

Country	Cost (US$)
UK	4.08
Italy	5.28
Germany	5.64
Netherlands	8.83
Belgium	10.23
Ireland	11.19

Source: OECD, 2009

REGULATION OF THE ICT INDUSTRY

The independent organisation that regulates the UK communications industries is Ofcom. Its responsibilities extend across telecommunications, wireless communication services, television and radio. For more information visit www.ofcom.org.uk.

Note: The content of this chapter is extracted from the UK Trade and Investment Information Factsheet for the industry, updated in March 2010. For further information and updates visit www.uktradeinvest.go.uk or E-mail: enquiries@uktadeinvest.gov.uk

3.9 NANOTECHNOLOGY
Jonathan Reuvid,
Legend Business

INTRODUCTION

Nanotechnology is a collective term for a set of technologies, techniques and processes, rather than a specific area of engineering or science; it is a high-technology industry that utilises materials science and its application at the nanometre scale (one billionth of a metre).

In effect, nanotechnology is a new, radically different approach to manufacturing. The manufacturing process at the nano scale is either:

- "top down", by machining to ever-smaller dimensions; or
- "bottom up", by exploiting the ability of materials, molecules and biological systems to "self-assemble" tiny structures.

Potential market opportunities reside in the conjunction of these two approaches: the meeting of physical and chemical/biological manufacturing. The large surface to volume ratio at the nanoscale leads to a significantly increased chemical reaction where the laws of physics give way to quantum effects generating unusual electronic, optical and magnetic phenomena.

Market size

Potential applications for the relatively new nanotechnology will continue to grow rapidly. By 2008, the value of the global nanotechnology market was estimated to be US$12.7 and forecast to rise to US$27 billion by 2013 (source: BCC Inc, 2008).

COMMERCIALISATION OF NANOTECHNOLOGY APPLICATIONS IN THE UK

There are more than 600 micro and nanotechnology companies in the UK (source: NanoKTN, 2010) including university spinouts and international investors, all developing commercial applications from nanotechnologies including Oxonica, Hitachi, Elan and Nanoco. The following are summary case studies of their activities in the UK:

Case Summaries

Oxonica is a spinout company from the University of Oxford, drawing on many years of research in applied nontechnology. The company specialises in the creation of nanoparticles. Using patented assembly techniques, the company produces materials that are only a few atoms in size and have innovative chemical and physical properties. Website: www.oxonica.com/

Hitachi Ltd is one of the world's leading global information and electronics companies. The Hitachi Cambridge laboratory carries out research in collaboration with the Microelectronics Research Centre of Cambridge University at the Cavendish laboratory. Recent successes include innovations in the fields of single electron memory and logic, coherent optoelectronic control and quantum information processing. Website: www.hitachi-eu.com/r&d/redcentres/cambridge.htm.

Elan Corporation plc has developed an important platform technology to enhance the clinical performance of water-soluble drugs by transforming them into nanometre-sized particles. The company's patented NanoCrystal system has wide application and the nano-form can be incorporated into all common dosage formats. Website: www.elan.com/

Nanoco Technologies. Nanoco was the first company in the world to ship production level quantities of a special type of quantum dot, named "NanoDots". This discovery has numerous commercial applications; for example, inks and dyes containing NanoDots can provide unique, visible light signatures to authenticate products. They can be triggered by light to release very exact doses of drugs or DNA to particular parts of the human body. Website: www.nanotechnologies.com/.

Few industries will be uninfluenced by nanotechnology in terms of applications. Some of the sectors and sub-sectors where nanotechnology will have a major impact are:

- nerve and tissue repair techniques;
- biocompatible materials;
- advanced pharmaceuticals;
- controlled drug delivery;
- targeted drug delivery and personalised treatments;
- nerve and tissue repair techniques;
- nanoscale devices for research, diagnostics and therapy;
- better skin care and protection;
- surface coatings;
- nanotechnologically coated and nanoelectronic implants;
- sensors for real-time recording of neurological activity; and other biological functions;
- catalysts;
- magnetic materiaals and devices;
- faster computers;
- batteries and electronic displays;
- data storage;
- telecommunications.

Further information about the commercial development of the nanotechnology sector in the UK and across mainland Europe may be found on the Nanotechnology Industries Association website at: www.nanotechia.org.

GOVERNMENT SUPPORT
The UK
The development of the UK nanotechnology industry has been strongly supported by the UK Government. Examples of innovative projects that have received UK Government support include:

- Bangor UK-LMC (University of Wales, Bangor) – helping UK industry and universities to exploit laser micro-processing and emerging nanotechnology applications;

- BegbrokeNano (Oxford University) – providing open access to the significant measurement and characterisation expertise at Begbroke Science Park;
- Bondcentre (Applied Microengineering Ltd) – providing open access to wafer-bonding technology to help build multifunctional products;
- Emirate (BioCity, Universoty of Nottinghsam) – focusing on the growth, synthesis and evaluation of materials for the pharmaceuticals industry;
- Innovation in Nanotechnology Exploitation (INEX) – a microsystems and nanotechnology facility for industry, based at Newcastle University;
- MicroBridge (Cardiff University) – manufacturing micro-devices for the semiconductor market;
- NanoForce (Queen Mary College, London) – research and commercialisation of new nanomaterials including fashion, architecture, film, art and design;
- SemiMEMS (Semefab Ltd) - developing integrated sensing technology for interactive products of the future; and
- UK-MMT-BNC (Imperial College, University College London) – helping companies to develop and commercialise biomedical products.

In addition, the Technology Strategy Board, an Executive body sponsored by the Department of Business and Skills (BIS), has established a Nanotechnology Knowledge Transfer Network to support the exploitation and commercialisation of micro and nanotechnologies by informing, linking and facilitating innovation and collaborations between suppliers and users. (Visit: www.nanotechnologyktn.com for further information).

The EU
For the period from 2007 to 2013 the European Commission (EC) is implementing a programme to invest almost ?5 billion across Europe in nanotechnology research. Key areas to benefit from the EC's research funding are:

- Nanosciences and nanotechnologies
- Materials
- New production methods
- Integration of nanotechnologies for industrial applications.

Further information EC research funding can be found on:
http://cordis.europa.eu/home_en.html

UK RESEARCH CENTRES AND UNIVERSITIES

The UK's nationwide network of research institutes and universities have a world class reputation in nanotechnology research with numerous scientists focusing on nanotechnology research.

Research Institutes

Key research institutes include the 12 following centres:

- The Institute for Nanoscale Science and Technology (INSAT) and its commercial arm INEX at Newcastle. www.inex.org.uk
- Centre of Process Innovation (CPI) at Newcastle. www.uk-cpi.com
- University of Durham – Centre for Molecular and Nanoscale Electronics. www.dur.ac.ik/molecular.electronics
- Nanotechnology and Advanced Materials Research Institute (NAMRI), University of Ulster, Northern Ireland. www.namri.ulster.ac.uk
- Kelvin Nanocharacterization Centre, Glasgow. www.knc.gla.ac.uk
- The Nanoelectronics Research Centre, Glasgow. www.elecgla.ac.uk/groups/nano/welcome.html
- The Institute for Integrated Micro and Nano Systems, Edinburgh. www.see.ed.ac.uk/~SLIg
- Manchester Centre of Mesoscience and Nanotechnology, Manchester. www.cs.man.ac.uk/nanotechnology
- Nanoscale Physics Research Laboratory, Birmingham. www.npri.bham.ac.uk
- The Centre for Integrated Photonics (CIP), Ipswich. www.ciphotonics.com
- The Centre for Excellence in Metrology for Micro and Nano Technologies (CEMMNT), Loughborough. www.cemmnt.co.uk
- XGEN, Cardiff. www.xgen.org.uk

UK Universities

There are also over 35 universities listed below in alphabetical order throughout the UK currently undertaking nanotechnology research projects, either in conjunction with a research institute or through their own research programmes:

University	Areas of research
Birmingham	Nanostructured surfaces; size-selected
www.bham.ac.uk	nanoclusters and nanotools; molecular

manipulation and attosecond physics; nanofabrication and nanoelectronics.

Bradford
www.Bradford.ac.uk

Micromoulding; supramolecular materials science; modelling and design of drugs and delivery methods.

Bristol
www.bristol.ac.uk

Nanoparticle research for metal and plastics; biomedicine.

Brunel
www.brunel.ac.uk

3D Silicon Detectors.

Cambridge
www.cam.ac.uk

Spin detection in molecules; spin-dependent transport; nanotubes; nanofibres; nanowires; nanotribology; nanomagnets; magnetic logic; microscale sensors; scanning probe microcopy (SPM); electron beam lithography.

Coventry
www.coventry.ac.uk

Biosensors; protein derivatisation; gas sensors; gel.

Cranfield
www.cranfield.ac.uk

Ferroelectric ceramics, powders and composites; deposition of ferroelectric thin and thick films; piezoelectric ultrasonic motors; thermal IR pyroelectric detectors.

Durham
www.durham.ac.uk

Film deposition; focused ion beam milling; electron beam lithiography; atom force microscopy; magneto optic Kerr Effect; molecular nanostructures.

Edinburgh
www.edinburgh.ac.uk

Hybrid ECM-EDM, USM-EDM, Laser-ECM; system-on-chip design; system architectures; microstereolithography; silicon novel structures.

Exeter
www.exeter.ac.uk

Molecular engineering of structures and composites; molecular biosensors; biocatalysts; development of molecular switches for data storage and display applications; modelling and molecular design of fullerene derivatives.

Glasgow
www.glasgow.ac.uk

Molecular genetics; nanoelectronics; optoelectronics; molecular beam epitaxy: bioelectronics; silicon sensors; dry etching and plasma processing; device modelling and simulation.

Huddersfield www.huddersfield.ac.uk	Surface topology.
Hull www.hull.ac.uk	Particulate and stabilised emulsions; surfactant and colloid chemistry; nanochemiocal and biological reactions; nanophysics; laser ablation.
Imperial College London www.imperial.ac.uk	Nanoceramics; sensors and catalysts; carbon nanotubes; experimental solid state; quantum devices; electron, probe, ion beam w/SIMS; failure in composite structures: NEMS.
Kings College, London www.kcl.ac.uk	X-Ray and EUV optics; bio and nanophotonics.
Leeds www.leeds.ac.uk	Characterisation and design of new materials; colloid and surface chemistry; self-assembly; nanoparticular applications; nanomanufacturing; nanofluids in miniaturised devices; fibre optics; semiconductor materials and devices; properties of proteins; bionanoscience.
Leicester www.leicester.ac.uk	Instrumentation; devices; self-organised nanostructures; quantum theory of semiconductor nanostructures.
Liverpool www.liverpool.ac.uk	Nanoelectronic; magnetic nanostructured materials; sensor technology; functional materials; biomedicine; computational modelling.
London South Bank www.lsbu.ac.uk	Nanostructured functional coatings; photovoltaics.
Loughborough www.loughborough.ac.uk	Waterborne polymer composites; aqueous polymer colloids; advanced formulations for healthcare.
Manchester www.manchester.ac.uk	Molecular beam epitaxy growth; nanostructures and nanodevices; metal-semiconductor systems for fast electronic devices; microelectromechanical systems.
Newcastle www.newcastle.ac.uk	In vivo and in vitro cell chips; biomolecule engineering; self-assembly, synthesis qnd tethering of biomolecules and biomembranes; tissue engineering, cell regulation and cell adhesion on

	material surfaces; microfluidics, microreactors, nanofiltration, process intensification; micro and nano-device/systems engineering; nanoelectronic and microelectronic devices, biomimetic computation; nanostructured materials – fabrication and characterisation.
Nottingham www.nottingham. ac.uk	Molecular manipulation; surface analysis; electron spectroscopy; fuel technology; colloidal nanochrystal patterns; quantum nanostructures; fullerenes molecules; biosystems; electrospray; instrumentation.
Plymouth www.plymouth.ac.uk	piezo-electric sensors; thin film magnetic materials; MR head design and magnetic materials; two dimensional constraint coding for PRML; error correction coding and signal processing and equalisation for PRML channels; giant magneto impedence, magnetic recording theory; mathematical modelling of MR heads; high frequency magnetic recording theory.
Queens University, Belfast www.qub.ac.uk	Microchip technology; gene therapy, life science and nanotechnology applications.
Queen Mary University www.qmw.ac.uk	Carbon nanostructures; scanning probe microscopy.
Royal Holloway, London www.rhul.ac.uk	X-Ray collimators; semiconductor nanostructures.
Sheffield www.sheffield.ac.uk	Fluid flow in microchannel architectures; nanoparticulate technology; semiconductor nanotechnology; bionanoscience; polymer electronics; nanopatterning; tissue engineering; soft polymers; photonics and optoelectronics; nanomaterials; nanoparticles and nanotubes.
Sheffield Hallam www.shu.ac.uk	Polymers, composites and surfaces; corrosion technology; surface engineering; measuring/ imaging at atomic scale; self assembling nanostructures; sensors

	technology and systems; Microsystems; structural integrity.
Strathclyde www.strath.ac.uk	Superconducting devices; laser-induced nuclear, plasma and accelerators; plasmas; photonics; optics; biomolecular and chemical physics; semiconductor spectroscopy.
Ulster www.ulst.ac.uk	Fabrication tools and characterisation; devices; bulk materials/films with nanofeatures; molecular nanotechnology.
University College, London www.ucl.ac.uk	Diamond electronics; superconducting nanoelectronics; field emission display; material processing.
Wales www.wales.ac.uk	Biosensors; laboratory on a chip; medical physics; polymer electronics; optoelectronics; quantum computation and communication; pattern recognition and fuzzy systems.
West of England www.uwe.ac.uk	Nanotechnological developments in the fields of biomedicine, materials and sensor k sciences.
York www.york.ac.uk	Proteinbinding DNA, biochemical turnover; self assembly; electron microscopy and spectroscopy; magnetic materials; nanopatterning; surface physics; nanofabrication and analysis; condensed matter theory; photolithography techniques; immunological techniques for meningitis; spin electronics in magnetic materials and devices (spintronics); nanofabrication.

Note: The content of this chapter is extracted from the UK Trade and Investment Information Factsheet for the industry, updated in March 2010. For further information and updates visit www.uktradeinvest.co.uk.

3.10 RENEWABLE ENERGY: A UK PERSPECTIVE

Neil Budd
Watson Farley & Williams LLP

Climate change is a key item on the political agenda in the UK and promoting renewable energy is one of the ways that the Government is seeking to reduce the national 'carbon footprint'. In this chapter we examine the regulatory framework in the UK for renewable energy developers and review the current market conditions in particular areas of renewable energy.

STRATEGIC OBJECTIVES

Under the current Renewables Directive[1] each member state has been given a target to ensure that a specified percentage of its energy consumption (which includes electricity generation, heat and fuel usage) comes from renewable sources by 2020.[2] In the case of the UK the target figure is 15%. This is a significant increase compared to the baseline figure for 2005 of 1.3% stated in the Directive.

The UK Low Carbon Transition Plan 2009 outlined the former Government's strategy for reducing carbon emissions. It set a separate target for 30% of the UK's electricity generation to be produced from renewable energy sources by 2020. The UK is significantly less developed in capitalising upon renewable sources for heat and fuel and therefore, the UK's energy consumption target of 15% will mainly be met through electricity produced from renewable sources.

1 Directive 2009/28/EC
2 Department of Energy and Climate Change Consultation Paper on Renewable Electricity Financial Incentives, July 2009, p.20

The Coalition Government, which came into office in May 2010, has stated in its Programme for Government a strong commitment to the development of renewable energy and included commitments such as increasing the target for renewable energy, creating a "green investment bank" which will include the creation of "green financed products", introducing an offshore electricity grid in order to support the development of new generation of offshore wind power and encouraging "community-owned renewable energy schemes where local people benefit from the power produced".

LEGISLATIVE TOOLS

The legislative tools for achieving the strategic objectives outlined above are as follows:

Renewables Obligation and ROCs

Under the Renewables Obligation Order[3] licensed electricity suppliers are required to hold a certain number of Renewable Obligation Certificates ("ROCs"). The Obligation applies until 2037. The long period of the Obligation is likely to be important in enabling renewable energy developers to obtain project finance. A typical financing for a renewable energy project is ten to fifteen years and lenders require a secure legislative framework to be in place for the period of the loan.

The way the system works is that suppliers demonstrate their compliance with the Obligation by submitting ROCs to the regulator (Ofgem).[4] A ROC is issued by Ofgem to accredited renewable energy generators in respect of the electricity that they generate. Suppliers can either purchase the ROC from a renewable generator from whom they purchase the electricity or they can purchase the ROC separately. ROCs are separately tradable from the electricity to which they relate and ROCs can be bought from ROC traders. If a supplier fails to provide to Ofgem the requisite number of ROCs to demonstrate compliance with the Renewables Obligation, it must pay a buy-out payment. The buy-out payment is of an amount set periodically by Ofgem and has the effect of providing a cap on the ROC price. Buy-out payments go into a buy-out fund administered by Ofgem and this fund is recycled back to ROC-holders in proportion to the number of ROCs they hold. This payment (known as a "smear-back payment") is factored into the ROC price that a supplier would negotiate with a renewable generator.

Thus renewable generators will receive, in addition to the price for the electricity that they generate, a price for each ROC sold which will include an

---

3 Renewables Obligation Order 2009 (SI 2009 No 785)
4 The buy-out price from April 1 2010 to March 31 2011 stands at £36.99 per MWh (see Ofgem's website: www.ofgem.gov.uk).

element for the smear back payment.

Prior to the implementation of the current Renewables Obligation Order, each type of renewable power plant was given one ROC for each megawatt-hour (MWh) of electricity generated. The Renewables Obligation Order 2009 implements a system of banding which enables different numbers of ROCs to be granted to different forms of renewable energy depending on how established they are. Emerging technologies such as wave, tidal and advanced conversion technologies such as gasification and pyrolysis are eligible for 2 ROCs per MWh. Some technologies such as offshore wind will now receive 1.5 ROCs per MWh. Some, such as onshore wind) will continue to receive 1 ROC per MWh, whilst established technologies (such as electricity generated from landfill gas) are considered not to need a substantial subsidy in the future and have had their ROC entitlement reduced.

Due to concerns at the high cost of developing offshore wind farms, the former Government decided to increase the number of ROCs for offshore wind projects for a limited period, from 2010 to 2014, to 2 ROCs per MWh, provided that certain criteria were fulfilled relating to the entering into of contracts for the supply of turbines and construction of foundations.

The Coalition Government has pledged in its Programme for Government to maintain banded ROCs, but also to establish a full system of feed-in tariffs. It remains to be seen how the two will operate in tandem.

Feed-in Tariffs for small- scale generators

The Energy Act 2008 provided broad enabling powers for the introduction of feed-in tariffs (FITs) for small-scale low carbon electricity generation with a maximum limit of 5 MW. FITs are already widely used by other EU states to support renewables and have been particularly successful in Germany and Spain. FITs provide generators with guaranteed grid access and long term contracts for the electricity they produce.

The aim of FITs is to encourage the development of small-scale renewable energy sources for which the ROC system is regarded as expensive and cumbersome. The technologies which will covered by the FITs scheme include anaerobic digestion, hydro, solar photovoltaics (PV), wind turbines and micro combined heat and power (CHP).

The basic structure proposed for the FITs include a fixed payment from a nominated electricity supplier for every kilowatt hour (kWh) generated (the generation tariff) and an additional payment for every kWh exported to the grid (the export tariff). Generators will be guaranteed a market for their exports at a long-term guaranteed price. The generator then has the option to choose whether to sell exported electricity to the supplier at this guaranteed export tariff or to negotiate a price in the open market.

Renewable Heat Incentive

Currently there is a need to develop alternative ways of generating heat to ensure the UK meets its EU renewable energy target of 15% by 2020. The Energy Act 2008 makes provision for the setting up of a Renewable Heat Incentive (RHI). The RHI will provide financial assistance to the generators of renewable heat and the producers of specified renewable heat such as biomethane. It is expected that the RHI will cover a wide range of technologies including biomass, solar hot water, air and round source heat pumps, biomass combined heat power (CHP), biogas produced from anaerobic digestion and injection of biomethane into the gas grid.

THE EXPERIENCE OF RENEWABLE ENERGY IN THE UK

It can be seen from the discussion above that a renewable energy generator can expect to receive a considerable premium in respect of renewable benefits over and above the market price of the electricity. This is obviously intended to encourage the growth of renewable energy development in order that the Government can meet its target under the Renewables Directive discussed above. In this section of the chapter we look at the experience of different types of renewable energy development in the UK over the last few years and assess their future prospects.

Onshore Wind

Onshore wind has undoubtedly been the most successful type of renewable energy in the UK. According to Renewable UK, in 2010 there were a total of 248 operational on-shore wind farms with a capacity of 3,449.95 MW with a further 212 on-shore wind farms either under construction or having received consents (totalling 4897.53 MW).[5] However, to set this in an international context, whilst there is a total installed capacity of 4,491.15 MW of onshore and offshore wind in 2010 in the UK, this compares to a total of 25,777 MW of wind energy which was installed in Germany by the end of 2009 whilst in Spain the figure was 19,149 MW.[6] So the UK, whilst doing well, still has a long way to go to catch up with its neighbours.

5 www.bwea.com
6 www.ewea.com

The economics of onshore wind are a clear driver to investment. The main barriers to investment in onshore wind have been difficulties and delays in obtaining planning permission and difficulties in getting connected to the grid. The difficulties with the planning system have been the lengthy and convoluted processes for getting planning permission and the fact that many local planning authorities, whilst conceding the benefits of onshore wind in general terms, have been unwilling to see what they regard as unsightly wind farms in their "back yard".

In the case of grid connection, the difficulties have been that some distribution network operators, particularly in areas where there have been a lot of onshore wind farm applications for connections, have given connection dates several years hence because of the need to carry out reinforcement works to their network in order to accommodate the additional capacity represented by the new project. It is likely that proposals will be put in place to speed up grid connection through a "connect and manage" system whereby generators would receive a fixed connection date and would be entitled to use the system from that date, without having to wait for the network reinforcement works to be carried out.[7]

Offshore wind

The former Government was keen to promote the development of offshore wind projects in the UK which are recognised as offering the potential for much larger-scale projects than onshore wind (the London Array project, for example, is a 1,000 MW project). It was also thought that offshore wind farms, particularly those far out to sea, are unlikely to encounter the same level of objections on planning grounds to onshore wind farms.

In 2001 the Crown Estate organised the first round of tenders for offshore wind projects (known as 'Round 1'). Eighteen projects were awarded for sites within the twelve nautical mile territorial limit around the UK. Round 2 followed in 2003 and was on a much more ambitious scale. Fifteen projects with a combined capacity of 7.2 gigawatts were awarded. In June 2008 the Crown Estate announced proposals for a Round 3 programme designed to deliver up to 25 GW of additional offshore capacity by 2020. This announcement sparked significant interest. Following the closure of the competitive bid process for licensing of the wind farms in March 2009, the Crown Estate had received 40 bids relating to the nine Round 3 development zones from 18 different companies/consortia, including international companies from at least nine different countries. In January 2010, The Crown Estate announced the successful bidders for each of the nine Round 3 offshore wind zones within UK waters.

---

7 Department of Energy and Climate Change paper: "Impact Assessment of proposals to improve grid access" dated 3 March 2010.

The focus thus far given to wind energy reflects its importance to the UK renewable energy sector. If all the Round 2 wind farms come on stream, at 7.2 gigawatts, along with the projections of up to 25GW generated by the Round 3 wind farms, that is likely to account for a large percentage of the UK's electricity supply. Nevertheless, other forms of renewable energy, though small-scale, are attracting the interest of investors and these are discussed below.

Biomass

Biomass includes wood, crops, animal waste (e.g. chicken litter) and food waste. Biomass-fuelled power plants can operate using combustion or an advanced conversion technology" such as gasification, pyrolysis or anaerobic digestion. Advanced conversion technologies have lower carbon emissions and in the UK are eligible for 2 ROCs per MWh.

Biomass plants can also be developed as combined heat and power (CHP) plants whereby the heat is used as well rather than being wasted (e.g. to heat adjacent industrial premises). CHPs are environmentally-friendly and a regular biomass CHP (i.e. not using an advanced conversion technology) is eligible for 1.5 ROCs per MWh. The Renewable Heat Incentive discussed earlier is likely to provide a significant boost for CHP plants.

In its Programme for Government, the Coalition Government announced its intention to *"introduce measures to promote a huge increase in energy from waste through anaerobic digestion"*.

Solar

The UK, unlike countries such as Spain which has been credited as Europe's fastest growing solar power market,[8] has not up to now seen widespread development of solar energy. This may change, at least for small-scale solar PV (up to 5 MW), due to the introduction of feed-in tariffs mentioned earlier, the rates for which are particularly generous for PV installations. It is likely that the installation of solar panels in rooftops of commercial and industrial buildings and possibly also of residential block of flats or housing estates will become common-place. The new feed-in tariffs are also designed to encourage house owners to install solar panels. Larger solar plants, on farmland for example, may also become a common feature of the countryside, particularly as flat panels on fields are likely to encounter less hostility from local communities, in terms of their obtrusiveness, than onshore wind farms.

8 Platts Renewable Energy Report August 4, 2008, pg. 20

Wave/Tidal

Tidal/water energy can also be harnessed and used. Even a slow flowing stream of water, or moderate sea swell, can yield considerable amounts of energy. The Marine Renewables Deployment Fund is a £50 million fund established to assist the continued development of wave and tidal stream technologies. The fund sets high criteria for eligibility, the idea being to help projects not from start-up stage, but from a stage where they have significantly proven themselves to have a real chance of development. One of the projects awarded funding is the south-west Wave Hub project for which £4.5 million has been earmarked.[9] The Wave Hub project is being promoted by the South West Regional Development Agency which wants the south-west of England to take a "prominent position in marine renewable energy".[10]

In November 2008 the Crown Estate invited initial proposals from developers for the UK's first commercial marine power sites, located in Pentland Firth, north of Scotland. In March 2010, the Crown Estate announced that agreements for lease had been entered into for six wave project development sites and four tidal ones. The total maximum capacity of these sites is 1200 MW, half of which is for the wave projects and half for the tidal ones. At the same time, the Crown Estate announced proposals for a further major tidal energy project at Inner Sound for which they would shortly be inviting expressions of interest.[11]

In its Programme for Government, the Coalition Government announced its intention to introduce measures to encourage marine energy.

THE FUTURE OF RENEWABLE ENERGY IN THE UK

Overall, the future for renewable energy in the UK looks bright. Relatively low operating costs and established infrastructure mean that onshore wind is likely to remain important in the near future, although problems remain. Slow and inconsistent decision making at both a national and local level remain key concerns in the onshore wind sector.[12]

Offshore wind is the technology that the Government has pinned its hopes on in attempting to meet the country's renewable energy targets and the positive response to the Round 3 tenders suggests that offshore wind will over the next decade become the dominant form of renewable energy in the UK. The support mechanism given to offshore wind projects through additional ROCs allocated under the new banding scheme should encourage new equipment suppliers to come into the market, thereby reducing project development costs.

9 www.decc.gov.uk
10 www.southwestrda.org.uk
11 www.thecrownestate.co.uk
12 "Onshore Mid-Year Planning Update: Where Are We Now?", BWEA publication 'Real Power' issue 13, July-Sept 2008

Biomass is very likely to develop, as will waste-to-energy using advanced conversion technologies.

New feed-in tariffs should give a boost to microgeneration and also to commercial-scale solar PV projects.

Whilst research has suggested that tidal energy technologies in the UK still require development in order to reach commercial maturity,[13] the successful bid process for the development of offshore wave and tidal power in Pentland Firth suggests that tidal energy in the UK has taken a vital step forward in its long-term development.

13 "Turning the Tide – Tidal Power in the UK", Sustainable Development Commission, October 2007

Part Four

4.1 FINANCIAL REPORTING AND ACCOUNTING: AN OVERVIEW

Bee-Lean Chew, Michael Bordoley
and Jitendra Pattani
Wilder Coe LLP

This chapter provides an overview of the financial reporting and accounting requirements of the majority of entities carrying out trading or investment activities within the United Kingdom.[1]

INTRODUCTION

All entities carrying out business activities within the UK have an obligation to produce accounts summarising the entity's financial activities and results generally at least once a year. The accounts prepared normally cover a period of 12 months, though this can be varied to a maximum 18-month period. The period-end date to which these accounts are prepared is known as the accounting reference date (ARD).

The following chapter summarises the various financial reporting requirements and practical accounting issues faced by any entity looking to carry out its business activities in the UK.

---

1 This overview does not, however, cover specially regulated entities such as charities and registered social landlords, which have specialised requirements.

FORMAT OF ACCOUNTS
Unincorporated entities: Sole trader/ Partnership

There is no formal requirement for sole traders or partnerships to prepare annual accounts in accordance with any pre-determined format. However, in submitting the annual tax return to HM Revenue and Customs (HMRC), it is expected that the entity is to provide backing accounts supporting the figures included in the tax return, and these accounts should be prepared in accordance with UK Generally Accepted Accounting Practice (UK GAAP).[2] As a bare minimum, the sole trader or partnership will be expected to submit a statement of income and expenditure for the year with their tax return, prepared in accordance with UK GAAP.

Incorporated entities: Companies limited by shares or by guarantee

The most common types of entities are companies limited by shares incorporated under the Companies Act 2006. In terms of corporate financial reporting, the UK is currently undergoing a transitional phase in terms of its financial reporting requirements to the extent that it is aiming to achieve convergence with international reporting standards.

On 1st January 2005, it became compulsory for all UK publicly listed companies preparing consolidated accounts to prepare them in accordance with International Financial Reporting Standards (IFRSs). This requirement is not mandatory for non-public companies, though these may opt for early adoption, and therefore there is currently a divergence in accounting treatment across companies in the UK.

Statutory financial statements contain:

(i)   a directors' report;
(ii)   an auditors' report (unless the company qualifies for exemption from audit and takes advantage of that exemption);
(iii)   a profit and loss account;
(iv)   a full balance sheet, signed by a director of the company;
(v)   notes to the accounts.

As for unincorporated entities, incorporated entities submit backing accounts with their annual tax returns. Again, there is no formal standard to which these accounts are prepared, and a detailed statement of income and expenditure will suffice.

2 As for most countries, entities engaging in business activities in the UK are required by national law or regulation to prepare financial statements that conform to a required set of generally accepted accounting principles. In the UK, the preparation of financial statements is governed by a combination of statute and standard Practice, the whole of which comprises UK Generally Accepted Accounting Practice (UK GAAP). The latter is codified by the Consultative Committee of Accountancy Bodies (CCAB) in the form of Financial Reporting Standards (FRSs). Prior to 1990, accounting standards were issued in the form of Statements of Standard Accounting Practice (SSAPs) – in so far as these have not been superseded by FRSs, the guidelines provided by SSAPs are still relevant in the preparation of financial statements.

Incorporated entities: limited liability partnerships

Accounting rules as applied to companies apply in the same manner to LLPs, where the format and regulations are as set out in the Companies Act 1985 (and 2006), as amended by the Limited Liability Partnerships Act 2000.

LLP accounts must include:

(i)   An auditor's report (unless the LLP is exempt from audit);
(ii)   A profit and loss account;
(iii)   A balance sheet, signed by a designated member; and
(iv)   Notes to the accounts.

In respect of taxation requirements, provided the LLP carries on a trade or profession and is not purely an investment vehicle, it is considered to be tax-transparent, i.e. the LLP itself is not taxed on its income or capital gains. Instead, the members are taxed on their shares of the LLP's profits and gains, in accordance with normal partnership rules.

AUDIT REQUIREMENTS

Of the different vehicles through which a business can be carried out in the UK, only limited companies and LLPs are required to have their financial statements audited.

Definition of an audit

An audit includes an examination of the financial statements by a registered auditor[3] who, on completing the audit, makes a written report to the shareholders. It also includes an assessment of significant estimates and judgement utilised by the directors in their preparation of the accounts, as well as the accounting policies adopted.

The examination is performed on a test basis on the basis of evidence relevant to the amounts and disclosures shown in the financial statements.

On completion of the audit, the auditor will provide an opinion as to whether the annual financial statements:

(i)   provide a 'true and fair view' of:
        - the state of the company's affairs at the balance sheet date; and
        - the profit or loss for the period under review;

3 For contact details of firms registered in the UK to carry out statutory audits: i) The Institute of Chartered Accountants in England and Wales, Gloucester House, 399 Silbury Boulevard, Central Milton Keynes, MK9 2HLwww.icaew.co.uk
ii) The Institute of Chartered Accountants of Scotland, ,CA House 21 Haymarket Yards, Edinburgh EH12 5BH www.icas.org.uk
iii)The Institute of Chartered Accountants in Ireland, 32 – 38 Linenhall Street, Belfast, County Antrim BT2 8BG www.icai.ie
iv) Association of Chartered Certified Accountants ACCA UK, 29 Lincoln's Inn Fields, London WC2A 3EEhttp://uk.accaglobal.com/

(ii)   have been properly prepared in accordance with the relevant financial reporting framework; and

(iii)   have been prepared in accordance with the relevant legislative require-ments.

Furthermore, the auditor will confirm that:

(i)   adequate accounting records have been kept;

(ii)   the financial statements are in agreement with the accounting records and returns;

(iii)   disclosures of directors' remuneration in accordance with relevant legisla-tive requirements have been made; and

(iv)   all information and explanations required for the audit were received.

In giving an opinion, the auditors state that they would have performed the audit with a view to obtaining reasonable assurance that the financial statements are free from material misstatement, whether caused by fraud, other irregularities or errors.

The opinion expressed within the audit report may be qualified should the audit uncover any areas of uncertainty or disagree with the directors' treatment of items within the financial statements, or encounter any deficiency in evidence required to support amounts and disclosures in the financial statements. The extent of disclosure included within the audit report would depend on the degree to which the shortcoming would affect the reader of the financial statements.

'True and fair' concept

This concept is a statutory requirement and central to the whole process of financial reporting in the UK. While there is no definitive guidance on what constitutes a 'true and fair' view, "[i]t is inherent in the nature of the concept that financial statements will not give a true and fair view without containing sufficient quantity and quality of information to satisfy the reasonable expectations of the readers to whom they are addressed."[4]

The 'true and fair' concept is essentially dynamic in nature, and constantly evolves in response to changes in accounting and business practice. These changes are constantly monitored, and codifications of such changes are con-tained within the Financial Reporting Standards (FRSs), Statements of Standard Accounting Practice (SSAPs) and, most recently, International Financial Reporting

---

4 Accounting Standards Board: *Statement of Principles for Financial Reporting*

Standards (IFRSs). For specialised activities such as charities and financial services, further guidance in the form of Statements of Recommended Practice (SORPs) are issued. While not statutory, the guidance provided in FRSs, SSAPs, IFRSs and SORPs is generally taken to be authoritative in the UK. Any departure from these principles would have to be clearly explained and justified in the financial statements.

Finally, to emphasise the fundamental nature of this concept to UK financial reporting, it is important for anyone involved in the preparation of financial statements to note that the 'true and fair' concept can override the application of all FRSs, SSAPs and IFRSs, and the reasons for the override need to be disclosed in the financial statements.

Materiality

'Materiality' is an expression of the relative significance of a particular matter in the context of the financial statements as a whole. An item would be considered material if its omission would reasonably be expected to influence the decisions of readers of the financial statements.

Exemption from an audit

A company or LLP may be exempted from the statutory requirement to have its financial statements audited if it fulfils all the exemption criteria laid down by statute. The entitlement to audit exemption is based on three criteria: turnover, gross assets and the size of the company. All criteria have to be fulfilled to qualify for audit exemption. As at the time of writing, the thresholds for audit exemption are as shown in Table 4.1.1.

Table 4.1.1 Thresholds for audit exemption

	Single company/ LLP	Group of companies*
Turnover	< £6,500,000	< £7,800,000 gross** < £6,500,000 net**
Gross Assets	< £3,260,000	< £3,900,000 gross** < £3,260,000 net**
Size***	Small	Small

A company/ LLP will constitute part of a group where there is common ownership and control across all companies/ LLPs within the group
**'Gross' refers to the group's aggregate result, inclusive of intercompany transactions and balances. 'Net assets' comprise the group's consolidated results, i.e. exclusive of intercompany transactions and balances.*
***A 'small' company/ group is defined as one which fulfils at least two of the following conditions:*

	Company	Group
Annual turnover	< £6,500,000	< £7,800,000 gross < £6,500,000 net
Gross assets	< £3,260,000	< £3,900,000 gross < £3,260,000 net
Average number of employees	< 50	< 50

Note that a subsidiary company or LLP contained within a group of companies which fulfils the above criteria will not be entitled to exemption from audit, regardless of its individual financial results, unless the group as a whole fulfils the small group criteria as detailed in the table above.

The following entities will not be entitled to exemption from audit, irrespective of size:

- Public limited companies;
- Banking or insurance companies;
- Registered insurance brokers;

- Companies registered with the Financial Services Authority;
- Companies where the Articles of Association specify that an audit is required;
- A member of a group of companies in which any member is:
  - A public company or entity which has publicly quoted shares or debentures;
  - Registered with the Financial Services Authority; or
  - A person who carries on insurance market activity.

Finally, shareholders controlling 10 per cent or more of any company can override the audit exemption size criteria rule by exercising their statutory right to require an audit.

PRACTICAL ACCOUNTING ISSUES

Any entity intending to carry out business activities within the UK should also be aware of the following issues:

Filing Deadlines for Financial Statements

Depending on the nature of the entity, financial statements must be filed with the relevant authorities within a specified timescale of Table 4.1.2:

Table 4.1.2 Timescale for filing financial statements

Business vehicle	Filing authority	Filing deadline
Sole trader/ partnership	No requirement to file annual accounts	
Company – private	Registrar of Companies	Within 9 months after the ARD
Company – public	Registrar of Companies	Within 6 months after the ARD
Limited liability partnership	Registrar of Companies	Within 9 months after the ARD

The filing deadline for companies and LLPs will change where the entity alters its ARD, for example, if a company changes its ARD, the filing deadline will be the later of the original filing deadline and 3 months after the application to extend the filing deadline. Late delivery of accounts to the Registrar of Companies will result in an automatic late filing penalty, and is, technically, a criminal offence for which directors can be prosecuted.

Filing Deadlines for Tax Returns

All entities carrying out business activities within the UK are required to submit tax returns to the HMRC on an annual basis. Filing deadlines for submission of the annual tax return for the various entities are identified in Table 4.1.3, as follows:

Table 4.1.3 Filing deadlines for tax returns

Business vehicle	Filing deadline
Sole trader/ partnership/ LLP	By 31st January following the business's ARD
Companies	By 12 months following the business's ARD

Value Added Tax (VAT)

In the UK, there is a tax imposed on consumer expenditure called Value Added Tax (VAT). Most business transactions involve the supply of goods or services and VAT is payable if the supply is made:

(i)   in the United Kingdom;
(ii)   by a taxable person; and
(iii)   in the course or furtherance of business and is not specifically exempted or zero-rated.

The regulation, monitoring and collection of VAT is currently undertaken by HMRC.

Forms detailing the breakdown of an entity's VAT liability must be submitted on a periodic basis to HMRC, as well as payment of net VAT due. An entity can opt to submit VAT returns monthly, quarterly or annually. Submission of the periodic returns is due by 30 days after the period-end. Payment of VAT is due 14 days after the submission deadline.

It is compulsory for an entity which makes taxable supplies exceeding £70,000 per annum to register with HMRC and submit VAT returns. Notification to HMRC must be made within 30 days of the end of the month in which the value of taxable supplies first exceeds £70,000.

The rate of VAT imposed on a supply depends on the type of supply made. There are three categories of supplies:

(i)   Exempt
(ii)   Zero-rated
(iii)   Standard-rated

The operation of VAT has become increasingly complicated over the years since its introduction, and it is important to seek professional advice in the following situations:

- importing and exporting goods or services
- supplies made by the entity are a mixture of different VAT categories
- retail schemes
- land and property transactions
- self-supplies

Finally, more detailed guidance on an entity's responsibilities under the VAT regime is contained in Chapter 4.3 and on the website www.hmrc.gov.uk.

Payroll Taxes

Any person looking to pursue business activities in the UK will encounter payroll taxes if they are looking to employ staff.

Payroll taxes are under the remit of the HMRC, who publish various booklets relating to how the system for collecting taxes is operated and the legislation which has to be complied with.

In brief, the employer is responsible for reporting, collecting and remitting payroll taxes to the HMRC as well as operating the Department of Social Security's (DSS) sick pay, maternity pay and paternity schemes.

The employer must register with the HMRC to operate a payroll scheme. Upon registration the HMRC will provide the employer with guidelines on operating the scheme as well as copies of the necessary returns which have to be made to the HMRC over the course of the year.

Tax and national insurance contributions are payable to the HMRC by the 19th of the month following that in which the salaries were paid.

In most businesses, the directors, and often the employees, have benefits that are not immediately taxed through the payroll system in place. Returns detailing such benefits, and the national insurance contributions payable thereon are due on 19th July following the fiscal year in which the benefits are made available.

More detailed guidance on an employer's responsibilities for payroll operation is contained on the website www.hmrc.gov.uk.

Dividends and Distribution of Profits

A company may distribute its available profits to its members (shareholders) by way of dividend at any point in the course of a financial year.[5] Such distributions can only be made out of post-tax profits and must be in accordance with the rules and conditions laid down by the Companies Act 2006. The Companies Act does not provide who shall declare a dividend, and the usual practice in the UK is for the Articles of Association to specify that dividends be declared by the shareholders in general meeting. It is also possible to specify in the Articles that directors be given the power to declare dividends to the exclusion of general meetings.

An important point to note is that, before declaring an interim dividend, i.e. a dividend paid between annual general meetings, the directors must satisfy themselves that the financial position of the company warrants the payment of such a dividend out of profits available for distribution,[6] that is, net accumulated realised profits.[7] If the company does not have positive reserves at the time of declaration of the dividend, the dividend is deemed to be an illegal distribution, and the directors may be prosecuted under civil law.

The Companies Act imposes an additional capital maintenance requirement on public companies to ensure that the net worth of the company is at least equal to the amount of its capital. A public company can only distribute profit if:

(i)   at the time of the distribution, the amount of its net assets, that is the total excess of assets over liabilities, is not less than the aggregate of its called-up share capital and its undistributable reserves;[8] and

(ii)   the distribution does not reduce the amount of the net assets to less than the aggregate of the company's called-up share capital and its undistributable reserves.

A company should always prepare accounts reflecting its financial position at the date of the distribution of profits to avoid the illegal payment of dividends. For

5 This does not include distributions in the course of winding-up, bonus issues of paid-up shares, and certain types of share redemption or reduction of share capital.

6 A statutory code of profits in the legal sense appears in sections 841 to 846 of the Companies Act 2006.

7 Section 830(2) of the Companies Act 2006 lays down the basic rule which states that a company's profits available for distribution are its accumulated, realised profits (on both revenue and capital items) not previously distributed or capitalised, less its accumulated realised losses (on both revenue and capital items) not written off in a proper reduction or reorganisation of capital.

public companies, there is a statutory requirement that 'relevant accounts' be prepared to the date a distribution is made to ensure its legality.[9] For private companies, there is no such requirement but, from a practical viewpoint, this requirement should be adhered to. Note that, even if the annual accounts prepared at a later stage show an insufficient figure of distributable profits, a dividend paid on the basis of the interim accounts will still be considered lawful.

8 Undistributable reserves are defined as: i) the share premium account ii) the capital redemption reserve iii) the amount by which the company's accumulated unrealised and uncapitalised profits exceed its accumulated unrealised losses not written off, and iv) any other reserves which the company is prohibited from distributing by statute or its Memorandum or Articles.
9 Defined in section 836 of the Companies Act 2006.

4.2 BUSINESS TAXATION

Tim Cook
Wilder Coe LLP

INTRODUCTION
This chapter is divided into three parts:

- General Tax considerations relating to various types of business entity formed to trade in the UK
- Information as to the types of income, the payment of tax, and the rates of tax applicable.
- A description of how taxable business income and gains are determined, and the deductibility of certain revenue and capital expenditure.

GENERAL TAX CONSIDERATIONS ON UK BUSINESS FORMATIONS
In determining the method of trading in the UK commerciality must determine the vehicle to be used: corporation, branch, limited liability partnership (LLP) or general partnership.

Each type of entity has its own advantages and disadvantages. Below are some comments about the alternatives.

Representative Office versus Permanent Establishment
If the intention is not to create a taxable entity or legal presence in the UK, then

care has to be taken to ensure that any presence in the UK is purely representative without the creation of a permanent establishment (PE).The comprehensive list of double tax agreements (DTAs) between the UK and other trading nations will set out what will contribute to the creation of a PE and therefore bring the foreign entity within the UK tax regime.

The basic difference between the two and what establishes whether or not there is a PE, is whether the overseas entity is trading with the UK, or is trading in the UK.

From 1st January 2003 under provisions in Finance Act 2003(FA2003) non-resident companies are only liable to corporation tax in the UK if they carry on a trade through a PE. Otherwise they will be liable to income tax.

Under the FA2003 provisions a company has a PE if it has:

- a fixed place of business in the UK;
- an agent acting on behalf of the company who habitually exercises\ authority to do business on behalf of the company.

If a foreign company has a PE it is chargeable to tax on the profits wherever arising, which are attributable to that PE.

The losses arising in a PE may be available for offset against the profits in the main country of residence of the foreign company. As losses frequently arise in the initial periods of trading, PEs are frequently set up for the first periods of trading, with incorporation following at a later date. (See below).

Factors influencing the decision are complex and include the nature of the activities, the ability to enter into contracts or commit the foreign entity to a course of action. Care and advice are necessary.

Branch versus subsidiary

The UK branch of a foreign company is taxable on the profits arising in the UK. The calculation is as for a separate entity (e.g. a subsidiary) so that transactions will need to be on a proper commercial basis. Profits arising in the branch can be remitted to the head office without restriction and without any form of withholding tax.

Branches come within the normal corporation tax methods of calculation, and so if the profits exceed a certain threshold the branch will be liable to pay corporation tax in four equal quarterly instalments. In assessing this, the number of associated companies on a world wide basis has to be taken into account . (See below).

If the UK entity is a subsidiary then, subject to the appropriate DTA, withholding tax might be applicable, but only on certain specific types of income. There is no UK withholding tax on the payment of dividends.

There is little or no difference from a UK taxation perspective as a result of trading through either a UK branch, or a UK subsidiary.

In both cases the rules relating to thin capitalisation will need to be considered. (See below).

A subsidiary is a separate legal entity in the UK and so, normally, any claims would go no further. A branch is part of the overseas entity and so any claim would ultimately rest with that entity.

Direct Investment versus holding company structure

Direct investment through a branch, corporation or partnership is easy to establish and will normally be the preferred method. There are usually no adverse taxation consequences of any of these routes, and ongoing administration and compliance can be kept to a minimum.

Sometimes, however, a UK holding company route can be appropriate. This is dependent upon the functions and activities of the UK business entity, the need for financing both in the UK and elsewhere, exit strategies, and the interaction with other non-UK entities.

Residence

Liability to taxation in the UK will come with residence here. Incorporation in the UK or elsewhere does not determine the residence status of a company. A simple, accepted guideline is that residence is where the 'central management and control' of the company resides. This is where the strategy and management of the company are formulated and actioned.

Value Added Tax (VAT)

The harmonisation of VAT within the EU means that, in general, goods can be moved around the region without VAT consequences.

When goods are imported from outside the EU, import VAT is payable. From that point onwards the goods are freely moveable between EU countries.

Any business investing or trading in the UK will have to consider whether or not it has a "business establishment" for UK VAT purposes. The rules for the creation of a "business establishment" are different from those used for determining the residence of the company. Other general VAT rules will also apply (See Chapter 4.3).

DIFFERENT TYPES OF INCOME

The UK tax system works on the basis that each type of income is subject to specific rules as to how it will be calculated. The main types of income are set out below with a general description of the method by which they are calculated.

Companies and branches

Trading income
Introduction
The starting point for the calculation of taxable business income is the profit shown in the accounts of the entity – the accounting treatment of expenditure is often the key to how the expense will be treated for taxation purposes. This will become more common in the future as international accounting standards become standardised on a worldwide basis.

The accounting profit is then adjusted to exclude certain expenditure not allowable under UK taxation rules, and the resulting figure is then reduced to take account of various taxation only allowances and reliefs that are not part of the accounting records. The calculations relating to general expenditure incurred in the UK apply whatever the nature of the entity in the UK. The treatment of charges from the foreign entity can differ in the UK depending upon whether the UK entity is a PE or a separate legal entity such as a limited company.

Some of the adjustments are set out below. This list is not exhaustive and advice should be taken in respect of any particular item of expenditure.

Not allowed:
- entertainment;
- certain legal and professional charges;
- capital expenditure or depreciation (see comments on Capital Allowances below);
- general provisions in respect of any expenditure;
- fines and illegal payments;
- gifts.

Allowed:
- All employee costs in the form of wages and salaries for services rendered to the business are generally deductible. However if the employee receives

a benefit – under UK tax law this can be quite complex – the employee may suffer an additional tax charge and the employer an additional National Insurance (NI) charge.

- Accounts depreciation is replaced by Capital Allowances under a complex but comprehensive system – allowances run from 4% up to 175% depending upon the nature of the expenditure. Capital expenditure otherwise disallowed for taxation purposes might obtain an allowance if it falls within the Capital Allowances regime (see above).
- Specific provisions for certain types of expenditure e.g. bad debts.

Deduction dependent upon nature of UK entity

- Although interest and royalty payments made by a UK Company will be deductible (subject to transfer pricing rules), payments to a head office by a PE will not be deductible. Relief could be obtained if the payments were to a foreign affiliate, in other words to a separate legal entity.
- Management charges can be deductible in both cases, subject to transfer pricing rules. In the case of a company the charge could be based upon the services provided by the offshore parent. In the case of a PE the allocation could be on a 'shared' basis of total costs, provided they can be shown to be used by the UK PE.

Land and property

Income from Land and Property is taxable under different sections of the Taxes Acts in the UK depending upon whether the property is situated in the UK or overseas. However the rules for calculating the profit are essentially the same.

Income and expenses from all UK sources are pooled and treated as a separate rental business, with a separate business in respect of overseas properties.

The calculation of the profits generally follows the rules for trading activities and accounts must be prepared on an accruals basis and in accordance with generally accepted accounting principles.

Where commercial properties are involved capital allowances may be obtained for certain capital expenditure, but no relief can be claimed for such expenditure on residential properties.

Certain other allowances might possibly be available for residential lettings, but this will depend upon the type of letting.

Losses from a commercial letting business can, in a company, be offset against other general income of the same or later accounting periods while the same trade is being carried on.

Interest

Interest is, as with other company income, usually taxed on an accruals basis. However certain types of interest under this heading have different treatment. Care has to be taken on the receipt of interest to ascertain the correct taxation treatment. The company regime differs from that for individuals mentioned below.

Capital Gains

Capital gains arising from the sale of assets are added to other profits for the year in the company and taxed at the same rates.

In calculating the gain costs of purchase and sale can be taken into account. If there have been improvements to the asset after original purchase, and the improvements are still reflected in the asset at the date of sale, the costs of the improvements can be deducted from the sale proceeds in calculating the gain.

The original cost, and any other allowable expenditure, is indexed upwards from the date the expenditure is incurred up to the date of sale. The date of sale is taken as the date of exchange of contracts binding seller and purchaser to the sale.

The indexation rates are announced monthly and are broadly the retail price indices.

UK Dividends

With the abolition of the imputation system no refundable tax credit is now given at the shareholder level. Individual shareholders do receive a notional tax credit which covers their UK liability unless they are liable to the higher rates of income tax, in which case UK residents will have a further liability.

Corporations receive no credit, but no further tax is due.

Individuals and partnerships

Income

The income from a partnership is allocated to the partners in accordance with the partnership agreement. The income so allocated, from each source or type of income is then assessed on the individual partner – be it a company or an individual.

An individual's income is calculated in the same way as for a company where there is a 'trading' element. The calculations and points made above with reference to Trading Income , Land and Property are therefore the same for individuals.

The other types of Income and Capital Gains are dealt with differently, and the differences are set out below.

Interest

In the main, for individuals, interest and other investment income will have been received after deduction of income tax at 20%. The income is assessed on an arising basis and not an accruals basis used for companies. Individuals liable at the higher rates of income tax of either 40% or 50% will have to pay the difference.

Capital Gains

The basis of calculation of the gain arising is exactly the same as for companies in respect of the deduction of costs from the sale proceeds. However there is now no relief due in respect of indexation.

A new capital gains tax regime was introduced from 6th April 2008. The tax is charged at a flat rate of 18% of the gain. In the budget statement on the 22nd June 2010 it was announced that this flat rate of 18% will only apply to basic rate tax payers. Higher rate tax payers will have to pay a higher rate of 28% on their capital gains. A special reduced rate of 10%, which is more correctly known as entrepreneurs relief, will be payable on the first £5 million of gains made in a taxpayer's lifetime, where the gain is made on qualifying business asset disposals. Thus the disposal of all or part of a business, or the disposal of shares or securities in an unlisted company, or the disposal of assets following the cessation of a business should all qualify for entrepreneurs' relief. There are a number of conditions which need to be met in order for entrepreneurs' relief to apply and these need to be checked carefully beforehand.

Land and Property

As indicated above, profits are calculated in the same way for companies and individuals. However if losses are incurred they are treated differently. The company position is as set out above. For individuals the losses, if they arise from the letting of commercial properties, can be offset against other property income of that year. Alternatively they will be carried forward and used against future income from the property business.

Where the losses arise from residential lettings they can only be carried forward, and not offset against other income.

Dividends

Dividends from UK companies and qualifying unit trusts received by a UK resident are deemed, for taxation purposes, to have had notional tax of 10% deducted before receipt. If the individual is not liable for tax at the higher rates the notional credit covers any liability due.

If the individual does not pay tax however, no refund of the notional tax can be obtained.

If tax is paid at the new highest level of 50%, which becomes effective only from 6th April 2010, a further 36.11% tax will be due on the net dividend received.

PAYMENT OF TAX

Companies

The corporation tax liabilities of companies are payable 9 months and 1 day after the end of the accounting period. Accounting periods generally run for a period of 12 months to the same accounting date each year. If the accounting period is extended or shortened special rules apply to the method of calculation of profits, capital allowances etc., and adjustments will be made to the tax payment dates.

Large companies pay corporation tax on account in quarterly instalments based upon an estimate of the current year's corporation tax liability.

The basic definition of a large company is one with profits in excess of £1.5 million. Various rules apply to companies in the first years in which they come within the large company definition to ascertain in which accounting period they have to start the quarterly payments.

When there are associated companies, the £1.5 million lower limit is divided between the number of companies. Associated companies include overseas companies so in large groups it is possible that the quarterly instalment procedures will apply at much lower profit levels.

Applicable tax rates

Table 4.2.1 identifies the rates that apply to all income and gains.

Table 4.2.1   Tax rates applicable to all company income and gains

	Taxable profits/gains	Tax Rate
Small Companies Rate	£0 – £300,000	21% reducing to 20% from 1st April 2011
Main Rate	> £1,500,000	28% reducing to 24% over the four years ending 2014

If profit is above the Small Companies profit maximum of £300,000, but below the Main Rate threshold of £1,500,000 a marginal calculation applies to the excess over £300,000. The effect is to bring the tax at £1,500,000 back to 28%. The result is that tax in the margin has an effective rate currently of 29.75%.

The Small Companies Rate threshold of £300,000 is divided between all associated companies. Thus if there are four associated companies each would be entitled to £75,000 of profit taxable at the 21% rate before going into marginal calculations. Associated companies include both UK and overseas companies.

Partnerships (General or LLP)

Applicable tax rates

Tax on partnership income is based upon the profits allocated to each partner. Each partner is responsible for his/her own tax liability.

If the partner is a limited company the rates are as shown above for companies.

If the partner is an individual the rates are those applying to individuals as set out in Table 4.2.2 below:

Table 4.2.2 Tax rates applying to partners who are individuals

Taxable Income	Tax Rate
Up to £37,400	20%
Between £37,400 and £150,000	40%
Above £150,000	50%

The above rates of tax are applied cumulatively and are for the year ending 5th April 2011.

Each partner will be entitled to offset their personal allowances and reliefs against their allocated share of the partnership profits.

Payment of tax

In respect of trading income from a partnership the tax is payable twice yearly, on 31st January within the year of assessment, and on 31st July following the year of assessment.

Special rules apply on commencement of trade.

Once the trade is running the payments are based upon the profits earned in the previous year.

As tax payments made in January and July are likely to be estimates of the final liability for a particular tax year adjustments are made to correct these payments on account in the following January .

The result of this is that where profits of a business are rising the January payment will always be the greater of the two. If profits are falling, so that it is expected that the tax due will be less than that paid for the previous year, claims to reduce the payments on account can be made. However, if the calculation is inaccurate, leading to an underpayment of tax interest will be charged. In extreme cases of abuse of the system penalties can also be imposed.

CAPITAL ALLOWANCES

The UK system of Capital Allowances is comprehensive and covers the majority of assets from general plant and machinery (which includes fixtures, fittings, computers etc.), to allowances on certain types of buildings, to intangible assets, patents, research and development expenditure etc.

The allowances are based upon the cost to the entity, and where connected parties are concerned (e.g. acquisitions from the Head Office in the case of a PE, or from a parent in the case of a separate company) the cost to the UK entity will broadly be as defined in Table 4.2.3:

Table 4.2.3 Cost basis for capital allowances

	Acquired from: Head Office	Foreign associate
Plant and machinery	Market value	Lowest of actual cost, book value or market value
Hotels/ industrial buildings	Calculated written down value for tax purposes	Calculated written down value for tax purposes
Intangible assets	Book value	Market value

New rates of Capital Allowances were introduced from 6th April 2008 for unincorporated businesses, and from 1st April for incorporated businesses. The main rate of annual Writing Down Allowance is now 20%, reducing to18% for accounting periods ending after April 2012, and 10%, reducing to 8% for accounting periods ending after April 2012, for assets classified as long life assets (ie assets which it is reasonable to expect will have a useful life of more than 25 years) and for assets that are integral to buildings at the time of purchase. In addition a new Annual Investment Allowance of 100% was introduced for expenditure on plant and machinery incurred up to a maximum of £100,000, reducing to £25,000 for accounting periods ending after April 2012,in any one year. Any excess expenditure, over £100,000 (or £25,000), will then qualify for Writing Down Allowances.

There are 100% capital allowances still available for expenditure on certain environmentally friendly projects such as natural gas and hydrogen refuelling equipment, low emission motor vehicles, waste water recovery and re-use systems, and certain heating, lighting and air flow energy saving technologies.

Although not necessarily a capital allowance relief, there are special allowances available to companies for expenditure on research and development. Dependent upon the size of the company relief of up to 175% of the revenue expenditure can be obtained. This relief is normally by deduction against profits, reducing the taxable amounts. In some cases, where the company has losses and so is unable to obtain immediate tax relief, cash credits can be paid to the company in place of the corporation tax deduction.

LOSSES

Trading losses are calculated in the same way as trading profits. Capital Allowances can increase losses or change a profit into a loss.

Once determined, a loss can be utilised in a variety of ways. Examples are:

- Offset against total profits, income and gains of the year in which the loss arises.
- Offset against total profits, income and gains of the year prior to the year in which the loss arises. A temporary extension has been introduced here so that a maximum of £50,000 of unused losses will be available to be carried back to two earlier years as well.
- Carried forward indefinitely against profits of the trade arising in later accounting periods.
- Surrendered to other UK group or consortium companies in the year in which the loss arises for offset against the income and gains of those companies in that year.
- The surrender to other group companies can include surrenders between PEs and subsidiaries.

Where a company is acquired with losses arising from trading activities, care has to be taken to ensure that those losses are available to the new owners of the company. Consideration has to be given to the way in which the trade will be carried on after the change of ownership in order to preserve the availability of those losses.

ROLLOVER RELIEF

Where a business disposes of a qualifying business asset (see below) and reinvests the proceeds in another qualifying asset, the capital gain arising on the sale can be deferred until the sale of the second asset. Rollover can continue being applied on all subsequent sales until the final sale without reinvestment takes place.

The main qualifying asset types are listed in Table 4.2.4, as follows:

Table 4.2.4 Types of asset qualifying for rollover relief

Class	Asset
1A	Land and buildings
1B	Fixed plant and machinery
2	Ships, aircraft and hovercraft
3	Satellites, space stations and spacecraft
4	Goodwill

Other, less common assets are also included.

THIN CAPITALISATION

Funding of a UK company must also be on a commercial basis, or adjustments can be made under the Transfer Pricing rules (already mentioned) or, where the UK company is a 75% (or greater) subsidiary of an overseas company, under the rules relating to thin capitalisation. There are requirements for appropriate debt/equity ratios, and of course if the lending is intra group, on the interest rates applied.

From 1st July 2009 there will be new rules introduced exempting most UK companies from paying corporation tax on receipt of foreign dividends. Dividends received from what are known as Controlled Foreign Companies, i.e. companies resident in low tax rate countries, will continue to be taxed under existing rules which charge them to corporation tax here with relief for foreign with-holding and underlying taxes suffered.

The reason for the legislation is to stop excess leveraging of a company allowing the profits to be extracted by way of interest charges. At the moment parts of the legislation are under review and discussion to ensure that they are in line with EU tax harmonisation rules generally.

STAMP DUTY LAND TAX/STAMP DUTY

From 1st December 2003 Stamp Duty Land Tax (SDLT) replaced the old Stamp Duty regime with respect to land and property transactions in the UK.

As with Corporation Tax and Income Tax in the UK SDLT is a self-assessment tax and the obligation to notify the Inland Revenue that a transfer has taken place falls on the person paying the tax – the purchaser.

Under Stamp Duty the tax was payable on the completion of the contract. This gave rise to various arrangements to postpone payment. As a result, although the SDLT is also payable on completion of the contract there are provisions which charge the tax on substantial completion of the contract. Under English Law this could be on the exchange of contracts. Substantial completion is not defined but is in broad terms when receipt of most of the consideration, taking possession of the property, and the entitlement to receive the rents or profits from the property.

Rates of Tax

The rate of SDLT depends upon whether the property is residential or commercial.

The rates of tax are not based upon slices of value. If a value is within one of the slices shown below in Table 4.2.5 the whole of the price is subject to tax at that rate; e.g. if the residential value is £175,000, no tax is payable; if the value is £175,001, the rate on the whole is 1%, or £1,750.01.

Table 4.2.5 Rates of stamp duty land tax (SLDT)

Residential property Consideration	%	Non-residential or mixed property Consideration	%
Up to £175,000	0	Up to £150,000 (depending upon whether or not an anuual rent of >£1000 is payable on a leashold property)	0 or 1%
£175,001 to £250,000	1	£150,001 to £250,000	1
£250,001 to £500,000	3	£250,001 to £500,000	3
Over £500,000	4	Over £500,000	4

Where transactions are linked the aggregate consideration determines the rate of the tax payable.

4.3 VALUE ADDED TAX (VAT)

Neil Warren
Wilder Coe LLP

INTRODUCTION

VAT is relevant to every single business in the UK. The majority of businesses have to become VAT registered, and charge VAT on the sales they make, but there are some entities that do not need to register. However, these businesses will still pay VAT on their expenditure and, because they are not registered and able to reclaim this VAT from the tax authorities on their VAT returns, this tax payment will become an additional cost to the business.

VAT is an EU tax, so is therefore adopted by tax authorities in all EU countries. The legislation is intended to be consistent in all countries, although there are variations on a number of issues which mean, for example, that certain sales might be exempt from VAT in one country, but subject to tax in other countries.

This chapter gives a brief summary of the key parts of the VAT system that could be relevant to a business that is investing in the UK. There are many special rules and schemes that cannot be covered in the chapter but further information can be obtained in a wide range of VAT notices published by HM Revenue and Customs, which administers VAT in the UK. The best contact point for information on VAT is to telephone HMRC's National Advice Service on 0845-010-9000. Further information is available on their website at www.hmrc.gov.uk

SALES SUBJECT TO VAT AND DIFFERENT RATES OF VAT

The basic concepts of VAT in the UK are as follows:

- it is chargeable on a supply of goods or services in the UK;
- the supplies must be made in the course of business ie not as a hobby etc;
- the tax is charged by VAT registered businesses but is effectively borne by the general public who buy goods and services but are unable to reclaim the VAT they are charged on these purchases;
- a business that is VAT registered is able to reclaim the VAT it pays on its expenditure (known as input tax) – but only if these expenses relate to its taxable rather than exempt sales.

There are three rates of VAT in the UK:

- standard rate of VAT – in accordance with EU law, this rate must be between 15% and 25%. The UK rate has been mainly set at 17.5% in the last 20 years, which is one of the lower rates of VAT in the EU but will now be raised to 20% from 1 January 2011.
- reduced rate of VAT – charged at 5%. The application of the 5% rate tends to be fairly limited, the most common example being that 5% VAT is charged on gas and electricity bills for domestic consumption
- zero-rate of VAT – 0%. If a business has all or mainly zero-rated sales, then it will be classed as a 'repayment' trader as far as VAT is concerned. This is because it will not charge VAT (output tax) on its income, but can still reclaim VAT (input tax) on its related expenses. Examples of business entities that usually reclaim rather than pay VAT include farmers, grocers, retailers of children's clothes, new house builders.

A business might receive income that does not involve a supply of either goods or services in the UK. In such cases, the income is classed as being 'outside the scope of VAT.' Examples include donations to a charity, most grants received by a charity or non-profit making body and, more commonly, sales of services to overseas business customers that are treated as being made in the country where the customer is based.

EXEMPT SALES

Some supplies made by a UK business are exempt from VAT. Common examples include:

- Many land related transactions – for example, property rental is exempt from VAT unless the landlord has made a special election with HMRC to charge VAT. However, this opportunity is only available in relation to commercial property.
- Insurance
- Postal services
- Betting, gaming, lotteries
- Finance
- Education
- Health and welfare
- Burial and cremation
- Subscriptions to trade unions and professional bodies
- Sport, sports competitions and physical education

There are other categories of exempt sales in the legislation but the ones listed above tend to be the most common examples.

An important point to recognise with the VAT system is that just because a business category is listed as being exempt, it does not mean that every single supply linked to that heading will be exempt. To give a simple example, supplies of education tend to be exempt if provided by a school or non-profit making body but subject to VAT if provided by a commercial company.

OUTPUT TAX

When a business makes a sale to a customer that is subject to VAT, then tax is usually added to the net price of the goods or services being supplied. However, in some cases, the price of goods or services might be set at a price that is dictated by the market, and this price will need to include VAT if the sale in question relates to a standard rated supply. For example, retailers tend to set their prices based on the competition they encounter from similar outlets.

The general principle is that a business will declare any VAT it charges on its sales on a quarterly VAT return. So VAT never belongs to a business, it is collected from customers on behalf of the tax authorities and paid over to the authorities when each VAT return is submitted.

Some businesses have special schemes for calculating output tax:

- A business that sells second-hand goods can account for VAT on the margin it makes on the sale, rather than on the full selling price. So if goods are bought for £200 and sold for £300, then the £100 profit margin will be treated as VAT inclusive.
- Retailers can use a number of special schemes, to recognise the fact that it is not practical for them to issue a tax invoice for every sale that is made.
- There is a flat rate scheme available for both farmers and small businesses which means that a percentage of total business income is paid in VAT, as opposed to the VAT shown on an invoice.

INPUT TAX

As explained above, a VAT registered business can claim the VAT it pays to suppliers on its expenditure, as long as the expense in question relates to a taxable part of the business, and is not related to any sales that are exempt. So to give a simple example, if a firm of accountants pays £10,000 plus VAT for an advert in a national newspaper, then it will reclaim the VAT element as input tax on its VAT return. But an insurance broker placing an advert in the same newspaper to promote its activities will not be able to reclaim VAT on the expense. This is because insurance services are exempt but accountancy services are taxable.

Input tax cannot be reclaimed on non-business or private expenditure. There must be a clear link between the taxable business and the expense. If an expense if partly used for business and partly for private purposes, then the input tax claimed must be apportioned on a fair and reasonable basis.

REGISTERING FOR VAT

The UK has one of the highest VAT registration thresholds in the EU. A business can make annual taxable sales of £70,000 before it needs to become VAT registered. This is a very generous limit when it is recognised that many EU countries adopt a zero threshold.

It is also possible for a business to register for VAT on a voluntary basis e.g. if it is making mainly zero-rated sales and wants to reclaim input tax.

The technical phrase in the legislation is that a 'taxable person' needs to be VAT registered if he exceeds the relevant threshold. A taxable person can be:

- an individual – sole trader
- partnership
- limited company
- limited liability partnership
- a club, association or other unincorporated body

An important point to recognise is that all activities of a person are included within a VAT registration, rather than one particular business. So if John trades as a plumber during the day and an accountant in the evening, then VAT would be relevant to both his activities if they were within the same legal entity.

RECORD KEEPING

Every VAT registered business must keep records that enable it to accurately calculate the amount of VAT that it owes on its quarterly returns. These records will include purchases and sales books, invoices, bank statements, takings records for retailers and cash books.

If a business makes a 'careless' error on a VAT return, it could be liable to a penalty if this error is an underpayment and is not disclosed to HMRC before they discover it. The penalty for an underpayment that has been deliberately made by a taxpayer will attract an even higher penalty. The onus is on a VAT registered business to submit returns and pay its tax on time.

HMRC carry out routine VAT visits to review figures declared by a business on its returns. These visits are also intended to help a taxpayer with his VAT accounting issues, possibly identifying expenses where he is entitled to reclaim VAT but has not done so in the past.

INTERNATIONAL TRADE – SELLING GOODS

A UK business that sells goods to other VAT registered businesses in the EU will not charge VAT. This assumes that two important conditions are met:

- the business acquires the VAT registration number of the customer and shows this number on its sales invoice;

- the business also holds proof that the goods in question have left the UK – this evidence could be commercial paperwork or transportation documents. It is important that this evidence is retained in the event of a routine VAT visit by HMRC.

A sale of goods to a private individual in another EU country will generally charge standard rated VAT, unless the goods in question are specifically exempt or zero-rated e.g. books or children's clothes. However, a business selling goods to private individuals in another EU country needs to be aware of the fact that it might need to register for VAT in that country (and submit VAT returns and pay tax to the authorities in that country) if its annual sales of goods in that country exceed:

- 35,000 Euros; or
- 100,000 Euros.

Each EU country makes its own decision whether it adopts the higher or lower threshold – in the UK, the limit is £70,000 if an EU business sells goods into the country because we are not in the Euro zone.

The above process is known as the 'distance selling' rules and is intended to create a level playing field across the EU, so that there are no big VAT advantages to be gained by setting up in business in a country with a low rate of VAT.

Another important point to be aware of is that in the case of goods being zero-rated when they are sold to a VAT registered business in another EU country, they are not actually escaping a charge of tax. The business receiving the goods must declare the VAT on its own VAT return (Box 2 of the return is described as 'acquisition tax') but it can usually claim the same amount of tax as input tax in Box 4 of the same return.

A sale of goods to a customer outside the EU is always zero-rated, irrespective of the status of the customer.

SELLING SERVICES TO AN OVERSEAS CUSTOMER
The VAT rules for selling services to an overseas customer tend to be very complicated. As a basic principle, if a service is being sold to a business customer outside the UK, then no VAT is charged. There are exception to this statement – for example, a service relevant to UK land (e.g. an architect invoicing a customer in Germany) will be subject to VAT because the sale is deemed to have taken place in the UK. The same principle applies to construction services e.g. the

services of a plumber, electrician, or bricklayer – it is where the land or building is based that is the deciding factor.

In contrast, the sale of many services to a non-business customer based outside the UK will be subject to UK VAT. There are a number of important exceptions if the customer is based outside the EU – for example, an accountant will not charge UK VAT for services rendered to an American individual for e.g. completing his UK tax return.

If a UK business sells services to an EU business customer without charging VAT, then the customer will account for the VAT on his own VAT return by doing what is known as a reverse charge calculation. This is similar to the entry for acquisition tax explained in the previous section, but entries are made in Boxes 1 and 4 of the VAT return, as opposed to Boxes 2 and 4. To ensure this process has been carried out correctly, the UK business must complete a quarterly return known as an EC Sales List. The ESL records the VAT registration number of the EU customer, and the value of sales (invoiced rather than paid) during each calendar quarter.

CONCLUSION

For many UK businesses, VAT accounting is straightforward. However, the experience of the author over many years has established that there are three particular aspects of the tax that produce numerous complications and problems, and where special care is needed:

- *land and property transactions* – particularly in relation to the situation where landlords can choose whether income from a property is exempt or subject to VAT (known as the 'option to tax' regulations);
- *international transactions* – as explained above, the rules concerning the buying and selling of services across borders can be particularly complicated;
- *partial exemption* – relevant to input tax recovery for a business that has some taxable income and some exempt income. The issue here is defined in the legislation as 'partial exemption' and produces a range of pitfalls and planning opportunities where care and attention to detail is very important.

The key theme about all of the three issues above is that large amounts of VAT are usually involved, so advance planning and specialist advice is crucial.

4.4 KEY BUSINESS TAXATION PLANNING POINTERS

Tim Cook
Wilder Coe LLP

INTRODUCTION

This Chapter carries on from the overview in Chapter 4.2. and sets out planning pointers, both in terms of taxation savings and also in avoiding an increased charge. It describes the taxation consequences of various courses of action.

TAXATION CONSEQUENCES OF OPERATION VIA A UK RESIDENT COMPANY

(i)   Profits will be liable to Corporation Tax (CT).

(ii)   The gain on the eventual sale of shares in a UK company is likely to be exempt from UK tax, if held offshore.

(iii) In several jurisdictions the sale by the resident company of shares in a non-resident company (e.g. UK company) will be exempt. In most jurisdictions individuals would have a liability.

(iv)   The timing and manner of repatriation of profits can be flexible and assist in planning in the offshore jurisdiction.

(v)   European Union (EU) parent companies might be able to claim that the UK loss-making subsidiary should be included in local tax consolidations.

(vi) Disclosures by UK companies are limited to the activities of the company itself. In the case of a Permanent Establishment (PE) the UK Inland Revenue might require information about non-UK transactions to determine and agree liabilities to CT.

(vii) Royalties and interest paid by a UK company to overseas associates are tax deductible if on arms-length terms. Payments made by a PE to its parent/head office are not deductible.

(viii) Any problems, if applicable, in setting up a PE and subsequently incorporating it are avoided. These might include a tax charge in the foreign jurisdiction on the transfer of assets from the PE to a foreign subsidiary. Generally there are no UK tax consequences on the incorporation.

KEY TAX PLANNING ISSUES

Purchase of shares

The acquisition of the shares of a company means that the purchaser inherits all of its assets and liabilities – both known and unknown. The company is a continuing legal entity and a change in its ownership does not affect its obligations from the past.

Because of this the purchaser normally requires the vendor to give indemnities in respect of the company's current and past liabilities, as well as future liabilities that may arise as a result of the acquisition.

It should be noted that the acquisition of the company means that there is no uplift in the value of the assets held by the company. Any gains on those assets remain in the company and will be taxable on the company on a sale of those assets. This inherent and contingent tax liability needs to be reflected in the price paid for the shares.

However, if the vendor of the shares is non-resident at the time of the sale , no capital gains tax will be payable by him on the share disposal and inherent gains will only be of concern in assessing the price to be paid for the shares.

Purchase of business assets

The purchase of the business assets from a company, as opposed to buying the company itself, does mean that they are purchased free of liabilities. The purchasing company will also have acquired the assets at current value and so there will be no inherent gains to take into consideration in the future. This can be of advantage where the assets might have to be sold prior to any future disposal of the company.

Tax grouping

The association of companies can have an effect in the UK on the rate of tax payable by both resident companies and branches. There are different types of tax grouping in relation to trading profits and capital gains, and also the surrendering of losses between companies with economic interests such as where a company is owned by a consortium.

Association normally comes from common control of companies. Thus if the same individual, or group of individuals, has control of companies those companies, for UK taxation purposes will be associated (and connected). This has effect in the following ways:

- Transfers of assets between associated companies must be at an arm's length value. Where this does not happen the Inland Revenue can deal with the calculation of tax as though it had been at arm's length by substituting the open market value for the actual transfer value.
- The number of associated companies will affect the rate of tax where the small company rate is involved (on profits up to £300,000). The limit of £300,000 will be divided between the associated companies.

Grouping comes from direct shareholdings of one company by another. The share percentages of such holdings are followed through.

If, for example, Company A held 80% of the ordinary capital of Company B, which in turn held 90% of the ordinary capital of Company C, then A would be held to have an interest in 72% (80% x 90%) of C.

If the percentages held are 51% or more, the companies are deemed to be a group for Capital Gains Tax purposes.

If the percentages are above 75% the companies are deemed to be a group for all UK corporation tax purposes.

The effect of a grouping >75% is to allow:

- Transfers of assets within the group without taxation consequence and without the need for open market values to be used.

- Trading Losses and Capital Losses to be surrendered between group companies, so that the tax rates can be averaged for best effect.

Transfer of a UK Permanent Establishment to a UK Company

As mentioned in Chapter 4.2 it can be the best solution, if losses are expected in the initial trading periods, to start trade in a UK branch by way of a PE so that the losses can be utilised in the overseas jurisdiction (subject to the taxation laws in that jurisdiction). When the entity becomes profitable the UK trade could then be transferred to a UK company.

The usual route would be for the foreign parent to incorporate a company in the UK and then transfer the trade and assets of the PE to that company at the appropriate time.

Using the group rules mentioned above the transfer in the UK would be achieved without taxation consequences. Care would have to be taken in considering whether the transfer triggered any offshore liability to the parent making the transfer.

Frequently, any losses incurred in the UK branch can be carried over into the subsidiary for use against future profits in the new company. One of the possible benefits from this route is that the losses initially arising in the UK branch can be utilised twice.

Sale of a UK Permanent Establishment

Unlike the situation for the sale of the shares of a UK company, mentioned previously, the situation with regard to the sale of the assets (including goodwill) of a branch or PE of an overseas company will differ. The PE is resident and trading in the UK and is thus taxable on the sale of its UK assets.

The foreign company (head office) will be taxable at 28%, reducing to 24% over the four years ending 1st April 2014, on the gain, subject to indexation relief (see Chapter 4.2).

Controlled Foreign Companies (CFC)

When considering the best structure, overseas investors will need to take into account the use of low tax rate intermediate countries for functions such as, holding, trading, financing or management.

Using such countries complicates the structure and detailed consideration of CFC rules in all countries affected by the structure will be necessary.

In using such low tax rate jurisdictions transfer pricing legislation will also become a factor for consideration (see below).

Investment in UK properties

If property is acquired in the UK by a non-resident individual, or a non-resident company, for rental return purposes coupled with capital gain on disposal the taxation position differs in terms of rates applying.

An individual, even though non-resident, will be taxable at the rates set out in 4.2. Thus the highest rate could be 40% (50% from 6th April 2010).

A non-resident company, however, pays tax on such income at a flat rate which is currently 20%.

Special administrative provisions apply in both cases in that, if there is not a collection agent in the UK, tax will have to be deducted at source on the gross rental by the tenant. The individual or company would then have to claim a refund in respect of any expenses available to offset against the income.

Repatriation of Profits

In general there are few UK taxation implications on the repatriation of profits to the parent company or head office.

There are no taxes on distributions so a remittance of retained profits, in any form, does not attract a liability.

There is no withholding tax on UK dividends paid to offshore shareholders.

As mentioned in Chapter 4.2, there is a notional tax on dividends and for non-resident individuals this is deemed to cover their UK liability.

Non-resident companies receiving dividends from UK resident companies are similarly protected from additional UK tax.

Under the provisions of certain tax treaties a refund of 50% of the tax credit can be paid where the shareholder is a company holding 10% or more of the UK Company.

However other provisions provide, in most cases, for a 5% UK tax to be deducted from the grossed up dividend (the cash dividend plus the tax credit refund). The effect of this is to almost cancel out the benefit of the refund – probably leaving the refund at only 0.2% of the UK companies pre-tax profits.

Transfer Pricing

The UK legislation relating to transfer pricing can impact on any transaction carried out between the UK entity (whatever its nature) and any foreign associated entity. The rules are similar in most jurisdictions and any resulting double taxation can usually be resolved under the provision of double Taxation Agreements that may be in force.

The broad implication is that any transaction between a UK entity and its associated foreign entities will be on normal commercial terms and that no tax advantage will be obtained by the pricing method used. If it is not, the legislation allows adjustment to recalculate profits to what they would be under an 'arm's length' transaction. It also allows for the charging of penalties of up to 100% of the tax due.

The adjustments to recalculate the profits only apply if UK profits are understated. There is no adjustment if they are overstated.

Transactions which could therefore be affected include:

- Sales of products
- Services provided
- Financing
- Licensing
- Management fees
- Property leases and other transactions

The onus, under UK compliance rules for the submission of returns, is for the UK taxpayer to confirm that all related party transactions are carried out on an arm's length basis.

In cases where the transfer pricing determination of arm's length transactions might be very complex it is possible to agree arrangements and methods in advance under Advance Pricing Agreements with the Inland Revenue.

4.5 FINANCIAL OUTSOURCING

Robin Berry
Artiaus Ltd

INTRODUCTION

The term "outsourcing" is now commonplace in the world of business today, and there are some good reasons why this is the case.

Successful businesses are able to innovate and adapt to market conditions. This requires a sharp focus on the key drivers that underpin the business. This is the central role of the senior management team, who will possess the skills to achieve this.

Increasingly, other non-core activities are seen as an unwelcome distraction that may divert attention away from the growth of the business. Company directors must not, however, ignore their legal responsibilities, or the broader needs of their stakeholders.

Therefore it has become more common for companies to identify these areas and outsource work to external service-providers. Thus they are able to fulfil all of their duties while retaining focus on what is truly important.

THE BENEFITS OF FINANCIAL OUTSOURCING

There are many benefits in choosing to engage an external provider. Firstly, and perhaps most importantly, a UK-based outsource partner will be able to provide complete peace of mind that the business is UK tax-compliant. The regulatory regime has been strengthened in recent years and the cost of non-compliance has risen sharply. There are now myriad penalties and surcharges for late or incorrect filings for Income Tax, National Insurance, Corporation Tax, and Value Added Tax. These administrative matters can no longer be left at the bottom of the "in-tray"- it has become too expensive to do so.

A financial outsourcer will often be the client's primary source of pro-active advice to save money for the business. For example, there are many tax concessions and schemes available to businesses which can reduce or defer tax liabilities. This requires an up-to-date knowledge of the UK tax regime. It is virtually impossible to recruit individual staff members who possess all of this technical knowledge.

When a business first invests in the UK, it may also be difficult to hire the right calibre of finance staff. The UK business will be in its infancy, and comprise little more than a business plan, an outline sales contract and a lease agreement. It is likely that executives will be asked to fulfil a number of roles in this embryonic stage. An investor must consider they are able to attract the right type of person, possessing the right skill-sets at this point in time. Every new business venture will require a certain amount of low-level processing work, together with a certain amount of technical expertise. At the same time, the business will benefit from more circumspect financial advice. Outsourcing can deliver all of these features, and can do so economically.

It is also often very difficult for an overseas business to adequately assess the suitability of candidates when recruiting for UK financial controllers. Furthermore, it can be even more difficult to cover for staff illness and holidays. Outsource businesses naturally assume responsibility for such issues, and provide automatic cover so that the service continues without interruption.

Furthermore, most outsourcers operate web-based systems, allowing businesses to access their own financial records remotely and in real-time. This provides an added layer of visibility and accountability.

UK employment law is covered in the next chapter, Chapter 4.6, but there is an obvious contrast between the legal responsibilities of being an employer, and the contractual terms of an outsource agreement. Many providers are regulated by professional accountancy bodies. In addition, agreements with outsource providers can incorporate quality-control assurances, and of course ensure that the service-provider is legally accountable. This provides a level of assurance that cannot be matched by employing staff directly.

Employment law is complicated and employees, including part-time staff, receive additional legal rights after one year's service. Restructuring and redundancy must therefore be handled very carefully if time-consuming and costly legal disputes are to be avoided. Outsourcing allows a business to "buy-in" a variety of skills as and when needed, and allows onerous employment law to be side-stepped.

WHAT FINANCIAL SERVICES CAN BE EFFECTIVELY OUTSOURCED?

Setting Up of a Company:

- Formation of a UK business entity e.g. Private Limited Company with an agreed name.
- Dealing with all the statutory formalities including –
- appointment of Directors and Secretary (if required);
- provision of a Registered Office address;
- preparation of Annual Returns;
- maintenance of statutory books.
- Registering a company for Value Added Tax.
- Registering a company for Pay As You Earn taxes (this is a method of collection of Income Tax and National Insurance earned through employment).
- Arranging for UK Contracts of Employment to be prepared.
- Advising on appropriate accounting software and financial reporting.
- Preparing a Chart of Accounts.
- Compiling a business plan incorporating budgetary forecasts.
- Setting up credit procedures.
- Introduction to UK banks and assessing the formalities of opening a bank account.
- Introduction to Insurance brokers to ensure relevant insurance policies are in place.
- Introduction to marketing and PR consultants.
- Introduction to solicitors and HR professionals to draw up terms and conditions, apply for work permits etc.
- Treasury control – Internet banking, issuing and signing cheques on behalf of the company. Organising cheque signatories and procedures.

Once a Company is Established:

Acting as Administrative Office:-

- Stock and order processing.
- Pre-sales credit control.
- Preparation of sales invoices.
- Sending sales invoices to customers.
- Post sale credit control.

Maintenance of all Accounting records:-

- Sales Ledger (Accounts Receivables).
- Purchase ledger (Accounts Payable).
- Nominal ledger.
- Inventory control.
- Bank reconciliations.
- Payroll processing.
- Submission of VAT returns.
- Agreement / reconciliation of supplier statements.

Production of Management Information

- Weekly management information and flash reports.
- Monthly Management Accounts.
- Production and interpretation of Key Performance Indicators.
- Comparison of actual results with forecasts.

Liaison with Overseas Holding Companies

- Preparation of Accounts in accordance with overseas Head Office timetable and accounting policies.
- Reporting in depth using any format required on any accounting matters, complying with International Accounting standard.

Liaison with Government Bodies

- Dealing with all statistical returns for VAT purposes (EC Sales Lists, IntraStat).
- Dealing with all PAYE returns.
- Dealing with Corporation Tax Returns.
- Dealing with data as required by UK Data Protection Act.

Liaison with Statutory Auditors and Tax Advisors:-

- Prepare Year End file in format preferred by UK firms of Chartered Accountants.
- Provision of additional information and explanation to auditors.
- Ensuring that all group audit timetables are adhered to.

CONCLUSION

Outsourcing in the UK is a growing service industry, offering skills to businesses at an economic price, which those organizations could not readily acquire or control independently without incurring a significant financial and time cost.

The result is a fixed overhead that leaves the company free to concentrate upon their core activities knowing that the administration and financial side of the business will run smoothly, seamlessly and efficiently.

4.6 EMPLOYMENT LAW

Asha Kumar
Watson, Farley & Williams LLP

INTRODUCTION

Employment law in the UK has changed over the decades to reflect social and political changes, and has also been affected by the UK's membership of the European Union (EU). Any business considering operating in the UK needs to be aware of the employment and immigration laws that operate in the UK. Those investing in the UK will have to deal with different aspects of employment protection according to the mechanism used to invest in the UK, and it should also be noted that special protection is afforded to employees where there is a merger or acquisition of a business.

This chapter seeks to assist those unfamiliar with UK employment law by providing an overview of the rights and obligations afforded to individuals through the employment relationship.

EMPLOYMENT STATUS

In common with other European countries, UK employment law distinguishes between "employees", "workers" and the "self-employed". This status is important because it determines the statutory employment rights to which a person is entitled.

Significant rights are conferred upon employees who, traditionally, have been seen as individuals with full-time jobs working under indefinite employment contracts. Examples of rights afforded include:

● the right to claim unfair dismissal;
● the right to a redundancy payment in certain circumstances; and
● the right to maternity leave and statutory maternity pay.

However, as new working arrangements emerge, the UK has seen an increase in the number of individuals whose working arrangements fall outside the traditional pattern.

There is no statutory definition of "employee", and while case law has developed in this area, the actual finding of employment status depends upon the circumstances of each particular case. As a consequence, the growth of legislation that applies to "workers", a term wider than "employees", embraces certain types of self-employment. Examples of legislation that apply to workers include:

a. the Working Time Regulations, 1998;
b. the National Minimum Wage Act, 1998; and
c. the Part-Time Workers (Prevention of Less Favourable Treatment) Regulations, 2000.

An individual who is not a worker or an employee will not be entitled to any employment protection rights, although it is hard to define exactly who falls into this category.

CONTRACTS OF EMPLOYMENT

A contract of employment comes into existence as soon as someone accepts an offer of employment in return for pay. It is legally binding between the employer and employee, and can be written or oral, express or implied, or a combination of these. In addition, some employment terms are imposed into contracts by statute.

While employers are obliged only to provide a written statement of the main employment particulars (see below), it is recommended that employees are given a full written contract, as it provides certainty and may help to avoid later disputes. However, even a written contract may not necessarily reflect all of the terms that apply in an employment relationship, and terms are often implied into a contract. These may be necessary to make the contract workable or may reflect custom and practice. In addition, all employment relationships have an implied term of mutual trust and confidence. This is intended to prevent either party acting in a way that is likely to destroy or seriously damage the relationship of trust and confidence that exists between employer and employee.

A contract can be for an indefinite duration, terminable on an agreed period of notice, or for a fixed term. Protection is afforded to a fixed-term worker so that he/she cannot be treated less favourably than an equivalent permanent worker, unless the treatment is objectively justified. In certain circumstances, fixed-term contracts automatically become permanent contracts.

Written particulars of employment

The Employment Rights Act, 1996, obliges employers to provide employees with a written statement of employment particulars. The written statement is not necessarily a contract, but can provide evidence of the terms and conditions of employment. It must be provided to the employee within two months of the employment commencing and must contain certain basic information, including:

- the names of the employer and employee;
- the rate of remuneration and the intervals at which it is to be paid;
- the hours of work; and
- holiday entitlement.

An employee that has not been provided with the required particulars may make a complaint to the Employment Tribunal, which may award him/her between two and four weeks' pay. For these purposes, a week's pay is currently capped at £380, and this generally increases annually on 1 February each year.

Policies and procedures

Often written contracts are supplemented by the use of policies and procedures that describe the employer's more general employment practices, such as email and internet use.

MINIMUM STATUTORY PROVISIONS

In the UK, employees (and sometimes workers) are provided with minimum terms, which are aimed at providing decent minimum standards and promoting fairness at work. Many of the minimum standards were introduced in order to implement European directives, and consequently similar provisions apply throughout Europe. Minimum terms related to the following cannot be overridden:

- the national minimum wage;
- statutory sick pay;
- working hours;
- disciplinary procedures;
- notice periods;
- employers' liability insurance; and
- health and safety.

National minimum wage

The National Minimum Wage Act applies to almost all workers and sets minimum hourly rates of pay. The national minimum wage is reviewed annually. The rates vary for different groups of workers and as of 1 October 2009, were set as follows:

- £5.80 per hour for workers aged 22 and over (this will change to 21 and over from 1st October 2010);
- £4.83 per hour for 18-21 year-olds (this will change to workers aged between 18 and 20 inclusive from 1st October 2010); and
- £3.57 per hour for all workers under 18 who are no longer of compulsory school age.

From October 2010 these rates will increase to £5.93, £4.92 and £3.64, respectively.

Statutory sick pay

Eligible employees are entitled to receive statutory sick pay (SSP) for up to 28 weeks in one period, or more than one linked period, of sickness (periods with eight weeks or less between them are linked). A helpful SSP calculator can be found on the HM Revenue and Customs website.[1]

The rate of SSP is reviewed annually and is currently £79.15 per week. In certain circumstances, an employer may be able to recover some or all of any SSP they have paid to their employees.

---

1 http://www.hmrc.gov.uk/calcs/ssp.htm

As a matter of policy, employers may choose to pay employees full pay (inclusive of SSP) for a limited period; this is referred to as "contractual sick pay".

Working hours

The Working Time Regulations implement a European directive aimed at protecting the health and safety of workers by ensuring that working time does not adversely affect a worker's health. In summary, the regulations provide details of:

- the 48 hour week;
- rest breaks; and
- annual leave.

The 48-hour week

An employer cannot require an employee to work more than an average of 48 hours a week, although there are a number of exceptions to this rule for senior employees and certain other categories of employment. Unlike many other European countries, Britain has negotiated an opt-out whereby this limit does not apply if an employee agrees in writing with his/her employer that it is not to be applied. It should be noted that the employer cannot compel the employee to opt-out and that the employee can reverse this opt-out by giving appropriate notice.

Rest breaks

Workers have the right to an uninterrupted rest period of at least 11 hours between working days, and to a 24-hour period clear of work each week. Additional rest breaks must be provided to workers whose pattern of work puts their health and safety at risk. The regulations also provide the right to a rest break of at least 20 minutes after six hours of consecutive work. Special provisions apply to night workers.

Annual leave

Workers currently have the right to a minimum of 5.6 weeks' paid annual leave. This right applies from the first day of employment and accrues at the rate of one-twelfth of the annual entitlement per month worked. A "week" reflects the employee's working week. So, where an employee works a five-day week, he/she will be entitled to 28 days' annual leave, and if an employee works three days a week, he/she will be entitled to 16.8 days' annual leave. In practice, many employers offer employees the statutory minimum inclusive of bank holidays and will provide employees in senior roles with additional annual leave.

Grievance and disciplinary procedures

When resolving workplace disputes there is a requirement for both parties to comply with a code of practice developed by the Advisory, Conciliation and Arbitration Service (ACAS). The ACAS Code provides basic practical guidance to employers, employees and their representatives and sets out principles for handling disciplinary and grievance situations in the workplace. If an employee or employer is unreasonable in its failure to follow the new code of practice, employment tribunals will be able to order an increase or decrease in awards of up to 25 per cent.

Notice periods

The minimum legal notice periods to be given by an employer are:

- one week's notice if the employee has been continuously employed by the employer for at least one month but for less than two years; or
- two weeks' notice if the employee has been continuously employed by the employer for two years, plus an additional week's notice for each further complete year of continuous employment, up to a maximum of 12 weeks.

An employee's contract of employment may, however, provide for a longer notice period. An employment contract may be terminated without advance notice where the employee has committed an act of gross misconduct.

In the absence of any contrary contractual provisions, an employee who has been employed for one month or more must give their employer at least one week's notice to terminate their employment.

Employers' liability insurance

Every employer in the UK must have employers' liability insurance, which covers employers against damages and legal costs following injury or disease to its employees during their employment.

It is no longer necessary to display a hard copy of an employer's liability insurance, provided that an electronic copy is available.

Health and safety

In the UK, employers have legal obligations to ensure a safe workplace. The health and safety obligations are extensive and if breached may give rise to criminal liabilities. Further details can be obtained from the Health and Safety Executive's website.[2]

WORK/LIFE BALANCE

Over the years, legislation has been brought in to enable employees to achieve a better work/life balance. It has been particularly targeted at parents to enable them to spend adequate time bringing up their children by allowing them to work around their commitments.

Maternity leave

All pregnant employees are entitled to 52 weeks' maternity leave. All employment benefits, including non-contractual benefits connected with an employee's employment that are not "remuneration", continue to be provided for the full period of maternity leave. For parents with children born on or after 3 April 2011, maternity leave can be transferred to the father where at least 20 weeks from the child's birth has passed and the mother has returned to work.

Employees on maternity leave who are eligible are also entitled to receive up to 39 weeks' statutory maternity pay (SMP) at the rate set by statute. The first six weeks of SMP are earnings-related, and an employee is entitled to 90 per cent of her average weekly earnings with no upper limit. The remaining 33 weeks are paid at a lower rate, which is currently £124.88 (or 90 per cent of earnings if this is less).

Employees who are not eligible for SMP are entitled to a Maternity Allowance for up to 39 weeks. This is currently £124.88 per week (or 90 per cent of earnings if this is less) and is claimed from the Department for Work and Pensions. Similar provisions to those set out above apply on the adoption of a child.

Paternity leave

Eligible employees whose partners are expected to give birth will be entitled to time off at or around the time of the birth. They are entitled to take either one or two consecutive weeks' leave as paid paternity leave. Statutory paternity pay is either 90 per cent of an employee's weekly earnings or the prescribed amount (currently £124.88), whichever is the lesser. Fathers may also be eligible for transferable maternity leave (see "Maternity leave" above).

2 http://www.hse.gov.uk

Parental leave

Parents who have at least one year's continuous employment may take up to 13 weeks' unpaid parental leave for each child up to that child's fifth birthday (or fifth year of adoption). Parents of disabled children are entitled to up to 18 weeks' leave until the child's 18th birthday.

Time off to care for dependants

In the UK, all employees have the right to take a reasonable amount of time off, without pay, to care for dependants. The right to time off is intended to enable employees to deal with an emergency in the short term and/or, where necessary, to make longer-term care arrangements.

Right to request flexible working

Employees who have at least 26 weeks' continuous employment may be able to make a request for flexible working, which will allow them to work modified hours of employment, if they either:

● have responsibility for the care of a child under the age of 17; or
● care for an adult.

Proposals have been formed to extend this right to all employees.

Part-time working

Protection is also afforded to those who work on a part-time basis. Regulations have introduced provisions that prevent part-time workers from being treated less favourably than equivalent full-time employees, unless this is justifiable. Part-time employees should also have access to the same rights and benefits as full-time employees, albeit on a pro rata basis.

EQUALITY PROVISIONS

The law in this area has been consolidated by the Equality Act 2010 which comes into force in October 2010. In general, the UK outlaws discrimination on the grounds of sex, race, disability, sexual orientation, religion or belief and age. Generally, the law recognises the following types of discrimination:

● Direct discrimination: this is where someone is treated differently because of their sex, race, etc. It is not necessary to show an unlawful motive; it is the reason for the treatment that matters.

- Indirect discrimination: this is a less obvious form of discrimination. It occurs where certain requirements, conditions or practices imposed by an employer, although applied equally to all employees, have a disproportionately adverse impact on one group or other.
- Harassment: this is where one person subjects another to unwanted conduct related to their sex, race, etc., which has the purpose or effect of violating the other's dignity, or creating an intimidating, hostile, degrading, humiliating or offensive environment for them.
- Victimisation: this is where a person is treated less favourably because they have started proceedings, given evidence or complained about the behaviour of someone who has been harassing them or discriminating against them.

Special provisions apply to disability discrimination and age discrimination. Under the disability discrimination provisions, an employee with a particular condition may receive additional protection where this amounts to a "disability" as defined under the legislation. The most recent form of anti-discrimination legislation is on age discrimination. The UK has a default retirement age of 65, which is soon to be abolished. It is important to note that compensation for acts of discrimination is uncapped.

MISCELLANEOUS MATTERS

"Whistleblowing"

Protection is given to employees who disclose or "blow the whistle on" wrongdoings at work. Employees are protected if they blow the whistle and, if they are dismissed or receive detrimental treatment as a result of their action, they can present a claim in an employment tribunal. Compensation for whistleblowing is uncapped. Whistleblowers are protected where they disclose in good faith something that relates to:

- the commissioning of a criminal activity;
- failure to comply with a legal obligation;
- a miscarriage of justice;

- a health and safety issue; and/or
- damage to the environment.

Data protection

The UK has data protection or "privacy" laws. Data transfer to companies outside the EU is permitted only when the receiving country has data protection laws that are considered "adequate" by the European Commission. UK data protection laws may give individual employees access to information held on them by their employer, provided that certain conditions are satisfied.

Reporting and consultation requirements

The Information and Consultation of Employees Regulations 2004, (ICE) give employees the right to be informed and consulted about the business they work for, including information on the employer's activities and any possible threats to their employment. ICE applies to all undertakings with at least 50 employees. The aim of ICE is to encourage people to develop their own voluntary arrangements tailored to their particular circumstances.

TERMINATION OF EMPLOYMENT

In the UK, employees have the statutory right not to be unfairly dismissed. Generally, after one year's service, an employee can only be dismissed for a "fair" reason. The reason will only be fair if it comes under one of the six prescribed reasons, namely:

- capability;
- conduct;
- avoidance of a legal enactment;
- redundancy;
- retirement (although this will no longer apply when the default retirement age of 65 is abolished); or
- some other substantial reason that justifies dismissal.

Even though a fair reason may be established, the employer is also expected to follow a fair procedure when dismissing an employee, and the parties are required to comply with the ACAS Code.

Where a dismissal is found to be unfair, an employee can recover compensation up to a current maximum of £65,300. There are, however, a number of circumstances, including in the event of whistleblowing or discrimination, in which an employment tribunal can ignore the cap on compensation and award unlimited compensation. If the reason for dismissal is redundancy, an employee is generally entitled to a statutory redundancy payment, up to a current maximum of £11,400.

Employers should note that there are special rules concerning redundancy. An employer who proposes to make 20 or more employees redundant must consult with the relevant trade union or employee representatives beforehand. Failure to do so may result in compensation of up to 90 days' pay for each affected employee.

Breach of contract

In addition to statutory rights that apply on dismissal, if an employer does not comply with a term of the employment contract, this may be a breach of contract. An employee can bring a claim for damages or "wrongful dismissal" if they do not receive their notice entitlement under their contract of employment. A fundamental breach of contract will also usually entitle an employee to resign and claim unfair "constructive dismissal". Similar principles apply where an employee breaches their employment contract.

When awarding compensation for breach of contract, UK courts will seek to place the innocent party in the position they would have been in had the contract been properly performed.

MERGERS AND ACQUISITIONS

Where a business or part of an entity is transferred to another by way of a business transfer, the employees in the transferring part are given significant legal safeguards under the Transfer of Undertakings (Protection of Employment) Regulations, 2006. These safeguards apply only when there is a transfer of assets and not where the employing entity is the same, as might be the case where the transfer is of shares in the company. These special provisions also apply in certain outsourcing situations. The special protections include:

- appointment of employee representatives who must be informed (and possibly also consulted) in advance of the transfer;
- inheritance of past (undischarged) liabilities of the employer by the buyer;

- changes to an employee's terms and conditions of employment being rendered unlawful; and
- dismissals in connection with the transfer being rendered unlawful, unless they are for certain specified reasons.

CONCLUSION

It might seem at first sight that employers in the UK are subject to a considerable amount of legislative requirements. It should, however, be borne in mind that many of the provisions, particularly in the area of equal opportunities, were introduced as a result of European directives and thus apply to all EU member states. Further, in many areas the UK has managed to water down the impact of the legislation by opting out of certain provisions. In summary, the UK employment law continues to strikes a healthy balance between ensuring that employees receive adequate protection in their working arrangements and allowing employers the freedom to run their businesses so that they can compete successfully in the global market.

4.7 PENSIONS, INSURED BENEFITS AND OPTION PLANS

Liz Buchan and Rhodri Thomas
Watson, Farley & Williams LLP

Introduction
In the UK it is usual for an employer to provide its employees with a mix of benefits including one or more of: pension arrangements, insured benefits and/or stock/share options, in addition to basic salary. This chapter summarises these types of benefits.

PENSIONS
Occupational pension plans v personal plans
Pension plans can either be occupational or personal. Broadly, occupational plans are annuities provided by employers for their staff in order to provide an income in retirement. Occupational pension plans vary in size from large arrangements that have many thousands of members and assets worth many millions of pounds down to individual arrangements set up for single executives.

Occupational pension plans operate on a triangular basis. They are established by the employer and administered by a board of trustees who act in the interests of the third party – the beneficiaries. The employer and the trustees will agree the terms of the constitutional documents. In addition to these documents, the plan has to be run in accordance with UK legislation and HM Revenue & Customs ("HMRC") rules.

Personal pensions are different in that the primary legal relationship is between the employee and the personal pension plan provider, such as a life insurance company, a bank or another authorised institution.

Defined benefit v defined contribution
What differentiates between types of occupational plan is how they are funded. Some are funded on a defined benefit basis and others on a defined contribution basis. There is a significant difference between the two.

Defined Benefit
Here the pension which is provided for the employee is calculated according to a variety of factors which might include length of service, amount of salary at the retirement date and the "accrual rate" (often specified as a fraction, e.g. one-sixtieth for each year of service). To the extent that there is a difference between the amount of contributions made by the employer and the employee, the employer will be responsible for making up this shortfall.

Defined Contribution
These plans take contributions from the employee and from the employer and invest them in such a way as to optimise returns with a view to purchasing an annuity for the employee at their normal retirement date. The investment risk falls on the employee, not the employer and this is the funding method chosen by most companies starting out new occupational pension plans.

Combined
On rare occasions a mix of the two or a "hybrid" plan is chosen. This may be a defined contribution plan with a defined benefit underpin (or vice versa) or a plan which permits a change from one to the other at a given age or service period. The uncertainty of cost and complexity of running such plans makes them rare choices.

Problems with defined benefit plans
Many companies have closed their defined benefit pension plans to new entrants to try and cap the under funding problems that such plans have caused.

Personal Pension Plans

The main other type of plan used by employees to provide for their retirement is known as a personal pension plan. A personal pension plan is the only type of HMRC approved pension arrangement that can currently be initiated by an employee who is not eligible to join an occupational pension plan.

A personal pension plan is a very simple form of pension contract. It is a defined contribution contract issued by a provider to an individual employee. The provider takes contributions from the employee, and invests them, with the contributions receiving certain tax privileges. Employees can take their benefits from age 50 (which will go up to age 55 in 2010) and the value of the fund that an employee accrues over their period of membership (including investment income) will be used to purchase a pension.

Employers can also make contributions to the arrangement.

Group Personal Pension Plans

Many employers offer a group personal pension plan. This is, essentially, a branding exercise and the "group personal pension" is merely a collection of personal pension policies arranged by the employer through its financial advisor. This does not change the fact that, for legal purposes, this is an arrangement between the employee and the provider.

Stakeholder Pension Plans

Since October 2001 all UK employers who employ five or more employees and who do not offer employees membership of an occupational pension plan or make contributions of at least 3% of basic salary to a personal pension plan have had to comply with the stakeholder access requirements.

These obligations are not as onerous as they may sound. They merely require an employer to nominate a stakeholder pension plan, after consulting with its relevant employees and any organisations representing them, and then to provide employees with certain information about the stakeholder pension plan.

Employers do not have a legal obligation to make employer contributions, but if an employer does not comply with the access requirements the penalty is a fine of up to £50,000.

The vast majority of stakeholder pension plans are merely personal pension plans which meet minimum requirements prescribed by statute. The particular feature of stakeholder plans is that the maximum charge that can be levied on a stakeholder pension plan cannot initially exceed 1.5% of the funds under management, dropping to 1% after 10 years.

INSURANCES
Introduction
In addition to pension benefits, it is also very common for employers to provide employees with insured benefits, such as life insurance, private medical insurance and permanent health insurance. These benefits are summarised below.

Life Insurance
This benefit pays out a lump sum in the event of the death of the insured employee. Typical arrangements will provide for a lump sum payment based upon a multiple of the insured employee's annual salary, sometimes up to a maximum salary level. Where an employer provides this benefit through a group life insurance plan (see below), the level of cover that can be provided is capped at four times an employee's annual salary.

Where life insurance is provided as an employee benefit, this will usually be done by the employer establishing a group life assurance plan for which the employer pays the plan premium. Individual employees can then be entered into the plan.

The provision of life insurance by an employer (where the group policy meets certain HMRC requirements) does not constitute a taxable benefit in the hands of an employee who is entered into the policy.

Private Medical Insurance
This benefit provides cover to meet the costs of treatment of short-term curable illness or injury of an employee, and consequently ensures that the employee has access to such treatment with as little delay as possible. Certain conditions may, depending on the scope of the policy, be excluded from the cover provided (for example, any conditions pre-existing on commencement of the policy will often be excluded).

Similarly to life insurance plans, group private medical insurance may be arranged by an employer, and individual employees may then be entered into the plan. This will usually decrease the 'per capita' cost of cover, as the employer is able to obtain lower premiums for the group policy than would be available to an individual. However, the value of the premiums paid by the employer in respect of an employee is a taxable benefit for the employee, and the employee will therefore be required to pay income tax on this amount (at the employee's prevailing marginal rate) to HMRC.

Permanent Health Insurance (PHI)

Where an employer provides this benefit to an employee, in the event that the employee becomes unable to work due to illness or accident, the insurer will pay a percentage (usually between 50 and 75%) of the employee's salary for the duration of the employee's incapacity. PHI policies will usually provide either that an employee must be unable to perform his or her own occupation, or that the employee must be unable to perform work of any kind, in order to receive benefits, although other forms of policy are available.

Payments will begin after a deferment period during which time the employee must be incapacitated (within the meaning prescribed in the policy). Deferment periods of six months are common, although the period may be longer or shorter. Shorter deferment periods will increase the premium payable on the policy.

Often the employee will be eligible to receive company sick pay from the employer for some or all of the deferment period, following which the employee may become eligible to receive benefits under the policy.

Where an employer provides PHI as a benefit to employees, it will normally do this by establishing a group plan, into which individual employees may be entered. Where an employer sets up a plan in this way, the provision of PHI cover to an employee is not a taxable benefit in the hands of the employee. However, should an employee become eligible to receive benefits under the PHI policy, those benefits will be taxable as income (this is in contrast to where an individual arranges PHI independently, where any benefits received will not be subject to tax).

EMPLOYEE SHARE PLANS
Introduction

There are various types of share and share option plans that an employer can establish as another tax efficient way of rewarding and incentivising its employees.

The choice of plan or plans will depend on the needs and objectives of the employer. An employer will need to decide whether it wishes to put in place an option plan, (in which case Company Share Option Plans (CSOP), Savings-Related Share Option Plans (SAYE), and Enterprise Management Incentive Plans (EMI) may be of interest), a share plan, (in which case Share Incentive Plans (SIP) or

Long-Term Incentive Plans (L-TIP) may be of interest or a cash based plan which replicates an option or share plan (in which case a "Phantom" Plan may be of interest).

An employer does not need to adopt an approved plan or grant approved options. It can adopt an unapproved plan or merely grant unapproved options outside of, or in addition to, any formal plan. Further details in relation to share option plans may can be found on HM Revenue & Customs' website, at www.hmrc.gov.uk/shareschemes.

"Approved" and "Unapproved" Plans

Share and option plans are often categorised as "approved" or "unapproved" which indicates whether or not they are approved by HMRC.

Broadly, an employee who is granted an unapproved option will not normally be charged to income tax on the grant of the option itself nor when the option becomes exercisable. Income tax will, however, be charged following an exercise of an option on the excess (if any) of the market value, at the time of acquisition, of the shares acquired over the amount paid by the employee to acquire the shares. Capital Gains Tax ("CGT") may also be payable on any increase in value between the date of exercise and the date of disposal, although reliefs may be available to minimise any charge. There may also be PAYE and National Insurance implications for the employer on grant or, more likely, exercise of the option.

By contrast, options granted under the terms of an option plan "approved" by HMRC may, subject to conditions, be exercised without giving rise to a charge to income tax. The employee is still likely to be liable to CGT when he ultimately sells the shares, but certain approved plans do offer CGT benefits.

Company Share Option Plans (CSOP)
Summary

In a CSOP an employee is granted an option allowing him to buy a fixed number of shares in the employer at a price fixed at the date of grant during a set period of time. The price of the shares must not generally be less than the market value of the shares at the time of grant. To qualify for favourable tax treatment, options must be exercised by the employee not less than 3 years and not more than 10 years after the time of grant.

Under a CSOP the employer is, broadly, free to set its own rules as to the circumstances in which the options may be granted or exercised, provided that the performance-related conditions are objective and not subject to the exercise of a discretion by any one person.

Participation and Limits

The employer can decide on a discretionary basis which of its employees or full time directors can take part in its CSOP. There is, however, a limit of £30,000 on the maximum value of shares over which approved options granted under a CSOP may be held by an individual at any one time.

Further information on CSOPs can be found at:
www.hmrc.gov.uk/manuals/essum/ESSUM40000.htm

Savings Related Share Options Plans ("SAYE Plans")
Summary

SAYE plans are capable of approval as approved plans. Employees are given a share option to buy a certain number of shares at a fixed price at a particular time. The shares can only be purchased using amounts saved under a special Save As You Earn (SAYE) savings contract. Employees are required to make savings contributions out of net income over a number of years.

At the end of the fixed period the SAYE contract pays back the contribution and a bonus, out of which the shares can be purchased. If employees do not exercise their options, they will still receive the proceeds of their SAYE contract, including the bonus.

Participation and Limits

SAYE plans are all-employee plans under which all qualifying employees and directors must be eligible to participate on similar terms. The employer may specify a qualification period of up to 5 years' employment. Participants may choose to exercise their options at the end of fixed 3, 5 or 7 year terms and monthly savings must be between £5 and £250.

Further information on SAYE Plans can be found at:
www.hmrc.gov.uk/manuals/essum/ESSUM30000.htm

Enterprise Management Incentive Plans (EMI plan)
Summary

EMI plans are aimed at smaller trading companies. EMI plans can be established by independent trading companies that have gross assets not exceeding £30 million. Certain trades (such as property development) are excluded. While EMI plans offer attractive tax benefits, there is no approval mechanism, although an employer can get prior confirmation that it is eligible to grant EMI options.

Participation and Limits

There are no restrictions on the number of employees who may participate in an EMI plan. Options over shares worth up to £120,000 at the time of grant can be issued to each employee. However, there is an overall limit on the value of unexercised options at any time of £3 million. There are no rules about when the options may be exercised (although options must be exercised within 10 years of grant to obtain tax and National Insurance relief) or about the price at which options may be granted. Tax relief is limited if the options are granted with an exercise price of less than market value at the time of grant.

A qualifying employer under an EMI plan must have fewer than 250 employees, must not be under the control of any other company and must be carrying on a qualifying trade wholly or mainly within the UK. Please note, however, that further to the UK June 2010 Budget it is anticipated that this requirement will change to a requirement that the employer must have a permanent establishment in the UK.

Individuals, whether they are new recruits or existing employees, must work for the employer for at least 25 hours a week, or if less than 25 hours, for at least 75% of their working time, to qualify for EMI. The purpose of the grant of the option must also be to recruit or retain an employee and not for the purpose of tax avoidance.

Further guidance on EMI plans can be found at:
www.hmrc.gov.uk/manuals/essum/ESSUM50000.htm

Approved Share Incentive Plans (SIP)
Summary

All shares acquired under a SIP must initially be held in a UK resident trust, whose trustees hold shares in the employer on behalf of the employees who join the plan. Once established by the employer, a SIP must be approved by HMRC before shares are awarded. In order to obtain the full tax benefits, employees must normally leave their shares in the plan's trust for at least 5 years. An employer makes cash payments to trustees who then buy shares in the employer which are then appropriated to each employee in the plan.

There are four ways by which an employee can obtain shares:

- **Free Shares:** An employer can award up to £3,000 worth of free shares per annum (with a choice of performance related awards).
- **Partnership Shares:** An employee can buy shares out of pre-tax remuneration. The maximum percentage of salary which can be used to buy the shares is 10% with an overall limit of £1,500 per annum
- **Matching Shares:** An employer can match the partnership shares bought by the employee by awarding up to two free shares for every partnership share issued.
- **Dividend Shares:** An employee can use up to £1,500 of any dividends from the plan shares each year to reinvest in further plan shares.

Participation and Limits
Employers offering free shares have to offer a minimum amount of free shares to all eligible UK tax resident employees on "similar terms" based on objective criteria such as level of remuneration or length of service. Between that minimum amount and the plan maximum they can offer free shares on different bases to different employees (although there must be no deliberate weighting of rewards in favour of directors or more highly paid employees).

Further details in relation to SIP's can be found at:
www.hmrc.gov.uk/manuals/essum/ESSUM20000.htm

Long-Term Incentive Plan ("L-TIP")
Summary
This is a flexible, unapproved plan whereby employees receive a deferred right to shares or to exercise an option to acquire shares at nil cost. Rights are generally made conditional upon the employer attaining pre-set performance targets. The plan is intended to afford incentives for future performance over a period of (usually) 3 years. Many plans also provide that at the end of the period over which the performance is measured, the employees' rights to sell the shares are deferred for a further period of another 1, 2 or 3 years (i.e. up to 6 years in total). The plans are often aimed at company executives to encourage them to become long-term shareholders in the employer.

When shares are ultimately transferred to (or sold on behalf of) the employee under an L-TIP, they receive the full value of those shares, not merely, as in the case of a traditional share option, the growth in the value over the option period. This is because, should the targets be met, shares are usually transferred to the recipient at no cost.

Participation and Limits

Any employee may participate in the plan at the discretion of the directors/shareholders. Since L-TIPs are not capable of approval, there are no limits on the amounts up to which individuals may participate in the plan.

Tax Treatment for the Employee

The tax treatment for the employee will be as described above in relation to "unapproved" plans, the employee generally being liable to income tax when shares are received. There may be PAYE and National Insurance considerations for the employer, which generally do not apply to approved plans.

"Phantom" Share Options ("Phantoms")
Summary

Phantoms are a type of deferred cash bonus arrangement. As it is merely a method of calculating a cash bonus it is not subject to HMRC approval. The amount paid as a bonus is calculated by reference to the increase in the market value of a fixed number of shares over the "option period". The employee is granted a right to call upon the employer to pay him a cash sum calculated as the amount of the difference between the "exercise price" (usually the market value at the time of grant) and the market value of those shares at the time of exercise.

Participation and Limits

Any employee or director at the discretion of the directors/shareholders is able to participate in the plan. As phantoms are not capable of approval there are no restrictions on the amount of shares or on individual participation.

Tax Treatment for the Employee

The cash bonus paid forms part of the employee's emoluments and is subject to income tax and National Insurance Contributions.

ABI Guidelines

Listed companies are subject to various additional guidelines and codes of best practice relating to the adoption and amendment of employee share and share option plans. In particular, listed companies are expected to conform to the Guidelines for Share-Based Incentive Schemes issued by the Association of British Insurers. The guidelines are designed to provide a framework to enable companies to operate the full range of employee share plans within prudent limits, which avoid undue dilution of the interests of existing shareholders.

4.8 A GUIDE TO INVESTMENT IN UK COMMERCIAL PROPERTY

Gary Ritter
Watson, Farley & Williams

INTRODUCTION

Historically, the UK has had one of the most dynamic and transparent property markets in Europe, with a broad variety of property options, stable rents and flexible short term lease structures.

In *Marketbeat UK* , a report by Cushman & Wakefield, it stated that investment activity surged in Q4 2009 with transaction volumes hitting £9.7 billion according to Property Data.[1] In particular, within the London based office investment market, the majority of recent activity has been from new overseas purchasers, although there have been indications that traditional investors are beginning to return with the hope of taking advantage of perceived values in the current market.[2]

It would appear that international investors may be increasingly viewing the UK as being attractively priced. Indeed the strength of the Euro against the Pound is certainly one factor attracting European investors despite increased hedging costs.

This chapter will seek to provide a legal background for overseas entities or individuals considering investment in or rental of UK commercial property, either

1 Marketbeat UK Q1 2010, 'An Overview of the UK Property Market' – Cushman & Wakefield LLP
2 Central London Quarterly – Quarter 2 2009 – Knight Frank Research

to occupy themselves or for investment purposes. Importantly, subject only to tax implications there are no restrictions on foreign nationals or overseas companies buying or renting property in the UK.

As well as acquiring a property directly, there are a number of structures through which to invest in property including:

- Property companies;
- Partnerships;
- Joint Venture Vehicles; or
- Real Estate Investment Trusts (REITs): A REIT is a quoted company that owns and manages income-producing property, either commercial or residential which complies with certain conditions and may achieve certain taxation benefits.

OWNERSHIP OF LAND

The form of ownership and legal rights over a property can be very significant to an owner and/or occupier. Statute has established two forms of legal estate in land, with a recent addition, namely:

- A freehold estate – Where the property (both land and structures) is effectively owned by the freeholder in perpetuity. An investor may choose to own a freehold as this gives the most control, has a capital value and will enable the grant of leases to secure an income stream. Of course, freehold ownership may still be subject to certain covenants such as, for example, restricting the use of the property and/or rights of others, such as rights of way for third parties across the property.
- A leasehold estate (i.e. renting the premises) – Where the leaseholder's ownership of the land is contractually limited in time to the length of the term of the lease. The lease will be granted out of a freehold or superior leasehold estate.
- Post-2002 a new form of freehold tenure known as *commonhold* now exists. Essentially, this is where the freehold of the units and the common parts of a development are owned by a Commonhold Association and the owners acquire a unit, subject to the terms of the commonhold.

The English system enables the "legal interest" in the property to be split from the "beneficial interest," should this be desired. The legal title holder will be registered proprietor at the Land Registry or the legal owner on the title deeds, whilst the beneficial owner will be entitled to the pecuniary interest in the property and will receive the income. This would be of relevance in establishing structures for tax and accounting purposes.

As regards the beneficial interest, land can be held by more than one person in one of two ways; either as a joint tenancy or a tenancy in common. A joint tenancy is a form of ownership where, normally, should one owner die the property will automatically vest in the surviving owner(s), regardless of the terms of the deceased's will. A tenancy in common however, is a form of ownership where on the death of one of the joint owners, the relevant share in the property will form part of the deceased's estate and will pass to their beneficiaries by their will or intestacy.

LEASEHOLD
Key Elements
A lease is a contract between a landlord and tenant which creates a leasehold estate. It is characterised by the landlord granting the tenant exclusive possession of the property for a fixed time (i.e. for a specified term or a period which is capable of being brought to an end by notice).

If these criteria are not met, a personal licence may be created instead of a leasehold estate. This is significant in terms of whether third parties will be obliged to recognise the tenant's rights and also because statute contains substantial protection for tenants; for example, security of tenure for certain residential and business tenancies which is afforded by statute, but does not extend to licencees.

Main Types of Lease
- The ground lease: this is a long lease often granted for more than 99 years usually for a one-off sum, called a premium, with a nominal rent payable (sometimes called a 'peppercorn') throughout the rest of the term. A ground lease may be perceived to be closer in nature to a freehold owing to its capital value.
- The rack rent lease: this is the most prevalent form of commercial occupational lease usually granted for around 15 years. The tenant will pay a full-market rent often quarterly with rent review provisions and usually with no premium.

COMMERCIAL LEASES

Pre-lets

Companies can rent premises that are already available or may be entitled to enter into 'pre-let' agreements with developers to lease premises prior to the carrying out or completion of construction work (enabling the future tenant to specify the design, layout and fittings of the building).

Security of Tenure

In most cases where a tenant occupies premises for business purposes, statute grants them the right to renew their lease on largely identical terms (subject to a review of rent and length of term) at the end of the lease (the intention being to protect the tenant's goodwill at the premises established whilst in occupation). Certain rights to compensation, may also be available in the event that the landlord is able to rely on one or more of seven grounds to refuse to renew the lease (e.g. if it requires occupation of the premises for its own use or wishes to redevelop the property).

Nevertheless, it is common for the parties to agree to exclude security of tenure and right to compensation by contracting out. A contracting out agreement will only be valid where the landlord serves a prescribed notice on the tenant (in a strict timeframe) and the tenant makes a declaration that they have received the said notice or through the tenant making a statutory declaration to contract out in the presence of a solicitor if the full notice period is not given.

If the lease is contracted out then the tenant must vacate the premises when the lease expires with no protection from statute and no right to compensation.

Restrictions on Use

Leases usually restrict how the premises can be used. This is often linked to planning permission but sometimes e.g. with the leases of commercial units in shopping centres, the use stated may be very specific so as to ensure the landlord has a variety of businesses within the development.

Rent Review

Where leases are granted for more than 5 years, it is standard to provide for a rent re-calculation (review) every fifth year. These reviews can be based on the open market rent which would be payable for a lease of the property on similar terms, may be linked to the Retail Prices Index or (less commonly) on fixed increases. Such provisions generally provide for 'upwards only' reviews.

Full Repairing and Insuring Lease

The majority of leases of commercial premises in the UK are on a full repairing and insuring basis (FRI lease) which means that the tenant is liable for the upkeep and decoration of the property and the costs of the landlord in insuring the building.

Service Charge

Where a property is let to several different tenants the landlord will retain responsibility in respect of the structure and the common parts of the building. He will recover these costs from the tenant through charging a fee called a "service charge". The amount of service charge paid is generally proportionate to the size of the tenant's individual unit in relation to the rentable space in the whole building.

Break clauses

Some leases include break clauses giving the landlord and/or the tenant the option to end the lease before its expiry date. These clauses usually specify how much notice has to be given and may have financial implications.

Privity of Contract

Where a lease is transferred to a new party, the original tenant will be subject to different liabilities dependent on the date of the lease.

Leases signed before 1 January 1996 are subject to "privity of contract," which means that the original tenant remains legally responsible for the rent and other commitments for the duration of the lease, regardless of whether they transfer the leasehold interest to a third party.

Subject to certain exceptions, in leases signed after this date, the tenant will not remain liable unless the landlord requests the tenant to sign a guarantee (AGA), where the tenant will remain liable under the covenants in the lease during the ownership of the new tenant to whom he has transferred the lease, but not the new tenant's successors.

PLANNING

Prior to making alterations, erecting new buildings or changing the use of an existing building, businesses must contact their local authority's planning department in order to obtain planning permission. UK planning applications are administered by the local authority covering the area in which the particular building or site is located (contact details are available on most council websites).

The UK system is largely discretionary and therefore flexible, unlike many other European Union planning systems. The usual timeframe for a planning application to be considered is between 8 and 13 weeks from the formal application, depending on whether it is treated as a major application. The appeals system in the UK also follows a comprehensive process. (http://www.planning portal.gov.uk/england/public/planning/appeals/guidance)

REGISTERED LAND Vs UNREGISTERED LAND
Registered land

The majority of land in England and Wales is registered at the Land Registry. The register is a matter of public record. It contains information concerning the type of estate, the property description (through reference to a filed plan), current owner (known as the registered proprietor) and details of all third party rights which have been registered against the estate or protected by notice (e.g. mortgages).

Not all information relating to the property will be displayed on the register. Certain third party rights (overriding interests) will bind a purchaser of registered land regardless of whether they are recorded on the register, or whether a purchaser has any knowledge of them.

Unregistered land

Alternatively, where land has remained in the same hands for many years, there may not have been a trigger event requiring registration and the land may still be unregistered. In the absence of a register entry, a landowner can only deduce title by proving an unbroken chain of ownership by reference to the title deeds and documents relating to the property. In practice, for a landowner to prove a good root of title, the chain of deeds must go back at least 15 years.

HOW IS LAND TRANSFERRED?

A typical sale and purchase transaction is a two-stage process involving an exchange of contracts between the buyer and the seller followed by completion of the legal transfer. A seller's solicitor will issue a draft sale contract which will be negotiated and then exchanged with a deposit usually being paid. This is the point of no return, when both parties commit themselves to complete on a certain date. Up to this point, either party can withdraw without any liability to the other side. Following exchange of contracts, the transfer of the property is effected by completing the document which formally effects the transfer of the land from the seller to the buyer, and by complying with registration requirements. Completion is in effect moving day, when the money is paid to the seller's solicitors and the keys to the property are handed over.

Principle of Caveat Emptor

In UK conveyancing, the principle of "caveat emptor" (buyer beware) is key and places the responsibility for due diligence and searches relating to a property on the buyer. It is normally the task of a lawyer to consider the negotiation of legal documentation and discover as much information as possible about the property through a variety of searches and enquiries including but not limited to:

- Local Search – list of enquiries about property sent to local authority which includes questions about planning, highways, drainage etc.
- Preliminary Enquiries – questions about the property which are sent to the seller or landlord's solicitors requesting information about disputes with neighbours, use of property etc.
- Surveys – a survey of the property should be carried out and occasionally environmental studies of the land arranged.

TAX IMPLICATIONS OF ACQUIRING AN INTEREST IN PROPERTY
Value Added Tax (VAT)

Many commercial property transactions are subject to Value Added Tax (VAT). Whether it is subject to VAT will depend on a number of factors, mainly being whether it is regarded as a "new" property or an election to waive exemption from VAT has been made by the owner.

Stamp Duty Land Tax (SDLT)

SDLT is a mandatory tax payable by the buyer on the purchase price, payable on completion or substantial performance of the contract (which generally means occupation or a payment of at least 90% of the price), whichever is the earlier.

Current rates are available on the website of HM Revenue and Customs: http://www.hmrc.gov.uk/sdlt/intro/rates-thresholds.htm

SDLT is also payable on the grant of a lease upon both the Premium and rental payments. For more information on calculating SDLT please see:

http://www.hmrc.gov.uk/sdlt/calculate/calculators.htm

There are a number of transactions which may be exempt from SDLT, such as intra-group transfers within the same group of companies and the leaseback elements of a sale and leaseback.

Business Rates

Business rates are a property tax that business occupiers pay towards the costs of local government services. They typically range from £20 to £130 per square metre (approximately £2 to £13 per square foot). Details of business rates can be found at:

- England and Wales – http://www.voa.gov.uk/business_rates/index.htm
- Northern Ireland – www.lpsni.gov.uk/index.htm
- Scotland – http://www.scotland.gov.uk/Topics/Government/local-govern ment/17999/11199

This chapter provides a brief summary of the legal issues relating to investment in UK real estate; it does not take the place of advice from property experts.

An elevated view of MediaCityUK, as it will look in 2011

Get the full success story on England's Northwest

Few regions have the specialist skills and strengths of England's Northwest. The region is Europe's second largest media hub generating almost £16 billion GVA and employing 320,000 skilled professionals. This is before the arrival of five key BBC departments, and the completion of MediaCityUK – a 200 acre purpose-built development in Salford Quays, Manchester.

In low carbon, we're home to half of the UK's skilled nuclear workforce and two of the most advanced tidal energy proposals. We're also the UK's largest manufacturing region, with a host of global brands, including AstraZeneca, BAE Systems, Bentley Motors and Unilever, spearheading innovative R&D activity. To find out more about our success story, visit **englandsnorthwest.com**

Manchester — Liverpool — Cheshire — Lancashire — Cumbria

TheSourcingSolutions 游刃有餘

TheSourcingSolutions Ltd helps European and Chinese partners successfully grow their businesses together. We specialize in the automotive, medical and high-tech engineering sectors.

Our services include :

- Strategic advice on identifying the right partners
- Support in supplier development
- Project management for new product development
- In-market quality control inspections
- Shipping and logistics support
- Conference and event management
- Provision of training programmes

For more information, and a free consultation, please contact

TheSourcingSolutions Ltd
7200 The Quorum
Oxford Business Park North
Garsington Road
Oxford
OX4 2JZ
Tel +44 (0)1865487150
Email info@thesourcingsolutions.com

The Exchange; a new Business Innovation Centre under construction on Colworth Science Park a joint development by Goodman and Unilever with support from the East of England Development Agency.

Science Village a new 28,000 sq ft flexible laboratory building on Chesterford Research Park being developed by Aviva Investors and Churchmanor Estates Company.

Part Five

5.1 COMMERCIAL BANKING SERVICES

James Roberts
HSBC Bank plc

The information provided in this chapter and in Chapter 5.2 is drawn from the published material of HSBC but the services described are available from the other major banks offering commercial banking services in the United Kingdom. The commercial banking services available to international companies and UK banking practices are among the most reliable and sophisticated in the world.

INTRODUCTION

In common with most businesses, a company setting up in the United Kingdom for the first time wants to make payments to suppliers and receive payments from customers, and perhaps the parent company, quickly and efficiently in sterling and other currencies. It may also require a method of making and receiving routine planned payments in a cost-effective manner, acknowledging that they can often be 'bulked' and arranged in advance. To stay in control of cashflow, the business needs to keep track of payments made, to have rapid advice on receipts and to have transaction data available in an easily accessible form in the United Kingdom, in the parent headquarters and often at the offices of a third party that is undertaking back office, accounting and similar functions on its behalf. UK banks offer accounts in a wide range of currencies. However, the services described below may not be available in currencies other than sterling, the UK currency.

The starting point of the banking relationship for the customer is the opening of a business current account and, if required, the issue of a cheque book. Cheques remain one of the simplest forms of payment for low-volume transactions. However, cheque volumes peaked in 1990 and usage has fallen since then due to the wide range of alternative payment methods from card payments and direct debits to telephone and electronic banking services, as described in this chapter. Many suppliers in the United Kingdom such as landlords and utility companies will demand a direct debit in their favour and view this as part of their credit assessment of a new (to UK) business with no (UK) credit history. A direct debit is an instruction from a customer to their bank authorizing an organization to collect varying amounts from their account. The supplier must give the bank advanced notice of the collection. Direct debits save time, reduce costs and put cleared funds directly into the account of the collecting organization. There are a number of safeguards associated with direct debits to ensure that funds are not collected in error.

A business current account may be interest bearing but the interest rate will be low and for this reason it can be linked with a business savings account, enabling surplus funds to earn a better rate. Larger sums can also be placed in the money market at current rates and varying notice periods or fixed terms.

INTERNET BANKING

Internet banking allows 24-hour access to bank accounts and offers the following benefits, some of the benefits may be available on mobile devices such as Blackberry. Certain services may require the customer to take additional modules for superior services which are only available for a fee; however many of the services, such as balance information for sterling accounts, are often available without charge. Some services are subject to credit assessment by the bank. Some payments are only processed during office hours:

- real-time balances on business accounts;
- transaction details on individual accounts;
- Balance and transaction details on Business or Commercial cards;

- immediate transfers between customers' own accounts;
- payments of up to £100,000 per day using Bill Payments or BACS;
- sterling and currency payments by priority payment or CHAPS;
- save details of salaries or other beneficiaries to make repeat payments;
- forward date payments up to 45 days in advance;
- order a new cheque book or paying in/credit book;
- order a copy of a cheque or credit;
- viewing and cancellation of standing orders or direct debits;
- stop a cheque;
- apply for an overdraft;
- download application forms for other services such as a Commercial Card;
- initiate and monitor Trade Transactions;
- access market research and data and deal in foreign exchange and Money Markets;
- delegated access to the service to other company users;
- access to the accounts of your other businesses from a single logon, if required;
- download of transaction details to Quicken©, Microsoft Money© or spreadsheet packages; and
- security routines including unique 'one-time' passwords, automatic log-off after periods of inactivity and protected communication across the Internet using data encryption and digital certification;
- telephone support for the internet banking service is available, covering most of the day.

Most full-service banks offer a priority payment facility providing a simple, cost-effective way of making payments from a PC. These enable customers to initiate same-day sterling and euro payments in the United Kingdom and urgent payments to beneficiaries outside the United Kingdom. Templates with details of regular beneficiaries may be held and payments submitted for transmission around the world at any time of the day or night.

TELEPHONE BANKING

Telephone banking requires prior registration in order to provide a secure method of dealing with all queries by calling one simple number. Many of the key services offered with internet banking are available at the telephone. This service can be used as an alternative to electronic banking or as an alterrnative in emergencies or when electronic banking is not available.

MAKING PAYMENTS

For companies wishing to make payments, the services that will be the most appropriate will vary depending on whether payments are made in the United Kingdom or overseas and upon the volumes and speed of payments required.

Making payments in the United Kingdom

Services for customers in this category include cheques, various forms of debit or credit card and, increasingly, electronic payments through online or telephone banking. For a large number of payments each month with various payment times, the Automated Clearing House (ACH) (known in the United Kingdom as BACS), direct debits and credits are the norm. Software in the form of either easy-to-use dedicated Windows-based software packages that allow customers to make or collect payments direct from PCs within their organizations or an option in PC and Internet banking packages are provided by banks. The software has inbuilt security, allowing full control of the payment process through creation/generation, authorization and transmission. Each action can be allocated to a specific 'user' with relevant authority. This solution caters for fully euro-denominated credit payments within the United Kingdom and payments in a wide range of currencies to a growing number of countries through reciprocal banking arrangements. With the onset of ever-increasingly sophisticated Internet and PC banking services, most banks have now withdrawn fax payment services.

Payroll services, usually provided by third-party bureaus that interface with the company's bank, provide a full calculation facility, the printing of pay slips, management reports and payments direct into employees' accounts by wire transfer/BACS.

Card payments

The differing key features of three types of cards, available for both UK and overseas purchases as offered by HSBC, may be summarised as follows:

- **Business Credit Card** – a card for everyday business expenses and purchases:

- Up to 56 days' interest-free credit
- Accepted worldwide wherever the Visa symbol is displayed
- Separation of business from personal expenses with itemised monthly statements
- Individual credit limits (minimum £500)
- Facility to permit cardholders to withdraw up to £500 per day from Visa cash machines around the world (for a small charge) and subject to local currency regulations
- Allows telephone and Internet purchases with 'Zero Fraud Liability'
- No transaction fees on purchases
- Chip and PIN-enabled card combines new technology in a chip card with the security of a four-digit PIN

- **Corporate Card** – a credit card for companies with a large travel & entertainment (T &E) budget:

  - Provides easy payment methods and extensive expense management for a mobile workforce
  - Up to 56 days' interest-free credit
  - Can be used worldwide wherever the Visa symbol is displayed
  - Company chooses number of cards and maximum spending limit on each card
  - Itemised monthly statement for each card with a choice of statement date
  - Chip and PIN-enabled card combines new technology in a chip card with the security of a four-digit PIN

- **Debit Card** – available to sole traders, partnerships and limited companies with sole signatories in place:

  - Chip and PIN-enabled card combines new technology in a chip card with the security of a four-digit PIN
  - Saves the time and bother of writing out cheques
  - Use the card to purchase goods and services wherever the Visa symbol is displayed
  - Enables cash withdrawal up to £500 per day, balance enquiries

and inter account transfers through a network of self-service
machines
– Cashback is available from many shops, supermarkets and other
retailers in the UK up to £50

Card linked to an HSBC Business Current Account

Making payments overseas

Companies making payments overseas and needing same-day or next-day payment are recommended to use their bank's priority payments facility, which provides a fast and secure method of payment that can be sent to most countries in
any tradeable currency. Payments to Eurozone countries will be received within
one day. Payments outside the Eurozone will normally be received within four
working days. This service can be accessed by the Internet or PC banking or by
physically giving instructions to a branch in person. Most banks require these
instructions to be provided on a pre-printed and security-marked bank form.
Some banks, including HSBC, now accept payment instructions by telephone if
prior arrangements are made.

Payments to all European Union (EU) and European Economic Area (EEA)
countries will require Bank Identifier Code (BIC) and International Bank Account
Number (IBAN) numbers for the beneficiary. Elsewhere SWIFT and branch and
account number will be required

Payment instructions include:

- by credit to a specified bank account;
- by payment to the beneficiary at a stated address; or
- collected by the beneficiary upon production of appropriate identification.

If payment times of between three and six days are acceptable, HSBC offers to its
customers its 'Worldpay' solution for the cost-effective transmission of low-value
payments abroad from the customer's local HSBC bank branch. Worldpay
involves one simple document only and instructions received before 2.30 pm will
be acted upon the same day. There is a fixed fee with no deduction of fees by the
payee's bank. The system is available for payments of £2,000 or less in local
currency and may, for example, be used to pay salaries, fees and expenses to
employees abroad and pay subscriptions to trade organizations and publications.
The 21 countries, to which payments by this means may be made, are Australia,

Austria, Belgium, Canada, Cyprus, Denmark, Finland, France, Germany, Hong Kong SAR, Ireland, Italy, the Netherlands, New Zealand, Poland, Portugal, South Africa, Spain, Sweden , Switzerland and the United States. Other high street banks offer a similar service through their local branches.

The recent introduction of SEPA Credit Transfers within the 32 countries of the Single European Payments area (SEPA) offers a significantly cheaper method of making non-urgent transfers. However not all European banks are yet participating and individual banks offer different methods of access to these transfers.

For non-urgent payments overseas or non-urgent payments in euros within the United Kingdom, international drafts are an appropriate alternative, offering the customer the following advantages:

- low cost;
- ability to attach relevant documentation and correspondence;
- no time limit within which a draft supplied by the bank has to be sent; and
- drafts available in sterling and most currencies.

Cards provide an alternative payment method

Receiving payments within the United Kingdom
In addition to payment by cheque, direct debit, direct payment into their account via Internet Banking or cash, companies wishing to receive payment from customers in the United Kingdom may consider three further alternatives:

- Banker's draft – This provides a near certainty of payment upon presentation and is therefore attractive for the receipt of large sums, particularly where immediate delivery of goods or the transfer of title to property is concurrent.
- Electronic card processing – An efficient and swift system for dealing with sales transactions, which accepts all major debit and credit cards via terminals provided by the bank and software providing monthly statements showing the previous month's card transactions.
- Companies preferring to outsource their invoice payments and collections may consider using their bank's credit management service. This is outsourced sales ledger management through an integrated invoice finance solution – described more fully in Chapter 5.2

Receiving payments from abroad

Inward payment
Companies that request a wire transfer from the sender against full banking details may take advantage of their bank's inward payment service. Banks in all EU and EEA countries will require BIC and IBAN numbers for the beneficiary. Elsewhere SWIFT and sorting code and account number will be required. The bank applies the appropriate exchange rate in force at the time of the transaction on receipt of a payment in currency that is to be credited to the customer's sterling account and effects the credit. An advice with all details of the receipt, including exchange rate and commission, is mailed to the customer on the next working day.

Cheque negotiations
Most banks offer a cheque negotiation scheme to clear cheques received that are payable outside the United Kingdom, foreign currency cheques payable in the United Kingdom or sterling cheques drawn abroad. The proceeds of cheques credited to a customer's sterling account are immediately made available subject to recourse, while costs are much lower than those incurred with cheque collection. This service is offered at the bank's discretion and may be subject to credit assessment by the bank. A forward value date is applied when crediting a foreign currency account with funds of the same currency. The cheque negotiation scheme is also the only way in which the proceeds of travellers' cheques payable outside the United Kingdom can be paid.

Cheque collections
Businesses receiving cheques payable outside the United Kingdom, foreign currency cheques payable in the United Kingdom or sterling cheques drawn abroad and wishing to be sure that the cheque is paid when funds are received can take advantage of their bank's cheque collection scheme. Proceeds of cheque collections are made available to the customer only when the funds have been received by the bank, unlike a cheque negotiation where the proceeds are made available before the cheque has been cleared. This service will be offered if cheque negotiation is not appropriate for the customer and is not available for cheques drawn on all countries. As a part of the service:

● The collection process can be accelerated by requesting the bank to send cheques to the drawee bank by courier for an extra fee.

- The bank's international cheque-processing department monitors progress of each transaction and will chase for the proceeds or an advice of non-payment.
- Since receipt of proceeds usually means that a cheque has been paid, customers can use the cheque collections mechanism to withhold the release of goods or the provision of services where advance payment is an agreed term of business.

Foreign cheques can be paid in at any UK branch of most commercial banks.

US dollar and European lockboxes
If a company's goods or services are bought by customers in the United States, prompt and efficient processing of cheques receivable is paramount. For example, HSBC provides a US Dollar Lockbox service whereby funds are credited up to 10 days faster to customers' accounts by processing all cheques through the US clearing system rather than with traditional cheque negotiations. There is no need to open accounts with different banks in the United Kingdom and the United States, charges are fixed, paperwork is kept to a minimum and the documentation sent by the US customers is returned to the company.

There is an equivalent Euro Lockbox system to process all cheques from customers based in continental Europe through the relevant European clearing system. Use of this system will result in the earliest possible crediting of cheques to accounts, up to five days earlier than with traditional cheque negotiations. The transaction information provided can be linked to new or existing electronic balance reporting and payments services.

CASH MANAGEMENT

Physical cash management
Standard physical cash management services include the time-saving facility to place payments in self-sealing packets that can be handed over at branch counters and secure enquiry positions or deposited in automated paying-in machines to be verified later, and a range of solutions available to bank customers receiving over £10,000 in cash every week. These include cash collection services by secure carrier from the customer's own premises with delivery to

the bank and cash in transit services where the collections are delivered to one of the bank's network of cash centres across the United Kingdom.

At many banks there is a parallel bulk cheque service for organizations receiving more than 100 cheques per week whereby cheques are collected by an authorised carrier from the customer's outlets/premises and delivered to a cheque-processing centre within the UK network, which processes all branch and commercial cheque items.

Outsourcing payment collection

Finally, for companies preferring to outsource payment collection there is the option of using their bank's credit management service. Credit management is one of the three service elements of invoice finance (see Chapter 5.2) linked to credit protection and sales-linked finance services. For companies selling on credit terms to other businesses in the United Kingdom or overseas, full-service banks offer a credit management service providing consistent, professional credit control and efficient collection, which strikes a balance between the customer's need to be paid and the maintenance of good public relations.

OPENING A UK BANK ACCOUNT

Account opening formalities will vary in detail from bank to bank. However, in general the requirements for both UK registered and overseas registered companies will be:

1. **Business Customer Application Form**
● Giving details of the business requiring an account, its activities and ownership and details of the services required as well as instructions as to mailing addresses and other contact details.

2. **Mandate**
● Incorporates the resolution to open an account and gives signature instructions.

3. **Registration of company**
● A search is usually undertaken to confirm registration of a UK company, and sight of the Certificate of Incorporation or other proof of registration

is usually required. For businesses registered overseas a certified copy of a Certificate of Incorporation or its equivalent or a certified extract from the relevant companies register will be required.

4.   Bank statements
●   If the company already has a bank account it is usual for a bank to review recent bank statements. For new businesses, bank statements of the parent company or directors/beneficial owners may be requested.

5.   Audited accounts
●   Banks vary in their requirement to see accounts. Although these are not always required, for account opening, if the company wishes to borrow and is subject to audit the latest audited accounts for all businesses established for 18 months or longer are required. If the company is not subject to audit requirements unaudited accounts will be accepted.

Identification of key officials

It is usual to require verification of the *identity* and *personal residential address* for at least *two signatories* on the account, one of whom must be a director. UK banks are also required to identify the beneficial owner(s)[1] and/or principal controller(s)[1] [if any] of the company if they are individuals and not one of the directors. If beneficial owners are corporate entities, a structure chart is required and there may be a need to identify key officials and beneficial owners of those entities in due course.

Each signatory and/or beneficial owner and/or principal controller to be identified must provide original copies of a passport or National Identity Card and a separate proof of address such as a recent credit card statement or utility bill (not mobile phone). If any officers of the company are not resident in the United Kingdom, banks may also need a reference from their own bank.

Certification of documents

In all cases it is usual to require presentation of original documents/ID. However, arrangements can usually be made for these to be presented to and certified by bank branch offices or other officials such as a British Embassy, Consulate or High Commission, or a notary, lawyer, or attorney. Practices vary from bank to bank and potential account holders should take time to ensure that they will be able to meet their chosen bank's requirements.

---

1 Individuals, shareholders with 25 per cent or more shareholding, a public quoted company or an individual providing significant financial support, influence or control.

OTHER SERVICES

UK banks provide a wider range of services than banks in some other countries and owners and directors of businesses establishing in the UK are encouraged to keep their Branch or Relationship Manager up to date with the progress of their project. They should not be surprised if a variety of services and business solutions are offered by their bank and are encouraged to seek specific advice about ways in which the bank can assist their business.

Services include:

- **Insurance**

  By law, all busineses are required to insure agaisnst certain kinds of risk such as Employers' liability insurance. Public Liability Insurance should also be considered when dealing with customers and the public. Packaged products for various businesses are available and include these insurances plus insurances particular to their needs which may, for example, cover certain types of property, equipment , product liability or buiness interruption. HSBC offer the following packages:

  - Tradesman Insurance
  - Professionals Insurance
  - Retailers Insurance
  - Office or Surgries Insurance
  - Pubs, Inns and Rstaurants Insurance
  - Property Owners Insurance
  - Residential Landlords Insurance
  - Homeworkers Insurance
  - Whlesalers and Manufactuers Insurance

  Specialist Business Insurance can include:

  - Trade Credit Insurance
  - Cargo Insurance
  - Keyman Insurance
  - Shareholder or Partnership Protection
  - Solicitors Professional Indemnity
  - Business Vehicle Insurance

- **Pensions for Employees**
  Working closely with Pensions advisers defined contribution solutions are available to employers from large trust based occupational schemes to the smallest stakeholder scheme.

- **Trade & Supply Chain**
  Most British banks offer the services of Trade Specialists who will advise how Overseas trade may run more smoothly by using a range of international services including Import and Export Documentary Collections, Import and Export Bills and Guarantees and Foreign Exchange Risk Management.

- **Franchising**
  Successful businesses may consider entering the UK market by franchising their business. Due to initial capital expenditure the costs may be high – but once appointed, franchisees will pay a fee, reimbursing costs. There are some very clear advantages and disadvantages of franchising your business and major banks have specialist departments that can:

  – provide an insight into the franchise sector in the UK;
  – signpost/introduce relevant franchise professionals ;
  – explain how banks view franchising in the UK, the basis on which financing is carried out and what sort of information would be sought;

- **Asset Finance**
  Most UK banks provide a range of products to finance business assets including loans and leasing products. The facilities will be structured to reflect the working life of the asset and the business's cashflow.

- **Business Tools and Information**
  Information which is often web based or in news letters is available on a wide variety of current topics from Country Guides for Exporters to Economic Reports and advice on Employee Relations. HSBC, for example, offers a 'Knowledge Centre', Business Network and 'Tools and Resources' site

CASE STUDY

A privately owned Melbourne-based software company specializing in systems for financial services organizations and with a growing portfolio of clients in the United Kingdom decided to create a UK subsidiary to handle further UK and European sales and to provide technical support close to its clients and in the same time zone. Additional support and in particular accounting was to remain in Australia.

The company's bank in Melbourne did not offer a full service in the United Kingdom and the decision was made to open an account with a UK bank. Of primary importance was the ability to view and operate the account from Melbourne and there was a clear understanding that most transactions both in and out would be electronic.

After consulting the UK bank a 'pack' was created including the following documents:

- Business current account application form
- Business Internet banking application form
- Business telephone banking application form
- Mandate authorizing any one of two Melbourne-based owner/directors (of the UK company), a UK-recruited director and the Melbourne-based finacial controller to sign cheques and authorise other transactions up to and including £2,000 and any two of those designated to sign cheques and authorise transactions above £2,000
- Latest accounts of the parent company (unaudited as no Australian requirement for audit)
- Certified copies of:

- UK company Certificate of Incorporation;
- Bank statements of three months from the parent company;
- Passports of two founders of the parent company each with a 40 per cent interest in the parent and thus the wholly owned UK subsidiary;
- Driver's licence of one founder and recent credit card statement of the other;

As the founders are also directors of the UK company and signatures on the account, no further identification or address verification was required. The 'pack' was couriered to the UK bank and after making its own credit checks the account was opened four days after receipt of the documents.

Since opening the account, business cards have been issued to the UK director and three sales staff. The company has also leased cars for the UK-based sales staff from the bank, arranged insurance for employers' liability, buildings contents and equipment and a 'Key Man' insurance policy for the UK director (an appointment considered pivotal in pushing the company forward in Europe). The company is currently discussing a stakeholder pension scheme with its pensions advisers and the bank. With more and more European business in prospect, a Euro account will be opened and the bank is demonstrating a multi-currency upgrade to its Business Internet Banking Service.

5.2 FINANCE FOR COMPANIES

James Roberts
HSBC Bank plc

FUND-RAISING REQUIREMENTS

Most businesses will need to raise finance at some stage in their development either to fund growth or to enhance short-term cashflow. Raising finance wisely and taxing efficiently can make a major contribution to a company's profitability, whereas badly planned inappropriate finance may be burdensome. The first step in identifying appropriate financing solutions is to clarify the purpose for which a company needs to raise funds. Broadly, there are four main reasons for a company to seek external funding.

To assist cashflow

In practice companies investing abroad for the first time rarely seek this type of working capital finance in the early stages of a project, preferring to fund from the head office. However, after a certain period that differs from company to company, the decision is invariably made that the new business should now be self-sufficient. Prudently, this decision will coincide with the point at which the parent considers the subsidiary to have developed a strong enough balance sheet to enable it to approach bankers in reasonable expectation of a positive response.

The need for external support may be driven by the fact that your order book is increasing in volume and/or value, you need to take on more staff/buy more stock, your customers are demanding credit terms, your suppliers can offer you good early payment discounts or you may want to diversify in response to customer demand. Easily accessible solutions range from invoice financing services to an extended overdraft or the use of a bank business card or loan.

To finance international trade

International trade can put a strain on a company's cashflow and expose the business to a variety of risks. A number of specific solutions are available, depending on whether a company is engaged in import or export trade or both.

To acquire fixed assets

The acquisition of new premises and the expansion or improvement of existing buildings may all require funding of a longer-term nature for which there are several solutions. Equally, a number of funding options are available for company acquisitions of equipment and business vehicles.

To fund business growth

Companies needing a cash injection to facilitate growth should be sure to choose an option that supports their expansion plans constructively. The needs of a business planning to expand by organic growth may be very different from those of an enterprise expanding through franchising or a company growing through acquisition.

Alternative solutions for all these funding scenarios are discussed in the sections that follow. As for Chapter 5.1, the range of solutions is drawn from published HSBC material but all full-service UK banks offer a similar range.

ASSISTING CASHFLOW

Companies trading within the United Kingdom have access to a variety of financing services through the commercial banks.

Overdraft

Often the most convenient way for a company to pre-arrange the working capital it needs to ride out the troughs in its business cycle is to arrange an overdraft facility with its bank. An overdraft is flexible in as much as you decide how much you use and interest is only paid on what you use and not what is available. It is usually available from 1 to 12 months and subject to regular review. Overdrafts are repayable on demand. The company will need to satisfy the bank as to why the money is needed, how much is required and for how long. Subject to a favourable credit assessment and agreement on the overdraft limit, the bank will confirm arrangements by a facility letter including details of arrangement or renewal fees. The bank may require tangible security, which may incur security fees, or the support of the parent company by way of guarantee or bank guarantee or standby documentary credit. Interest is charged at a variable rate, usually a margin over the bank's base rate and is calculated daily and debited monthly or quarterly to suit the customer. A negotiated arrangement fee will apply initially and at renewal.

Business card

The business card facility identified in Chapter 5.1 as a payment method can be used as a means of easing cashflow by taking advantage of an interest-free credit period in paying for everyday expenses. Many banks also allow borrowing on business credit cards. A minimum monthly repayment typically of about 3% of the account balance is required and balances over and above this amount are rolled over at a published interest rate making this a useful and flexible way of borrowing relatively small amounts.

Invoice finance (factoring)

Invoice finance is the collective name for a range of service elements – sales-linked finance, credit management and credit protection – invoice finance improves cash flow by freeing up cash from invoices as soon as they are issued, provides relief from the time and resource burden of chasing customers for payment and safeguards against bad debt for businesses selling in the United Kingdom or overseas on credit terms. This full service is sometimes referred to as Invoice (or debt) factoring. Typically, up to 90 per cent of an invoice's value can be advanced the next working day. Using this facility it may be possible to obtain more favourable terms from suppliers by paying earlier.

Invoice finance is suitable for most businesses that sell business to business on credit terms with a projected sales turnover of £100,000 or more and is available to businesses recently set up in the UK. Invoice finance grows with your business and there is no need to keep increasing your borrowing facilities. This enables businesses to react quickly to market opportunities while keeping debtors under control. Other non-bank invoice finance houses offer services usually up to lower limits.

Invoice discounting

Invoice discounting differs from invoice factoring only in as much as you manage debt collection and credit control. Credit protection remains an option. Businesses seeking this type of finance must have an annual turnover exceeding £1,000,000 and a proven track record and must be able to evidence profitability.

FINANCING INTERNATIONAL TRADE

Loans and overdrafts

Loans and overdrafts are the first source of finance for international trade, as in the normal course of domestic UK business. For longer-term needs, fixed or variable rate loans in sterling or foreign currency are available from full-service banks with the repayment terms structured to suit a company's business cashflow.

Foreign currency loans on fixed terms are an attractive option for companies involved in international business. By taking out a loan in any major currency, a company can reduce its exposure to fluctuating exchange rates and is enabled to make and receive payments in the overseas currency without the cost and effort of conversion back into sterling. It opens an appropriate foreign currency account in the United Kingdom, which is simpler and may be more cost-effective than opening an account abroad. Foreign currency loans can be medium or short term and the borrower can have the option to repay in single or multi-currencies to suit its requirements.

Where these facilities are not suitable and either the lender or the borrower requires more structure, the following services are available from those banks that specialise in the finance of international trade.

Discounting/negotiation of Export Documentary Credits

Also known as letters of credit, Export Documentary Credits are a popular method of reducing the risks in overseas trade and are in global usage. They provide a measure of security for both the buyer and the seller. Having given credit to an overseas customer using an Export Documentary Credit, an exporter may find that the cashflow becomes tight during the credit period. If compliant documents have been presented to the bank, in most cases the bank will be able to give the exporter immediate value for the documents under the Documentary Credit, less a discount/negotiation fee.

Import Usance Documentary Credit

By asking their bank to issue Documentary Credits on their behalf to buy goods, an importer reduces the risk of non-payment for the exporter and may enable itself to negotiate a period of credit, such as 30, 60 or 90 days, from the supplier, thereby giving itself the opportunity to sell on the goods before having to pay for them.

Import loans for traders

There are two basic types of import loans. The first addresses the situation where a company has imported goods under an Import Documentary Credit, but has not received sufficient supplier credit to allow collection of any proceeds from selling on the goods. In this instance, an import loan can be used to pay the Documentary Credit on the due date. The loan is repaid when the proceeds are received from selling on the goods.

In the second instance, import loans are taken out to cover situations where a company wishes to import goods without using trade finance instruments, but still needs structured borrowing. The bank will require some assurance that the proceeds from selling on the goods will be used specifically to repay any debt associated with the original purchase of the goods. Therefore, the bank will probably provide an import loan for each transaction, with a repayment date set to match the expected date for receipt of proceeds from any onward sale of the goods.

Export loans for manufacture

If a company is the named beneficiary under an Export Documentary Credit advised to it by its bank, but needs working capital to manufacture the goods to be sold, an export loan may be appropriate. The Export Documentary Credit and the export loan will be repaid once compliant documentation has been presented to the bank, with any surplus being credited to the exporter.

Financing export sales

International commercial banks provide a range of services that allow companies to offer attractive open account terms to overseas customers, while protecting their business from the associated risks of severely delayed payment or non-payment.

Export factoring is the finance (factoring) of export invoices and the terms are described in the paragraph on Invoice Finance (above). Additional advantages of this service include the ability to offer open account terms to overseas customers helping them compete with local suppliers. You can choose to invoice in one currency and be paid in another. The bank will use UK-based linguists, its own network and correspondent invoice factoring providers abroad to collect your payments.

Such services iron out the risks of currency fluctuation, give professional assistance in assessing creditworthiness of potential customers and allow exporters to focus on negotiating the most appropriate terms.

Advances against export collection

Documentary Collections are an alternative to the relative complexity and cost of Documentary Credits and provide a cost-effective, more secure alternative to trade on open account. Basically, the method relies on using the overseas customer's bank as an intermediary. The exporting company sends the shipping documents to its own bank, which forwards them to the customer's bank, with instructions to only release them in return for payment or a promise to pay at a later specified date. The exporter's bank can advance funds against the subsequent collection of payment.

ACQUIRING FIXED ASSETS

Property purchases

The commercial mortgage is the most commonly used financial package to purchase existing or new owner occupied business premises or to extend premises acquired previously. Mortgage finance is available from a number of financial institutions including life assurance companies and pension funds. Mortgages are also available from commercial banks, typically up to 70 per cent of the purchase price for new or existing buildings or the professional valuation – whichever is the lower. There are no set maximum amounts but typically there is a minimum amount for the sum borrowed.

Loans from HSBC are for a minimum period of 2 years and a maximum period of 30 years. For loans up to £100,000 rates can be fixed or charged at a margin over the bank's base rate and for those of greater value variable rates linked to the London Inter-bank Borrowing Rate (LIBOR) are also available.. Interest is applied monthly with an optional moratorium on capital repayment of up to two years from drawdown. For loans over £250,000 it is possible to buy protection against interest rate rises.

Property-associated purchases

The small business loan
A quick and easy way to fund the refitting of premises or the purchase of new business equipment, such as PCs, which will minimise the effect on cashflow, is through a small business loan. Small business loans available may typically be for any amount from £1,000 to £ 25,000. To assist budgeting, the interest rate is fixed from the start and loan repayments therefore remain the same even if bank base rates should rise. Repayment schedules can match the expected lifespan of the items purchased and may be spread over 12 months to 10 years.

The flexible business loan
A similar type of facility is the flexible business loan, which HSBC offers to limited companies at variable rates for amounts over £10,000 and to all businesses at fixed or variable rates for amounts over £25,001 as a cost-effective way for a company to finance fixed investment in the business or, indeed, business expansion. There is no maximum to the amount for which a loan application can be made. There is an option to pay interest either monthly or quarterly. Security may be required, which may in turn incur security fees and an arrangement fee will apply.

Repayments may be spread over up to 15 years (10 years for fixed rates), although, in the case of equipment, the length of the loan is expected to match the useful life of the asset. For loans over £25,001 a capital repayment holiday of up to two years may be taken. On certain types of loan, an option is granted to defer up to two monthly payments a year.

Vehicle acquisitions
A range of alternative financing arrangements is available for the acquisition of vehicles and equipment, which are inappropriate for other fixed asset purchases.

Contract hire
Contract hire gives a business the use of a new car or light commercial vehicles for a pre-determined period of between two and four years based on an agreed

mileage, at a fixed cost. The finance company will purchase the new vehicle at the beginning of the agreement and take on the risks associated with reselling it at the end and for budgeting purposes a fixed cost maintenance package may be added to the agreement. The finance company will pass on the benefit of its buying power as both vehicles and maintenance are sourced and purchased at our preferential rates. Replacement vehicles are usually available in the event of an accident or breakdown, and tailored to suit your company's needs and reduce 'down time' for your drivers. A comprehensive Accident Management service is usually offered, covering the sourcing and processing of fast, high-quality accident repairs, with the minimum of involvement from your company or your drivers.

This service offers balance sheet efficiency as you do not own the vehicle during the contract, which improves the balance sheet ratios and the value added tax (VAT) recovered on purchase by the finance company is reflected in lower rental costs. Even if you have no tax shelter of your own, you will still benefit from the finance company's ability to claim Writing Down Allowance, passed on through lower rentals. Contract hire is tax efficient in that it is usually allowable as a trading expense. Treatment of VAT varies according to whether the vehicle is also used for private purposes. The lender can give advice.

Sale and leaseback

Sale and leaseback is an agreement under which a fleet of vehicles is sold to a finance company that then leases them back on a tailored, fixed-term basis using contract hire, allowing the immediate advantage of the savings and the security of contract hire. Each individual vehicle in a fleet is valued at a fair market rate. The finance company pays you this value and the vehicles are transferred onto a contract hire agreement. This agreement can be tailored to meet your individual business requirements. A fixed monthly payment covers the costs of regular servicing and maintenance and eliminates all residual value risk. Valuable capital can be released for more profitable use elsewhere in the business and the risks associated with selling and maintaining vehicles can be transferred to the finance company.

Equipment finance

Hire purchase

Finance packages are available from a variety of lenders including the equipment finance subsidiaries of commercial banks for the purchase or lease of equipment.

Hire purchase enables a company to select its own supplier and negotiate its own deal, acquiring ownership of the asset at the end of the agreement. The minimum HP term is two to seven years, the term is agreed with you at the start. Hire purchase allows you to fund the asset without the long-term outlay, and make repayments over a period that suits your cash flow. Fixed or variable interest rates are available.

For tax purposes the asset is deemed to belong to the company allowing it to claim any tax allowances available.

Leasing

Operating and finance leases enable a business to have the use of an asset over a predetermined period without leading to ownership. At the end of the contract the rental can be extended for a fair market rental or in the case of a finance lease, a nominal rental or the lessee can sell the asset and retain a part of the proceeds. The principal difference between finance leasing and other forms of medium-term finance is that the bank retains legal ownership of the asset and claims the capital allowances against tax, which are reflected in reduced rentals. This form of finance can be particularly beneficial for businesses that are unable to benefit from the tax allowances themselves. As previously noted, a small business loan or a flexible business loan can also fund the purchase of equipment. The type of assets suitable for this type of finance is limited and early consultation with the financial institution to discuss the most suitable form of finance is recommended.

Asset Loans

An asset loan allows the finance of up to 80% of new or existing and already paid for equipment for periods of two to seven years, although longer periods may be possible, at fixed or variable rates of interest and with repayment terms tailored to your cash flow requirements. You can claim capital allowances and the interest element can normally be set off against taxable profits. Once a purchase is made, the loan is advanced and the bank or finance company takes a chattels mortgage over the asset as security. It is also possible to agree the terms that all future business of this nature is conducted by agreeing an 'Asset Masterplan' with the lender. In this way:

- The borrowing limit is set at the outset.
- Assets can be acquired for a minimum cash outlay.

- Goods can be selected from your chosen supplier.
- A comprehensive monthly statement is provided for each individual agreement.

FUNDING BUSINESS GROWTH

The most suitable finance product to help fund a company's growth is based on its expansion plan. For example, a company planning to expand through franchising may need a bank Franchise Support service. Companies operating in the field of new technology will have special needs, while professionals wishing to buy into a partnership may require a Partnership Capital Loan.

In each of these scenarios bank customers will require the attention and advice of a specialist service that leading banks are organised to provide. At a later stage, well-managed companies with ambitious long-term plans may require to raise equity capital to support their organic business expansion, to fund management buyouts or to provide the cash consideration for acquisitions.

Enterprise Finance GuaranteeIntroduced early in 2009 to replace the Government backed Small Firms Loan Guarantee this could be the right solution for start up, expanding or diversifying businesses needing to increase working capital funding. It is designed for businesses with an annual turnover of up to £25 million that have a sound business proposal but are unable to obtain a bank loan due to lack of adequate security. Most sectors of the UK economy involving manufacturing, miscellaneous services and wholesaling of tradeable goods are eligible for EFG support. Key features and benefits are as follows:

- a government guarantee which secures bank loans, covering 75% of each qualifying loan;
- available to limited companies for sums of £10,000 to £1 million;
- available to sole traders and partnerships (not LLPs) for sums of £20,001 to £1 million;
- individually negotiated interest rates and fees;
- choice of fixed or variable rates;
- a quarterly premium is payable to the Department for Business Innovation and Skills (BIS);
- the repayment period is from 3 months to 10 years;
- each customer can take out an unlimited number of loans to a maximum

aggregate of £1,000,000;
- the Government announced that new lending under this scheme is available until March 2011.

Structured finance

Major commercial banks provide a range of complementary financial products giving structured solutions for complex financial needs. Funds are generally available from £1 million to £100 million to established companies with a proven record of cash generation. The structured finance may serve a variety of purposes from management buyout to acquisition of a business or company or for a specific working capital requirement.

The three main types of finance product available are term loan facilities, revolving credit facilities and overdraft facilities. Term loan and revolving credit facilities both provide funding for a specific purpose, which is then repaid from the future cash flow of the corporate borrower. In previous sections of this chapter, overdraft facilities and a range of commonly used asset-based solutions have already been described.

Venture capital and equity funding

The anatomy of venture capital and private equity finance in relation to specific niche market opportunities is discussed at length in Chapter 5.6. For established companies with an eye on stock market flotation and both institutional and private funds, a stock exchange main market listing may be available while a more detailed account of the requirements for listing on the stock exchange's Alternative Investment Market (AIM), which offers a cost-effective alternative for smaller companies with proven management to raise capital is given in Chapter 5.3.

INTEREST RATE RISK MANAGEMENT

Interest rate volatility can affect your bottom line profit if you borrow on a variable rate and interest rates rise increasing your cost of funds. If on the other hand you hold cash investments and interest rates fall, your return on these funds will be reduced.

There are a range of approaches to interest rate management, which could include fixing your rate with a fixed rate loan as described in this chapter or using interest rate swap. More flexible approaches can protect you against adverse movements in rates but allow you to benefit when rates move favourably. If your borrowings (including borrowings with other financial organizations) are in excess of £250,000 HSBC could protect you against increased interest costs if UK interest rates rise. By understanding your risks and the options available to you most major banks will assist you to develop and implement an interest rate strategy.

Insurance

Banks usually offer a range of insurance products which may be linked to your borrowing requirements. They typically offer a range of life insurance products which can be used to protect the key individuals within the business. They can also insure your business assets, such as property, vehicles or equipment.

Exchange protection

- Bank experts can help you to manage your exposure to exchange rate fluctuations for a large range of currencies. London is one of the world's most important locations for currency trading.
- Exchange rate volatility can affect your bottom line profit in different ways. If you have committed to either selling or buying goods or services in a foreign currency and the exchange rate fluctuates, your overall profit from a particular deal can fall, or in low margin deals be wiped out.
- The transfer of funds between the UK company and an overseas parent company will also be affected by exchange rate fluctations.

5.3 THE AIM MARKET OF THE LONDON STOCK EXCHANGE

Christina Howard and Gareth Burge
Watson, Farley & Williams LLP

INTRODUCTION

The global financial crisis has had a significant and well-publicised effect on the world's equity markets. The AIM Market (AIM) is no exception and the past few years have been some of the toughest on record for London's junior market. However, there are now signs of improvement with companies and investors returning to AIM in 2010.

AIM

The London Stock Exchange (LSE) launched AIM in 1995, as an alternative market for smaller growing companies, targeting businesses that either did not yet qualify for listing on London's main market or were otherwise not ready for this step. The LSE wished to provide a route to capital markets for companies that were at a relatively early stage in their development and smaller in size and resources than companies on the LSE's main market. Consequently, they required a more balanced and less burdensome regulatory environment in which to operate than was available on other markets. AIM was therefore structured with a measured level of regulation and with limited entry criteria.

The intention was to create an infrastructure that would enable companies to focus on growing their businesses rather than having to devote an inappropriate amount of management time and resources to regulatory compliance. This had to be balanced with the need to ensure the continued integrity of the market and the maintenance and enhancement of its reputation as a safe and effective place to do business. The result has been a highly successful capital raising market that now enjoys a global reputation.

THE GROWTH OF AIM

From its modest beginnings, AIM grew steadily and, by the beginning of 2003, more than 1,000 companies had joined the market. During 2003, a further 162 companies were admitted. AIM then began to grow more rapidly with the number of admissions in 2004 jumping to 355 and, in 2005, a further 519 companies joined the market, taking the number of admissions to more than 2,000—double the number from the previous three years. In 2006, a further 462 companies joined and by mid 2007, more than 2,500 companies had been admitted to AIM since its initial launch 12 years earlier. During the economic downturn, the number of AIM admissions fell dramatically with 114 companies joining the market in 2008 and just 36 companies joining in 2009. However, AIM has seen increased activity in 2010 with 25 new admissions so far (as of 30 April 2010) and a number of further admissions expected. As of 30 May 2010, 1243 companies were listed on AIM, with a combined market capitalisation of approximately £64.5 billion.

AIM has matured significantly in recent years. Companies from all sectors are now represented on the market and the number of international (ie. non-UK) companies admitted to AIM has grown strongly. The increasing maturity of the market has also been demonstrated by the amount of funds raised by AIM companies. In 2004, the total amount raised by AIM companies by way of initial public offerings (IPO) or secondary fundraisings reached £4.6 billion—more than double the previous year's figure. In 2005, this figure was £8.9 billion and in 2006 a total of £15.7 billion was raised. This was even more remarkable in view of the slightly moderated admission and IPO numbers in 2006 compared to 2005—almost twice as much money was raised by a smaller number of companies. In 2006, AIM raised more money than NASDAQ for the first time. Fundraising in 2007 rose slightly again to £16.2 billion before reducing in 2008 (£4.3 billion) and in 2009

(£5.5 billion) as the effects of the global financial crisis became clear.

2008 and 2009 have been some of the toughest years on record for AIM as the domino effect of the global financial crisis took hold. As of 30 April 2010, there were 386 less companies listed on AIM than on 30 April 2007.

Figure 5.3.1 shows the growth in admission numbers and in the amount raised by AIM companies since the launch of the market in 1995, and the effect that the global financial crisis has had on AIM. However, Figure 5.3.1 does not show the increased activity on AIM in 2010 which is expected to lead to further growth.

Figure 5.3.1 Admission amounts and amounts raised annually

Figure 5.3.1 Admission numbers and amounts raised annually

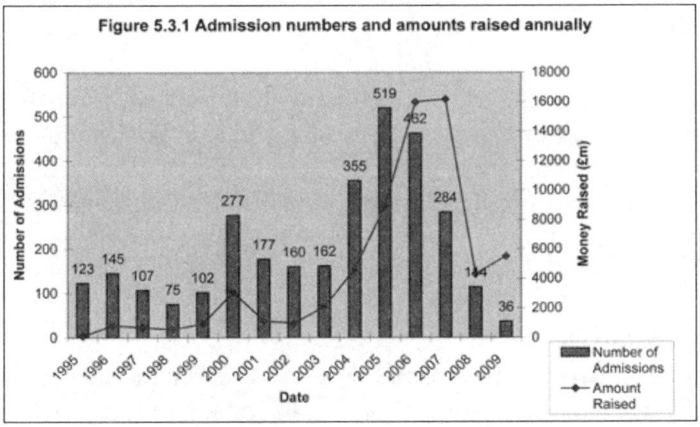

INTERNATIONAL COMPANIES

A significant development for AIM in recent years has been the growth in international admissions. As of 30 April 2010, there were 239 non-UK companies on AIM from some 30 or so jurisdictions, representing approximately 20 per cent of the market. However, this does not take account of businesses that have incorporated a UK holding company into their group structure—a strategy adopted by many companies in view of certain benefits in doing so. Taking these companies into account, the proportion of international businesses on AIM is considered to be much higher. Much of this growth in international business has been driven by companies from Australia, Canada, China and, significantly, the US.

As a result of the regulatory environment in the US, and the difficulties faced by small or mid-cap companies in the US to raise equity funds on its domestic exchanges, an increasing number of US businesses have elected to pursue an AIM strategy. As of 30 April 2010, there were 71 US companies listed on AIM—a substantial increase from around five years previously when just a handful of US companies were listed on AIM. The US Sarbanes-Oxley Act, 2002, has acted as a catalyst for this development, but it is rarely the principal or only reason for a business to choose AIM in preference to US markets; AIM is a market more suited to a smaller growing business than other exchanges, including those in North America.

AIM is attuned to the needs of these companies. Besides its appropriate level of regulation and relative ease of entry, AIM has a highly developed infrastructure of advisory firms focused on the market, specialising in this area. These include nominated advisers ("nomads") that:

- provide the corporate advisory function needed for such companies;
- assess the suitability of companies wishing to join AIM under delegated authority from the LSE; and
- in many cases, also provide broking and fundraising services for their corporate clients.

MARKET CAPITALISATION

AIM is home to companies with a broad range of market capitalisations. Many AIM companies have a market capitalisation of £5 million or less; however, most AIM companies have market capitalisations of between £5 million and £50 million. As of 30 April 2010, 54 AIM companies had a market capitalisation of more than £250 million, with 13 of these having a market capitalisation of more than £500 million. The distribution of market capitalisation across the value range is illustrated in Figure 5.3.2.

Figure 5.3.2 Distribution of companies by equity market value

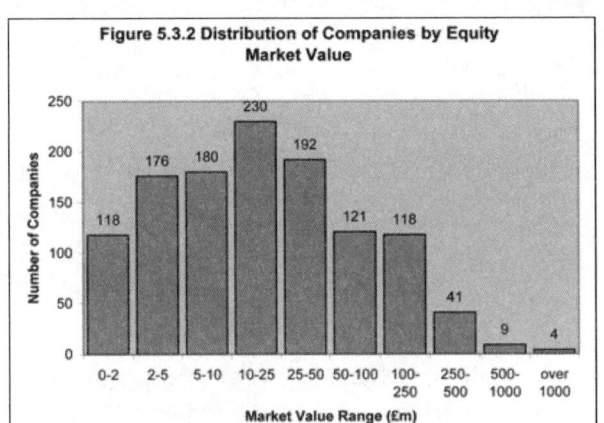

The average market capitalisation of an AIM listed company fell during 2008 to £24.3 million but rose significantly during 2009 to £43.7 million. By 30 April 2010 the average market capitalisation of an AIM listed company reached around £51.5 million, only slightly lower than the averages in 2006 and 2007 of £55.5 million and £57.6 million respectively.

REASONS TO SEEK A PUBLIC LISTING

There are a number of reasons for a company to seek a public listing. These include the following:

● accessing capital for growth;
● creating a market for its shares;
● obtaining an objective market valuation of its business;
● raising its profile;
● creating the ability to fund acquisitions with share capital; and
● providing incentives to employees through share ownership.

AIM provides all of the above benefits to a public company. In addition, AIM may be contrasted with other exchanges by virtue of the following:

● absence of onerous admission criteria;

- more straightforward admission process;
- simple secondary fundraising procedure;
- easier acquisition rules; and
- a more balanced regulatory environment.

AIM admission criteria

AIM imposes few eligibility criteria on companies wishing to join the market. In particular:

- there is no minimum requirement for a particular percentage of shares to be held in public hands;
- no trading record is required;
- admission documents do not require pre-vetting by a regulatory authority; and
- There is no minimum market capitalisation requirement.

Most other established exchanges require a particular length of audited trading history, a minimum market capitalisation and a certain percentage of shares to be held in public hands. In most cases, a prospectus or registration statement must be submitted to, and approved by, a regulatory authority in advance of listing, which can be onerous in terms of both timing and costs.

Although there are relatively few regulatory criteria for a company to qualify for admission to AIM, one of the essential foundations of AIM is the position occupied by the nomads, which act as the gatekeepers of the market.

ADVISERS
Nomads

Nomads are corporate finance advisers approved by the LSE. Their functions are to assist with the admission process and thereafter to advise on, and ensure compliance with, the ongoing requirements of AIM. The nomad's principal role in the admission process is to confirm that the company and its securities are suitable for admission.

Following admission, the nomad is responsible for advising the directors of the company as to their ongoing obligations, and for reviewing the company's actual trading performance and financial condition against any profit forecast, estimate or projection included in admission documents or published elsewhere.

In view of their responsibilities to the LSE, nomads are required to carry out extensive due diligence on their clients in advance of admission. In February 2007, the LSE introduced a new rule book for nomads, The AIM Rules for Nominated Advisers, which codified the role and responsibilities of nomads based on existing best market practice. While most nomad firms conduct their businesses in accordance with best market practice in any event, the LSE was keen to ensure that all firms adopted the same standards in their review of prospective AIM companies.

The system of delegated authority from the LSE to the nomads forms one of the bedrocks of the balanced regulatory environment upon which AIM is based. It is a system that has been accepted by investors and has worked extremely well. Investor confidence in the system is reflected in the amount of funds invested in AIM securities, and the moderate additional rules that AIM has introduced are likely to enhance investor confidence further.

Brokers

Every AIM company is also required to appoint and retain a broker at all times. Brokers are approved by the LSE. The function of these firms is to provide market support for trading in the company's securities and to undertake fundraising activities for the company. The broker will also generally provide research and institutional sales support for the company, and provide information about the company to the market.

In many cases, the nomad and broker functions are combined within the same firm, although in separate divisions. There is no requirement for a single firm to adopt both roles, and some companies prefer for their nomad to be independent of their broker.

Other advisers

In addition to a nomad and a broker, a company wishing to be admitted to AIM will need to engage legal counsel, reporting accountants and, in most cases, a public relations firm.

The role of legal counsel will be to advise the company on the legal and regulatory requirements for admission to AIM and on applicable securities laws, and play a principal role in the preparation and finalisation of the admission documents, working closely with the nomad in this regard. The legal counsel will also advise on:

● any required corporate reorganisation;

- any required amendments to the company's constitutional documents;
- the terms of directors' service contracts; and
- the duties and responsibilities of the directors under applicable UK law.

They will also undertake a legal due diligence review covering matters such as the company's contractual arrangements, employment agreements, and legal and regulatory compliance and litigation, as well as any other matters required by the nomad in order to satisfy itself that the company is suitable for admission to AIM.

The nomad and broker will also engage their own legal counsel to provide independent advice on legal matters in relation to the negotiation of the placing (or underwriting) agreement.

The reporting accountants, who are distinct from the company's own auditors, will:

- undertake a review of the company's financial position and financial reporting procedures
- generally produce a report containing the results of its financial due diligence review; and
- prepare with the directors a working capital report to demonstrate that the company will have sufficient working capital for at least 12 months following admission.

The role of the financial public relations firm will be to generate press and investor interest in the initial and any subsequent fundraisings, and to raise the profile of the company generally. The public relations firm will also work with the nomad, the company and its other advisers in agreeing the content of public statements.

ADMISSION PROCESS

Under the standard admission procedure, a company wishing to be admitted to AIM will be required to produce a formal admission document or prospectus that will include all relevant information on the company and its business. The content of the admission document is governed by The AIM Rules for Companies and is otherwise determined by reference to the UK's securities laws. Most AIM admission transactions are accompanied by a fundraising to institutional investors. If the fundraising constitutes a public offer of securities, is made to more than 100 persons in any member state of the European Union (EU) and is not otherwise exempted, a full prospectus under the EU Prospectus Directive will be required. Such a document will require pre-vetting and approval of the UK Listing Authority (UKLA) prior to admission of the company to trading on AIM. For this reason, it is rare for a company being admitted to AIM to seek to raise funds through a public offer, and the vast majority of transactions are undertaken by way of an institutional placing exempt from the full prospectus and UKLA approval requirements.

The admission document will provide the basis upon which investors subscribe for shares. The broker will undertake a fundraising exercise, generally based on a marketing presentation and a near-final version of the admission document. An AIM transaction is broadly similar to any other listing event, the principal difference being the absence of a regulatory approval process.

AIM has also introduced a streamlined secondary listing procedure, which is available to companies already listed on certain designated international stock markets. In such cases, companies can benefit from a streamlined regime under which the requirement to produce an admission document is replaced by an obligation to issue an expanded pre-admission announcement. The exchanges falling within the scope of the streamlined secondary listing procedure include the following:

● the Australian Stock Exchange;
● Euronext (a European stock exchange based in Paris, France);
● NASDAQ;
● the New York Stock Exchange;
● the UKLA's Official List; and
● the Toronto Stock Exchange.

Cost and timing

Although every AIM admission transaction is different, and while issues of both timing and cost will depend upon a number of factors, in most cases the admission process can be expected to take three to four months to complete. Some transactions are implemented in a shorter timescale, while others take longer, but this is a fairly reliable guide.

Similar variables apply in relation to the cost of an AIM admission. The largest single element of cost for an AIM admission with a fundraising is the commission payable to the broker or investment bank. This will generally be between 4 per cent and 6 per cent of funds raised. Other costs include the cost of legal counsel and of the reporting accountants and auditors. As a guide, companies would commonly expect the total cost of an IPO on AIM to be approximately 7–10 per cent of funds raised. This does, of course, depend upon the size of the fundraising.

POST-ADMISSION REQUIREMENTS

Once admitted to AIM, companies must comply with the AIM rules, as well as with applicable securities and other law. The AIM rules are written in plain English and are less prescriptively detailed than the rules on other major markets. AIM companies must provide certain information to the market on a regular basis and specifically upon the occurrence of certain events. To ensure that the market is kept fully informed, AIM companies are obliged to make similar ongoing disclosures to those required by companies on the other major exchanges, to ensure that the market is aware of the financial position of the company and its prospects.

Each AIM company is also required to publish accounts prepared in accordance with International Accounting Standards (IAS) for financial periods commencing on or after 1 January 2007 (prior to which the relevant standards were IAS, the UK Generally Accepted Accounting Practice (GAAP) or the US GAAP), as well as six-monthly interim results. Each AIM company is also required to notify the market of any changes in shareholdings of directors and to provide information to the market concerning substantial or related party transactions.

It should be noted that shareholder approval is generally not required for substantial transactions, which contrasts AIM with other markets. The only exception to this is in the case of a reverse takeover or a disposal resulting in a fundamental change of business, which requires the approval of shareholders in advance of the transaction.

Corporate governance

The UK has high standards of corporate governance applicable to public companies. The Combined Code on Corporate Governance is mandatory for companies listed on the Official List (which for reference periods commencing on or after 29 June 2010 is to be replaced by the UK Corporate Governance Code which will apply to companies with a premium listing on the Official List of equity shares regardless of whether they are incorporated in the UK or elsewhere). Although the Combined Code does not apply to companies trading on AIM, most AIM companies seek to adhere to the provisions of the Code so far as is practicable, including ensuring that the roles of chairman and chief executive are exercised by separate individuals and that there is a balance between executive and non-executive directors on a board. In 2007, the Quoted Companies Alliance (QCA) issued the Corporate Governance Guidelines for AIM Companies (a new edition is expected to be published in 2010), and although this guidance has no formal regulatory status, it does reflect a consensus position of the AIM advisory and investing community, as well as the key provisions of the Combined Code. The National Association of Pension Funds has also published corporate governance and voting guidelines for AIM companies and these are generally consistent with the guidelines published by the QCA.

Tax benefits

For UK taxpayers, an investment in shares traded on AIM can provide certain tax benefits by way of tax reliefs that may be available to them. These will include:

- certain reliefs on gains realised on the disposal of shares held by individual investors or trustees; and
- the holding over of certain gains made on disposal.

Such tax benefits and reliefs are designed to encourage investment in AIM stocks, which have generally been companies in the early stages of their development.

CONCLUSION

The global financial crisis has affected all international stock markets. As governments continue their work to rejuvenate markets across the world, AIM, with its balanced level of regulation and history of past success, is in good shape to recover its position as a leading international IPO market.

5.4 ROLES OF THE NOMAD AND THE BROKER ON AIM

Tony Rawlinson and Simon Sacerdoti
Cairn Financial Advisers LLP

INTRODUCTION

A company seeking admission to AIM is required by the AIM Rules to have a Nominated Adviser (referred to as a Nomad) and a broker. These advisers are so important to the life of a company on AIM that following Admission to AIM all AIM companies are also required to retain a Nomad and a broker at all times. Indeed, if a company finds itself without a Nomad, its shares will be suspended from trading on AIM, and if it is still without a Nomad after a month, its listing will be cancelled.

A Nomad is a corporate finance adviser which has been approved by the London Stock Exchange to act in the role of nominated adviser. It is responsible to the London Stock Exchange for ensuring that companies for which it acts adhere to the various rules and regulations applicable to AIM companies. The Nomad is privy to confidential, and often price sensitive, information on the company. Although its primary duty of care is to the London Stock Exchange, the Nomad's client is the company.

The function of the company's broker is to raise funds and manage the market in the company's shares. The broker may also make a market in the company's shares and produce research on the company, although these functions are not required by AIM. Brokers are dual facing with their corporate broking teams acting for AIM and other corporate clients and their private client or institutional sales teams acting for institutions or private individuals who invest in companies' shares and who are therefore not privy to confidential corporate information.

We examine the roles and responsibilities of both advisers in more detail below.

NOMAD

When the London Stock Exchange created AIM in 1995, it recognised the need to establish a flexible but effective way to regulate the market without overburdening the sort of younger, more entrepreneurial companies it wished to attract. The Exchange decided to do this by creating a new type of corporate finance adviser, the Nomad, which would have a responsibility to the Exchange for determining the suitability of a new applicant to AIM, and also an ongoing responsibility for monitoring the company and ensuring its compliance with the relevant regulations. Effectively the Exchange outsourced the regulation of AIM to the Nomads.

The London Stock Exchange itself acknowledges on its website that the reputation and success of AIM since its launch is largely due to the dedication and professionalism of the network of Nomads. The introduction of the AIM Rules for Nominated Advisers in February 2007 codified the role and responsibilities of a Nomad, as well as the process and criteria that must be satisfied by a firm in order to become and remain registered as a Nomad, which include demonstrating a certain level of recent relevant experience, and employing a minimum number of qualified executives each of whom must have the requisite level of relevant experience.

As well as acting as a regulator, Nomads offer companies the sort of advice that one would expect from a corporate finance adviser, and from a company's point of view, the role of the Nomad is to guide the company through the process of admission to trading on AIM, and through its life thereafter as a publicly-quoted company.

At the time of writing, there are approximately 63 firms registered as Nomads.

Obligations

The AIM Rules for Nominated Advisers set out the obligations of a Nomad in respect of companies for which it is the nominated adviser. The key responsibilities of a Nomad to the Exchange in respect of a company for which it acts are as follows:

General obligations

- To assess the appropriateness of a company on its application to AIM, and also when it takes on a company as its client. If a Nomad believes a company to which it is nominated adviser is no longer appropriate for AIM, it has a responsibility to contact the Exchange and discuss this;
- To comply with the AIM Rules for Companies, the AIM Rules for Nominated Advisers, and with any supplementary rules, procedures, notices, guidance, requirement, decision or direction issued by the Exchange; and
- To act at all times with due skill and care.

Nominated adviser responsibilities

- To advise and guide a company on its responsibilities and obligations both in respect of admission and on an ongoing basis. It must be available to give this advice and guidance to the companies for which it acts at all times and should allocate at least two appropriately qualified staff to be responsible for each such company.

Information obligations

- To provide the Exchange with any information that it reasonably requires, having first satisfied itself that the information provided is correct, complete and not misleading;
- To liaise with the Exchange when requested to do so either by the Exchange or by a company for which it acts;
- To seek the advice of the Exchange on any uncertainty on the application or interpretation of the AIM Rules, or on any concerns over the reputation or integrity of AIM;
- To advise the Exchange as soon as practicable if it believes that it or an AIM company has breached the AIM Rules; and
- To notify the Exchange in the approved manner on being appointed as Nomad to a company, or ceasing to act as Nomad to a company.

Independence and conflicts

- To demonstrate independence (both of the firm and its individual executives) from the companies for which it acts; and
- To avoid any actual or apparent conflict of interest.

Procedures, staff and records

- To follow the prescribed procedures, employ appropriately qualified staff and maintain sufficient records.

It is interesting to note that the stated responsibilities of a Nomad under the AIM Rules are all of a regulatory nature, and are owed to the Exchange rather than the company for which it acts. It may of course, subject to these responsibilities and obligations, also provide advice to these companies. It is the dual role of regulator and adviser that makes the relationship between a company and its Nomad such a unique one.

Responsibilities

A Schedule to the AIM Rules for Nominated Advisers contains a set of principles, with subsidiary actions, that a Nomad must follow in order to comply with its obligations. This codifies what had become best practice into required practice.
   The principles are as follows:

- In assessing the appropriateness of an applicant and its securities for AIM, a nominated adviser should achieve a sound understanding of the applicant and its business;
- In assessing the appropriateness of an applicant and its securities for AIM, a nominated adviser should (i) investigate and consider the suitability of each director and proposed director of the applicant; and (ii) consider the efficacy of the board as a whole for the company's needs, in each case having in mind that the company will be admitted to trading on a UK public market;
- The nominated adviser should oversee the due diligence process, satisfying itself that it is appropriate to the applicant and transaction and that any material issues arising from it are dealt with or otherwise do not affect the appropriateness of the applicant for AIM;

- The nominated adviser should oversee and be actively involved in the preparation of the admission document, satisfying itself (in order to be able to give the nominated adviser's declaration) that it has been prepared in compliance with the AIM Rules for Companies with due verification having been undertaken;
- The nominated adviser should satisfy itself that the applicant has in place sufficient systems, procedures and controls in order to comply with the AIM Rules for Companies and should satisfy itself that the applicant understands its obligations under the AIM Rules for Companies;
- The nominated adviser should maintain regular contact with an AIM company for which it acts, in particular so that it can assess whether (i) the nominated adviser is being kept up-to-date with developments at the AIM company and (ii) the AIM company continues to understand its obligations under the AIM Rules for Companies;
- The nominated adviser should undertake a prior review of relevant notifications made by an AIM company with a view to ensuring compliance with the AIM Rules for Companies;
- The nominated adviser should monitor (or have in place procedures with third parties for monitoring) the trading activity in securities of an AIM company for which it acts, especially when there is unpublished price sensitive information in relation to the AIM company; and
- The nominated adviser should advise the AIM company on any changes to the board of directors the AIM company proposes to make, including (i) investigating and considering the suitability of proposed new directors and (ii) considering the effect any changes have in the efficacy of the board as a whole for the company's needs, in each case having in mind that the company is admitted to trading on a UK public market.

The relationship in practice

In practice an AIM company's relationship with its Nomad is one of the most important adviser relationships it will have. The Nomad is available to advise the company, but can also be held accountable by the Exchange if the company does not comply with the AIM Rules, for example if it does not announce an announceable event or is late in posting its accounts.

Accordingly, there must be regular communication between the company and the Nomad on all matters, including the trading performance of the business, its budgets and plans and any milestones that are reached or expected to be reached, any issues relating to directors and shareholders. The Nomad will need to be provided with full information on the progress of the business. This will typically include receiving copies of budgets, board pack and regular management accounts; discussing any significant events in the business (both positive and negative); understanding any changes to shareholdings; and attendance at certain key board meetings.

BROKER

A broker is a securities house and must be a member of the London Stock Exchange. Its sole role under the AIM Rules is to use its best endeavours to find matching business if there is no registered market maker in a company's shares. However, in practice, the broker is a key adviser in the process of raising money in association with an admission to AIM or a secondary fund-raising, and in maintaining a sustainable market in a company's shares. The broker is normally responsible for running the fund-raising process, including advising on marketing materials, effecting introductions to potential investors, and coordinating the logistics of collecting funds and issuing shares.

Usually a company's broker also acts as a point of contact between the investment community and the company and, when requested, co-ordinates transactions in the company's shares with a view to maintaining an orderly market in those shares. It may also advise the Company on investment conditions and the pricing of its securities; and may produce research on the company for dissemination to the market.

Structure

Typically, a broker is divided into the company-facing corporate finance and corporate broking part of the firm and the market-facing part of the firm.

The corporate finance team advises client companies and is privy to confidential, often price sensitive, information on the company. It is focused on servicing the needs of the company, and its key function is to manage the broker's input into a flotation or other transaction.

The market-facing part of the firm includes sales people, who are engaged in selling the company's shares to institutional and other investor clients of the broking firm, and analysts, who are responsible for producing independent research on clients and other companies. This part of the firm is only entitled to receive information that is in the public domain, and once it receives information, it is deemed to be in the public domain.

Because these two parts of the broker have different objectives and are responsible to different clients (the company as opposed to the market), there are strict rules governing the interactions between them. These centre around protecting the confidentiality of information by the use of procedures that create and maintain a 'Chinese Wall'.

INTEGRATED HOUSE OR SEPARATE ADVISERS

Many city firms offer both Nomad and broker services, and it is quite common for a company to appoint such an integrated house to both roles. When this occurs, strict Chinese Walls separate the Nomad and broker functions, as in most cases information to which the Nomad is privy (in its role as quasi-regulator and corporate finance adviser to the company) must not be disclosed to the market-facing part of the broker.

Some companies prefer to keep the roles separate, choosing to appoint two distinct firms to fill these roles in order to safeguard the confidentiality of price-sensitive information and to ensure the independence of advice they are given.

FURTHER INFORMATION

Further information on the roles and responsibilities of Nomads and brokers may be found on the London Stock Exchange website: www.londonstockexchange.com, in particular in the AIM Rules for Companies and the AIM Rules for Nominated Advisers. Alternatively, please contact Tony Rawlinson or Simon Sacerdoti at Cairn Financial Advisers via their website: www.cairnfin.com

5.5 MERGERS AND ACQUISITIONS AND JOINT VENTURES

Tanvir Dhanoa
Watson, Farley & Williams LLP

INTRODUCTION

The phrase "mergers and acquisitions" (M&A) refers to the aspect of corporate strategy, finance and management dealing with the purchase, sale and merging of different companies and businesses. Unlike certain jurisdictions (notably the US), in the UK there is technically no concept of a true merger, in the sense of two or more separate entities combining to form one continuing entity (although the term M&A is used in the UK). The term "acquisition", also known as a takeover, is used to describe a wide variety of transactions involving the sale and purchase of either a business or a company. Through the acquisition of a UK target, an inward investor is able to gain immediate local presence, expertise and name recognition. The same principal issues are common to most acquisitions, whatever the size or nature of the parties or the entity being acquired.

The basic forms of business combination are:

- the purchase of shares of a target company;
- the purchase of the target's underlying business; and
- joint venture arrangements.

This chapter is divided into four sections: the first considers the private acquisition of companies and businesses; the second deals with the acquisition of public companies; the third covers joint ventures; and the final section provides an overview of merger control.

Private company and business acquisitions

There are generally two methods of acquiring a business: one is to buy the shares of the company that owns the business; the other is to buy the assets that make up the business. In either case, the buyer will achieve its commercial objective of acquiring the business that is being run by the target company, although the legal effects of the two types of acquisition are fundamentally different.

If shares in a company are purchased, all its assets, liabilities and obligations are acquired (even those that the buyer does not know about). The contract is made between the buyer and the owner of the shares (the seller). There is no change in the ownership of the business; it remains in the ownership of the company. Alternatively, the business may be purchased in its entirety as a going concern, together with all its assets and liabilities or, if appropriate, only those identified assets and liabilities that the buyer agrees to acquire.

A share sale is generally the quickest way to effect an acquisition because legally this only requires a share transfer. On a business sale, by contrast, transfer arrangements will need to be put in place for each asset being purchased. Tax issues will also play a central role in determining the best route to be followed.

Exclusivity

As an acquisition will involve a prospective buyer investing a substantial amount of time, effort and money, the buyer will often require the seller to agree not to negotiate with other parties for a given period while it conducts its due diligence exercise (investigation of the target business). An exclusivity (or "lockout") period for the buyer will often be agreed in a separate exclusivity agreement.

Confidentiality agreement

As most acquisitions will involve the buyer having access to significant information about the target business (and, to a certain extent, the seller and its group), some of which will be confidential, it is standard practice for a seller to ask any prospective buyer to enter into a confidentiality agreement requiring the buyer and its professional advisers to treat all disclosed information as confidential, and to agree that the disclosed information may only be used for the purposes of the acquisition or otherwise with the seller's consent.

Due diligence

For acquisitions subject to English law, the principle of *caveat emptor*, or buyer beware, will apply, which effectively means that there is only limited statutory and common law protection for a buyer under the law. It is, therefore, essential for a buyer to learn as much as possible about the target business and the issues that will be relevant to the acquisition as early as possible in the acquisition procedure through the process of due diligence.

Due diligence is intended to identify risks so that they can be allocated between the buyer and the seller. The review usually comprises legal, financial, tax and commercial due diligence, and will help to determine the contractual protections required from the seller, as well as the risks the buyer should avoid completely. The information-gathering process will aim to identify information that may impact upon the negotiation process and, in particular, on the price the buyer is prepared to pay. The buyer will seek to obtain contractual protection from the seller in relation to issues of concern to it and other risks in the form of warranties and indemnities in the acquisition agreement.

Warranties

In simple terms, warranties are contractual promises made by the seller to the buyer regarding the state of affairs of the target company/business.

Warranties serve two main purposes: one is to elicit information about the business from the seller by way of disclosure or qualification of the warranties—a process linked to the due diligence investigation discussed above; the second is to provide the buyer with a remedy (a claim for breach of warranty) if the statements made about the company/business later prove to be incorrect and the acquisition turns out to be other than as bargained for.

Indemnities

The buyer may seek further contractual protection in the form of indemnities included in the acquisition agreement (or sometimes in a separate deed). An indemnity is essentially a promise to reimburse the buyer in respect of a designated type of liability, should it arise in the future. The purpose of an indemnity is to provide a guaranteed remedy for the buyer, where a breach of warranty may not give rise to a claim in damages, or to provide a specific remedy that might not otherwise be available at law.

Stamp duty

Stamp duty is the tax payable when property or shares are transferred. Stamp duty land tax is payable when real property or land is bought, and either stamp duty or stamp duty reserve tax is payable when shares are transferred.

On an acquisition of shares, the buyer pays stamp duty at the rate of 0.5 per cent of the purchase price. On an acquisition of a business, the buyer pays stamp duty only on those assets that are taxable (essentially land and shares). On the purchase of commercial land, no stamp duty is payable if the value of the property does not exceed £150,000. Stamp duty on the purchase of real estate above this value is payable at varying rates up to 4 per cent.

Schemes of arrangement

A scheme of arrangement is a statutory procedure for business combinations effected under Section 895 of the Companies Act 2006, whereby a company may make a compromise or arrangement with its members or creditors. A company can effect virtually any kind of internal reorganisation, merger or de-merger restructuring under this section as long as the necessary approvals have been obtained, including the relevant shareholder approval and court approval.

Schemes of arrangement are becoming increasingly popular, and an inward investor should consider whether a conventional takeover offer or a scheme of arrangement would be the most appropriate method to acquire a target.

Public company acquisitions
The takeover market

The UK has a long history of takeover activity. Takeover activity has increased significantly since the Takeover Panel commenced work in 1968, and approximately three-quarters of all public takeover offers in the European Union (EU) occur in the UK. There are several reasons for this growth, including the fact that corporate balance sheets appear to be healthier than ever before and corporate earning expectations remain positive. In addition, the rising popularity of the AIM Market has continued and has generated significant takeover activity as companies on the market mature and consolidation of businesses becomes an attractive opportunity.

Regulation of takeovers

Transactions involving the acquisition of control of a public company (takeovers), and those involving the sale and purchase of public companies whose shares are listed on the London Stock Exchange, are subject to considerable additional regulation:

- The City Code on Takeovers and Mergers (the Takeover Code) is a set of rules developed by the Panel on Takeovers and Mergers (the Takeover Panel) and regulates takeovers in the UK. The Takeover Code applies to offers for public companies resident in the UK, the Channel Islands and the Isle of Man, irrespective of where their shares are listed or publicly marketed.
- The Listing, Prospectus and Disclosure Rules are made by the Financial Services Authority and regulate the process by which a company listed on the London Stock Exchange can make acquisitions or disposals.
- The Criminal Justice Act 1993, together with the Listing Rules, Disclosure Rules and Takeover Code, regulates insider dealings.
- The Companies Act 2006 contains the main legislation governing the formation and administration of companies.
- The Financial Services and Markets Act 2000 regulates the conduct of investment business and makes provision for the official listing of securities, public offers of securities and investment advertisement.
- Merger control provisions regulate the takeover of a UK company, which may require approval from the competition authorities of the EU or the UK.

Outline of a takeover

Takeovers are public transactions, and the Takeover Code prescribes a strict timetable to be adhered to. Unlike a private acquisition, it is not possible to simply announce the completion of a takeover. Under the Takeover Code, a takeover must be carried out publicly, and any takeover offer has to be held open for a fixed period of time. This in turn means that a potential rival bidder may make a competing offer to the target's shareholders.

In a "recommended bid", target shareholders are recommended to accept the offer by the target's directors. A "hostile bid", however, is an offer not supported by the target.

Joint ventures

A joint venture describes a commercial arrangement between two or more economically independent entities for the purpose of pursuing an agreed commercial goal, in which the joint venturers share in agreed proportions the financing and control of the enterprise, as well as the profits and losses it makes.

Joint ventures may be structured through limited partnerships, limited liability partnerships or unincorporated associations. However, the most common joint venture vehicle is a limited company.

International joint ventures

Joint ventures are vital to the development of international business, and an alliance with a local partner can provide an inward investor with:

● an important means of business expansion;
● access to new markets;
● distribution networks;
● greater resources; and
● the sharing of risks with a partner.

International joint ventures (where an overseas party combines with a local party to undertake joint business in that local jurisdiction) will require consideration of a number of issues, including choosing the type of legal structure most appropriate to the joint venture vehicle, tax considerations, restrictions on foreign participation, licensing issues and the requirement for governmental consents.

Contributions and funding

Initial finance may be injected into a joint venture company in a number of ways. One of these would be a straightforward subscription by the partners for shares in the joint venture company in consideration for a contribution of cash or non-cash assets. Alternatively, capital may be injected by way of loan, either from the joint venture partners or from third-party lenders. The parties will also need to consider in advance how future finance is to be provided to the joint venture company.

Management

It is common for the partners to retain some level of control and influence in the joint venture's decision-making process, either through representation on the board of directors or through requiring certain key decisions to be referred to shareholders. The level of each party's control will depend on their respective shareholdings. The management structure should be reflected clearly in the joint venture agreement.

The joint venture agreement

The written agreement between partners should set out the precise terms and conditions agreed between them, and provide a framework for the ongoing alliance. It should specifically cover:

- the structure of the joint venture;
- the objectives of the joint venture;
- the financial contributions that each partner is to make;
- the management and control of the joint venture (eg. the right to appoint directors and each partner's voting rights);
- how profits, losses and liabilities are to be shared;
- how any disputes between the partners will be resolved; and
- how the joint venture can be terminated.

Merger control

Merger control provisions exist under both UK and European law. Inward investors merging with, acquiring or entering into a joint venture with a UK company should be aware that the transaction may require notification to the Office of Fair Trading (OFT) to assess its effect on competition in the relevant markets. Although notification to the OFT is voluntary, the parties to mergers that meet or exceed the qualifying threshold criteria (see below) are well advised to notify their merger to eliminate the risk of investigation and possible sanctions.

A merger will be considered as "qualifying" for investigation in the UK where:

- two or more companies, at least one of which carries on business in the UK, cease to be distinct (brought under common ownership or control);
- the merging companies supply or consume goods or services that form part of the same market, and after the merger takes place, they will supply or acquire 25 per cent or more of those goods or services in the UK as a whole or in a substantial part of it; or
- the annual UK turnover of the company being taken over exceeds £70 million.

Larger mergers that have a "community dimension" will be reviewed by the European Commission under the European Community Merger Regulation (ECMR). For more details about merger control, please refer to the chapter on competition law.

5.6   VENTURE CAPITAL AND PRIVATE EQUITY

Mark Littlewood
The Business Leaders Network (BLN)

This chapter aims to provide a short overview of the private company funding landscape in the UK today, the types of funds that exist and for whom they may be appropriate, what investors expect from companies and some pointers towards maximising the likelihood of successfully closing a deal. It does not aim to be a guide to writing a business plan (most investors claim not to read them anyway). I hope it offers some useful information about the changing funding landscape in the UK and some insight into the way investors are thinking today.

TECTONIC SHIFTS
The last five years have seen significant changes in the venture capital (VC) and private equity (PE) industries in the UK and Europe. The near collapse of the global banking industry has significant implications for those firms that invest in private companies for their returns.

The turmoil in the global banking system has affected the venture and private equity industry in two ways: fund managers have become more cautious and picky about the investment vehicles that they back; and there has been a reduction in the amount of capital available, (asset allocation into venture and private equity funds is typically a percentage of the funds available). As the value of public market stocks falls, the overall value of funds available for alternative investments reduces too. Typically, fund managers allocate a small percentage (usually a maximum of 4-5 %) of their fund to 'alternative investments' – for the purposes of this discussion, venture capital and private equity investing.

The bad news is that the economic environment that we find ourselves in today is not very conducive to fundraising. VC and PE houses report that the price of deals is coming down, the quality of the teams that they spend time with is going up, the amount of debt available to support deals has evaporated and everyone, but everyone, agrees that the IPO window needs to open up soon.

The good news is that whilst the venture capital and private equity landscape has changed significantly over the past five years the UK remains one of the most attractive and benign environments for entrepreneurs. This despite significant changes around, for example, treatment of Capital Gains Tax for entrepreneurs implemented by the current UK government since May 2010 in an attempt to balance the books in the public sector. The UK still receives the lion's share of venture capital and private equity investments in Europe.

VENTURE CAPITAL DEALS IN THE UK AND EUROPE

Accurate and up to date information on venture investment is hard to come by wherever you are in the world. Private companies may wish to remain 'private' for many reasons and so there is no absolute source of information about the amount and number of venture deals. One index that we follow at the BLN is the Calibre One Index which offers a good sense of where money is being allocated by geography and by sector across Europe and the US. It does this by tracking reported deals and, where possible, amounts. It provides an excellent bellwether for the industry. Figure 5.6.1 illustrates what has taken place since the beginning of 2004.

Fig 5.6.1 Venture Investment, US vs Europe since 2004

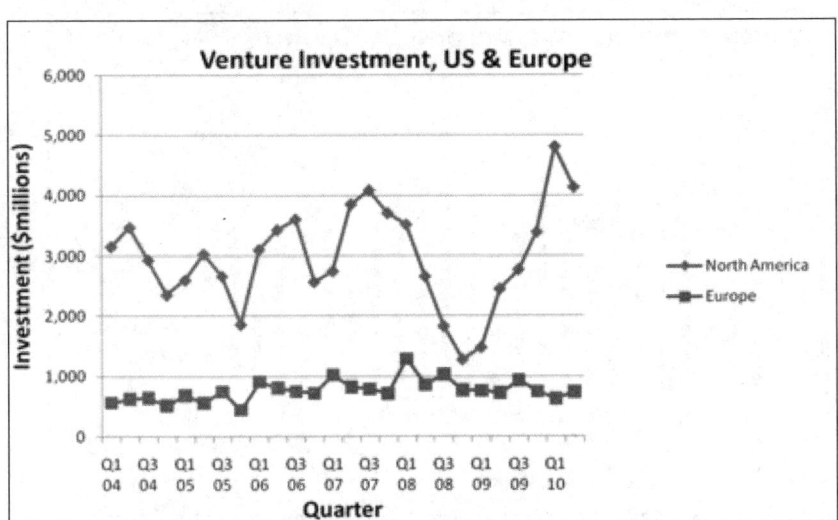

Source: The BLN from Calibre One Index

Europe overall only sees a small fraction – about a quarter – of the venture capital investment that is made in the US. While the amount of investment in Europe is lower, the US market is much more volatile and has tended historically to react strongly to changes in sentiment. This can be seen most clearly in 2008 when there was a drop off in European investment although this was nowhere near as violent a decline as that in US investment levels which almost intersected with European investment in the second half of 2008.

Figure 5.6.2 provides an analysis of venture investment in parts of Europe and Israel over the same period.

Fig 5.6.2   Venture Investment, Europe by country since 2004

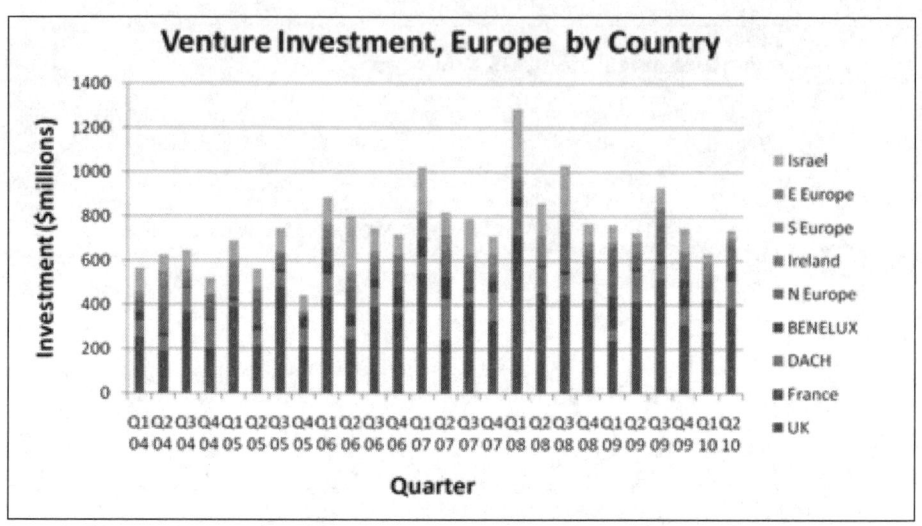

Source: The BLN from Calibre One Index

The UK has consistently been the most significant beneficiary of venture capital investment in Europe. The UK has rarely received less investment on a quarterly basis than any other country or region. The only countries to have ever received more investment in a single quarter over this period are France and Israel.

LANDSCAPE TODAY
Private companies cover a huge spectrum of types of business. A part-time trader buying and selling on eBay and an organisation like Alliance Boots are both 'private' companies.

Alliance Boots – Britain's Biggest Private Company

Shareholders: Kohlberg Kravis Roberts (KKR), Alliance Santé Participations
Nearly all Britons know the Boots name. The company's first shop opened in Nottingham in 1849, selling herbal remedies, and since then Boots stores have spread to almost every high street. The company has long been the market leader in Britain and more recently has become a big player in Europe. Its brands include No7 cosmetics and Soltan suncare.

The Boots brand may be synonymous with high-street chemists in Britain, but many consumers will be unsure of where the first word in the name Alliance Boots comes from. In 1977 Stefano Pessina founded Alliance as a pharmaceutical wholesaler in Italy and, 20 years later, merged it with Unichem, another pharmaceutical wholesaler, which had been founded in London in 1938. Alliance Unichem then merged with Boots in 2006 to form Alliance Boots, and a year later KKR, the private-equity giant, acquired the group in an £11 billion deal, including debt of £9 billion. It was the first time a FTSE 100 company had been bought by private equity.

Pessina said he wanted to turn Boots into a global brand and the task would be easier if the company was privately owned.

It was a bold move. Commentators speculated that this might have been a deal too far for private equity, and the transaction, Europe's biggest leveraged buyout, was completed just before the onset of the credit crunch and the recession. The results have been impressive, however, with revenue and profits growing each year since the deal. In 2010, revenue grew to £22.5 billion (including £3.8 billion from associates and joint ventures) and trading profit exceeded £1 billion for the first time, although it still carries debt of £8.4 billion.

The health-and-beauty businesses have 3,250 pharmacies and shops across 10 countries, while the pharmaceutical wholesale business supplies medicines and other healthcare products to more than 150,000 pharmacies and health centres in 16 countries.

Andy Hornby, formerly chief executive at HBOS, now leads the business from the group's headquarters in Switzerland. Pessina is the company's chairman.

The two men are focused on building Boots's brands into big global names in their own right, and alliances with companies such as Procter & Gamble are being forged to help with this. Waitrose recently started running test sales of Boots products in some of its supermarkets. In turn, Waitrose foods are being sold in some Boots stores.

The group has a higher turnover than all but the top 10 FTSE 100 companies, but a return to the stock market in the near future has been ruled out, with Pessina saying that the company may need five or six years to further reduce debt and continue to grow earnings before a flotation can be considered.

Source: Sunday Times Top Track 2010

Private companies of more than £1 billion revenue are very rare in the UK and are as likely to have listed on public exchanges as stayed private. Most investment into private companies is concentrated in a select group of businesses that are either early stage and offer significant growth potential (venture capital investment) or established entities that can use investment to move into new markets, acquire other organisations and consolidate their position in an established market (private equity).

This diversity of opportunity is also reflected in the vast range of investors in such companies. Investors look to make above average returns for their shareholders and to exit their investments at an appropriate time which usually rules out investing in lifestyle businesses or those with limited capacity to grow.

Sources of investment: Angel – Private Equity

The principal sources of investment capital available in the UK to private companies with an overview of the type of business for which they may be appropriate are listed in Table 5.6.1.

Table 5.6.1 Principal sources of investment capital in the UK

Investor type	Typical deal size	Advantages	Disadvantages	Suitable for
Lone Angel	£5-500k	Can make fast decisions Can bring industryexperience Ubiquitous if you can track them down	Often limited capacity to follow on Can be hard to find the right angel Angels may be able to capitalise a business fully or wish to exit before an entrepreneur in order to get a safe return	Smaller opportunities with limited capital requirements Entrepreneur who wants to have mentoring and support from experienced business person

Investor type	Typical deal size	Advantages	Disadvantages	Suitable for
Informal angel groups	£25k-£1million	Combine firepower and expertise of many angels Can make relatively quick decisions Easy to find	Can mean a company has multiple unofficial chairman Decision making process can be lengthy Professional investors can be put off from investing in companies with too many shareholders May wish to exit before business reaches potential to avoid dilution	Early stage businesses that would benefit from experience and connections from working with multiple investors Opportunities with growth potential and possibility of multiple rounds – some angel groups fund businesses through multiple rounds, some will actively encourage engagement with venture capital community
Angel fund raisers	£250k-£1million	Easy to find	A relatively recent phenomenon Usually require up-front payment from entrepreneur to be presented to potential investors Evidence of successful fund-raising activity is hard to establish success rates	It is generally accepted by the investment community that entrepreneurs should not pay up-front fees for introductions to angels unless all other avenues have been pursued

Investor type	Typical deal size	Advantages	Disadvantages	Suitable for
Early stage Regional VC Funds	£50k-£500k	Money is readily available, especially in those regions regarded as 'deprived' Multiple funds target deals in NE, NW, Wales and Scotland	Fund deployment rules mean that regional venture funds can have limited capacity to follow on May be viewed with suspicion by some top quartile investors Unclear what the future for these funds will be in new government given their investment track records	Particularly suitable for organisations that wish to locate all, or part of, their business in the regions outlined
Early Stage Venture	£250k-£2million	Can connect with sophisticated investors with deep knowledge of an industry sector Recent trend has been for successful entrepreneurs to set up small – c £20 million – funds to invest in sectors they understand	Active investors – those with funds to invest – change over time Significant dealflow usually means companies need to have exceptional potential and a clean history to secure funds	Most traditional early stage route to funds for businesses, particularly with a technology bias, with high growth potential

Investor type	Typical deal size	Advantages	Disadvantages	Suitable for
			Volume of good deal flow often means that entrepreneurs need to accept lower valuations than they wish	
Venture Capital	£1-20million	Large funds are often managed by individuals with significant entrepreneurial experience and strong industry connections themselves Securing investTment from a top tier firm can be a huge advantage in getting an organisation known Have experience and financial muscle to support growth of global businesses	VCs do not always provide the operational value they think they do VCs can end up controlling a business	Businesses with high growth prospects, high potential exit value and reasonably experienced management teams that can both drive the business and manage the requirements of the investor effectively

Investor type	Typical deal size	Advantages	Disadvantages	Suitable for
Private Equity	£5-500million+	Funds provide capital, governance and management expertise to companies and do not have to operate in the public eye PE firms perform very rigorous due diligence on potential investments and PE backed firms have shown significantly higher returns than other asset classes in the UK	PE funds have been accused of loading large amounts of debt into their investments that needs to be serviced from cash flow of the business Combination of debt and lack of liquidity can mean that companies struggle to exit at a time that they wish to Unlikely to offer significant operational expertise as they typically work on the premise that a company already has it	Private equity funds are useful to companies that want money for expanding working capital, funding M&A activity and strengthening balance sheet. They are not typically appropriate for early stage businesses
Venture Debt	£1-100million	Delivers additional working capital on top of the equity component in an investment	Debt providers typically require warrants etc that can give them control of a business should it fail to meet growth targets	Useful component of an equity finance package from top tier venture and private equity firms

PREPARING TO RAISE EQUITY FUNDING

Equity funding is not and should not, be the first place that a company goes to fund activities. If you are considering raising money for a business, there are a number of things that should be done before talking to a VC or PE firm. Many of these things need to be in place before an investor would invest and by having clear processes in place, the business will be stronger in the long term in any case.

As a minimum, ensure that there are clear guidelines and processes in place for the following to:

● Forecast and manage cash flow for business.
● Maximise sales revenues.
● Implement a rigorous credit control process.
● Plan supplier payments carefully.
● Minimise overheads.
● A clear plan for the development of the business.

Consider alternative sources of funds first; equity funding from institutional investors can be expensive and does not suit the majority of businesses:

● directors' funds;
● customers with vested interest in your success;
● commercial banks: loans, overdrafts;
● factoring;
● invoice discounting;
● grants, loans, regional assistance – especially in 'deprived' regions of UK.

Assuming these measures are in place, ask some hard questions that any investor will be asking of you.

● Does the company have high growth prospects or the potential to truly disrupt the market in which it operates?
● Do you have significant points of differentiation from competitors that give you a unique and competitive sales advantage?
● Can you demonstrate success and experience in the industry that you are in?
● Is the management team fully formed or are there gaps that need to be filled?

- Are you prepared to lose some control over the way the business is run?
- Are you and the management team ambitious and totally committed to growing the business fast?

The Investor View

While venture capital and private equity are both about investing in private companies, they do in fact operate as very different types of business. This is reflected in everything from the size of deals to the kind of deal structures they pursue: venture is typically a minority stake, often syndicated, in an early stage business; private equity deals typically involve a majority stake in a business where much of the cash invested comes in the form of debt from third party debt providers. This has meant over past few years that there have been differences in how investors view the markets that they operate in.

This can be seen in the divergent views on deal flow. (Deal flow defined as number of potential investable companies an investor sees rather than total number of companies). In talking to venture investors in 2009-2010, every active VC we spoke to reported seeing significantly higher percentage of high quality deal flow over this period. We can speculate that despite the downturn, this was due to three factors:

1. In a booming/bubble economy the market is saturated with a large number of potential deals, not just high quality propositions, but opportunistic propositions are less forthcoming in a downturn as many people assume that it is going to be impossible to raise money.
2. The counter argument to this is that people have lost jobs and so are turning to entrepreneurship out of necessity.
3. There are less funds in operating in the UK and so it is easier for active funds to be found by quality propositions.

The reverse is true for private equity where the number and size of deals that PE investors are assessing seriously has fallen through the floor in the first half of the year. One investor for example that did 6 deals in the £80-£200 million (with debt component) range in 2007 has not done a deal for more than £25 million in 2009-10 and only completed 3 deals in 18 months.

1. Difficulty in agreeing acceptable valuations to all parties in a deal (i.e. investors say management are dreaming; management say investors are

too aggressive).

2.	Absence of debt finance to pad out deals.

3.	No agreement about where the market is going and a fear that it could fall further.

In both cases, venture capital and private equity, funds are operating in a market that offers them significant choices about who they invest in. The bar to investment has undoubtedly been raised.

Fund Raising – the Investor's Guide to Success

Maximising your chances of getting investors engaged in your business is vital given the competition for their cash. Leaving aside the more obvious mechanical aspects of the fund raising process, we sought some advice recently from the investment community about how investors think entrepreneurs should approach them.

Of course the basic ingredient has to be there – you need an idea that will make enough money to give an investor a reasonable return. This should be obvious even to Homer Simpson although people often lose sight of the fact. Comments from investors about how they should be approached focused on softer stuff – here are the top three tips for raising money from investors in the UK:

- **Investors want honest conversations.**

  Investors need to feel that they are talking to people that they can do business with in difficult times as well as good. Growing a business is never a simple process and people behave differently in different circumstances.

  One VC confided over dinner that when they look at a company seriously, they will deliberately engineer a point of conflict in the discussion process. Investors look for obsession and experience in entrepreneurs and they can learn more about an entrepreneur in a high stress situation than they ever will in a nice friendly meeting. Be convinced your idea is excellent. Be committed to it and be committed to working together with your investors. This becomes much easier if you know them first...

- **Relationships.**

  Fund raising is a highly competitive process and very few companies can leave it until the last minute to get going. It is NEVER too early to make contact with investors.

Investors rely on trusted networks of people to get good ideas and you can increase your chances of fundraising by being a known entity in the first place. Find excuses to meet investors, talk to them about your market, ask their advice, get in their faces. It is incredibly valuable to be taking to investors at a point well before you have to raise funds. Take any opportunity you can to talk to them about your market your organisation and pump them for information. As a minimum, try to have three points of contact before you think about pitching. This time is never wasted and you should view this as being a two-way process. Use it to work out which investors you would want to work with.

Remember though, any contact with a VC counts. Drunk, sober, formal, informal, off the record, on a conference panel, any contact will count towards an investor's impression of you and your business. Developing relationships is easier if people in the ecosystem know what you do and can introduce you...

- Advisers networks.

    The best advisers and networks see a huge amount of entrepreneurs and have regular contact with the investor community. They have a trusted relationship with investors and can be very useful people to connect you with the right investors. Talk to them and work out which ones know what they are talking about (one good indicator is the number of deals they have worked on recently). Don't be afraid to ask for their advice over coffee or a beer but respect the fact that they make their money by selling their expertise. By spending time with you at an early stage, you are both investing in a relationship that will only work if it is of benefit to both parties.

USEFUL RESOURCES

Companies considering locating in the UK, particularly owner managed businesses should contact the UKTI Global Entrepreneur Programme whose team of experienced entrepreneurs is tasked with connecting quality businesses into the people that matter in the UK investment and entrepreneurial ecosystem. http://www.entrepreneurs.gov.uk/gep/aboutus/en-GB.html

You would be most welcome to join us at the Business Leaders Network at one of our regular entrepreneur/investor networking events. http://thebln.com/

Part Six

6.1 THE UK UPSTREAM OIL AND GAS SECTOR: OFFSHORE EXPLORATION AND PRODUCTION

Mark Evans and Benjamin James
Watson, Farley & Williams LLP

INTRODUCTION

First oil was produced from the United Kingdom Continental Shelf ("UKCS") in the 1960s and it is now a mature oil & gas producing region. Production peaked in 1999 and is now in decline as easily accessible reserves are depleted. However, substantial reserves remain and, as recently as 28 June 2010, Encore Oil plc announced that it had discovered possible reserves of up to 300 million barrels of oil equivalent ("boe") in the Catcher and Catcher East fields.[1] The current best estimate published by the Department of Energy and Climate Change ("DECC") of total remaining recoverable hydrocarbon resources from the UKCS is around 20 billion boe.[2]

The UK Government[3] is committed to a lower carbon future,[4] but recognises the importance of security of supply in relation to all energy policy during the transitional period.[5] The economic extraction of remaining UKCS oil and gas reserves, to avoid over-reliance on imports and excessive movement in the price of hydrocarbons, is a key element in ensuring that security of supply.

---

1 See http://www.londonstockexchange.com/exchange/prices-and-news/news/market-news/market-news-detail.html?announcementId=10549152

2 See: https://www.og.decc.gov.uk/information/bb_updates/chapters/Table4_7.htm for further details. Information last updated August 2009 and to be updated August 2010.

3 References to the "Government" or "UK Government" in this article are to either the Labour Government before the general election in May 2010 or the Coalition Government formed after that date. Energy policy is not expected to alter radically following the election, but details of the new Energy Bill 2010 had not been announced at the time of writing.

Ongoing economic extraction will require both new exploration and further development of existing fields. Whilst the Government recognises that the scope of future UKCS activity will be dictated by "geological inheritance" (that is, the amount and accessibility of oil and gas remaining in the UKCS) and global oil prices, it is conscious of the need to present flexible, attractive and predictable regulatory and fiscal regimes to encourage new investment from existing and potential participants.

This chapter presents an overview of the main regulatory issues facing potential participants in the UKCS offshore oil and gas market.

LICENCES

UK legislation provides that all rights of "searching and boring for and getting" petroleum in the UKCS are vested in the Crown.[6] The Secretary of State is empowered, on behalf of the Crown, to grant licences to such persons and on such terms and conditions as he thinks fit.[7] The legislative structure giving discretion to the Secretary of State in this manner has remained unchanged throughout the active life of the UKCS. Although this has led to some historical complexity, it has also allowed the licensing regime to adapt quickly to commercial change.

There are currently four types of licences allowing for intrusive exploration and production of licence areas (known as "blocks") and one type of licence allowing for non-intrusive exploration of areas not currently covered by any other production licences. Details of the different types of licence are set out below.

Seaward Production Licences

Seaward production licences are split into three periods, known as "terms", the duration of which depends on the type of licence. The initial term usually involves exploration of a licence area pursuant to an agreed work programme (including drilling or another similarly substantive activity). A prescribed proportion of the licence area must be relinquished before the second term (see column 2 of the table below), which involves the carrying out of a development plan. An extended third term (following relinquishment of all areas not included in development plan) is intended for the production phase.

The four types of Seaward Production Licences and their main features are set out in Table 6.2.1 overleaf:

---

4 See: http://www.decc.gov.uk/en/content/cms/publications/lc_trans_plan/lc_trans_plan.aspx for a copy of the UK Low Carbon Transition Plan.

5 See paragraph 2 of the Government's response dated 19 October 2009 to the House of Common's Energy and Climate Change Committee's first Report of Session 2008-09, UK offshore oil and gas, HC 341-I, published 17 June 2009 at: http://www.publications.parliament.uk/pa/cm200809/cmselect/cmenergy/1010/101002.htm

6 Section 2(1) Petroleum Act 1998.

7 Sections 3(1) and (3) Petroleum Act 1998.

1. Licence	2. Duration of term			3. Relinquishment	4. Comments
	1	2	3		
Traditional Licence	4	4	18	50% (term 1)	Most common form of licence. In use since 1960s. Competence of licensee proved before grant.
Promote Licence	4	4	18	50% (term 1)	Aimed at small and start-up companies. Applicants awarded licence before proving competence within 2 years of grant. Annual rental rate (see below) reduced by 90% in first two years.
Six-Year Frontier Licence	6	6	18	75% (3 years) then 50% of remainder (term 1)	Extended first term allows extensive exploration in large areas with numerous potential prospects. Competence proved before grant.
Nine-Year Frontier Licence	9	6	18	75% (3 years) then 50% of remainder (term 1)	Designed for harsh areas West of Scotland. Requires "drill or drop"[8] decision after 6 years and extensive seismic acquisition. Competence proved before grant.

On all licences, licensees are required to pay an annual rental rate based on the area covered by the licence (per square kilometre). The rate increases over time as the field moves towards production, which provides an incentive for licensees to relinquish unused or unexplored areas.

Seaward Exploration Licences

Companies which do not intend to drill for or produce oil and gas can apply for a Seaward Exploration Licence, which will allow them to carry out non-intrusive exploration in any acreage not covered by a Production Licence at any particular time. Seaward Exploration Licences are aimed primarily at companies who collect seismic data for sale. Seaward Exploration Licence holders are able to explore acreage covered by Production Licences with the consent of the Licence holders.

Model Clauses

The standard terms applicable to petroleum licences, known as "Model Clauses", are set out in secondary legislation and incorporated (historically by reference but now set out in full) into each licence. The Model Clauses which apply to a licence are those which were in effect on the date of the grant of the licence (so the terms of a licence do not change during its term).

There is one set of Model Clauses for all 4 types of Seaward Production Licence,[9] and one set for Seaward Exploration Licences.[10]

APPLYING FOR LICENCES

The majority of Production Licences are awarded through competitive licensing rounds. Applications are invited yearly and the latest round (the 26th Seaward Licensing Round) closed on 28 April 2010. Very few companies are willing or able to take on the entire risk and expense of being the sole licensee on a Production Licence, so companies often bid for licences together (the bid is usually coordinated by the intended operator as described below).

From time to time, DECC will also consider "Out of Round" applications. A company wishing to apply Out of Round must make submissions to DECC, persuading it to invite such an application. Such applications are only considered in situations where there is some urgency for a company to acquire a licence and where there is little chance that there would be any competition for it (for example where the only company that would have a genuine interest in acquiring a licence would be

---

8 A "drill or drop" licence requires a licensee to commence operations by a specific date or to surrender the licence.
9 The Petroleum Licensing (Production) (Seaward Areas) Regulations 2008 (SI 2008/225)
10 Petroleum Licensing (Exploration and Production) (Seaward and Landward Areas) Regulations 2004 (SI 2004/352)

the licensee of an adjoining licence).

Applications for Seaward Exploration Licences can be made at any time.

ACQUISITION OF LICENCE INTERESTS

Parties can also acquire interests in Production Licences by buying a percentage interest from an existing licensee.

Companies acting together on a Production Licence usually do so by way of an unincorporated joint venture pursuant to a joint operating agreement (JOA). The JOA will specify the percentage interest that each party has in the licence and will regulate the relationship between them. Subject to consent from DECC, each party is entitled to assign some or all of its interest to a third party, which provides opportunities for new entrants to buy in to the licence. Interests are sold at every stage of the life of the licence, which allows incoming companies to assess the appropriate level of risk.

DECC regards a large volume of transfers of licence interests as a positive thing, both to enable new entrants to the market and to allow existing participants to realign their interests. The market has, in conjunction with DECC, taken steps to facilitate licence transfers. Standard transfer documents such as the Master Deed[11] and the Approved Model Deed of Assignment[12] are aimed at cutting advisory costs and giving certainty to transferors and transferees alike. DECC expects, however, that companies will acquire interests for the purposes of development and does not intend that they become tradable assets.

LICENSEES

Given the different types of operations which are necessary to fully exploit remaining UKCS reserves, DECC is keen for a wide range of companies to participate in UKCS activities. It does, however, require that participants, whether applying for a licence or acquiring a licence by way of assignment, meet certain minimum criteria, both to ensure that they are financially and, where relevant, technically capable of operating in the UKCS, and to ensure that the UK Government can access the tax revenue generated by such companies.

Financial capacity

All companies seeking to be included on a licence must demonstrate that they have sufficient financial capacity to meet the actual costs which may reasonably

---

11 The Master Deed provides a voluntary mechanism for licencees to transfer licence interests on pro-forma terms and without the need to collect signatures from all licencees on all transfer documents. See:
http://www.masterdeed.com/masterdeed.cfm for further details.
12 See: https://www.og.decc.gov.uk/upstream/licensing/LicguideApp4.doc

be expected to arise (although note that for a Promote Licence, the requirement on the grant of the licence is to show financial viability (a lower threshold) only – financial capacity need only be demonstrated after two years (see Table 6.2.1 above)).

The level of financial capacity required is not prescribed and will depend on a number of factors. DECC's primary concern is that the presence of a particular licensee will not prevent or delay work being carried out pursuant to a licence.

The evidence required for a particular licensee will depend entirely on its funding strategy, and the net worth of larger oil companies alone may be sufficient to demonstrate financial capacity. Where the potential licensee is small, any larger parent company with significant assets will be required to provide a parent company guarantee in a form prescribed by DECC.

Technical capacity

Licensees entering into a JOA are required to designate one of their number as the operator under the licence. The operator has day to day control of the exploration or production activities being carried out under the licence. Although the JOA usually operates to ensure that the operator does not accept significant higher financial risk than the other participants, DECC requires that the party acting as operator demonstrates that it has the necessary technical capacity to carry out the role. DECC will review the track record of potential operators, including any track record from other jurisdictions, in deciding whether a particular company is a suitable operator.

Environmental capacity

Licensees are also required to show environmental competence in relation to their proposed operations through detailed submissions to DECC in relation to, amongst other things, arrangements for pollution liability and environmental management. The timing of such submissions depends in each case on the type of licence and stage of development of the field.

Oil and gas operators are subject to extensive environmental regulation,[13] and following the major oil spill caused by the explosion on and subsequent sinking of BP's Deepwater Horizon rig in the Gulf of Mexico, the Government announced a doubling of rig inspections and a further review of deep water procedures prior to the commencement of deep water drilling West of Shetland.[14] The Oil Spill Prevention and Response Advisory Group was also set up to assess the findings of the US investigation into the Gulf of Mexico spill. Although the UKCS has a good

13 See: https://www.og.decc.gov.uk/environment/environ_leg_index.htm
14 See: http://www.publications.parliament.uk/pa/cm201011/cmhansrd/cm100614/debtext/100614-0008.htm

safety record and robust regulation (largely introduced in response to the Piper Alpha disaster in 1988), it is possible that further regulation may result from this incident.

Residence

All companies with interests in the UKCS must have a place of business within the UK, which means:

(i)   it is a UK registered company; or
(ii)   it is a UK registered branch of a foreign company; or
(iii)   it has a staffed presence in the UK.

Parties to licences in producing fields must have a staffed presence in the UK or be a UK registered company. Operators must further demonstrate that they have sufficient proximity to the licence area to adequately control operations.

DECOMMISSIONING

The UK Government is required, under international law,[15] to remove all offshore installations or structures on the UKCS which are abandoned or disused in accordance with generally accepted international standards.[16] The Government is permitted some discretion as to whether installations are removed in their entirety, but OSPAR Decision 98/3[17] clarified that derogations from the basic principle would be limited to concrete installations, concrete anchor bases and the footings of large steel installations which are over 10,000 tonnes, or other exceptional cases.

These obligations rest with the UK Government, which passes them on to UKCS licensees through Part IV of the Petroleum Act 1998. The act empowers the Secretary of State, by written notice, to demand an "abandonment programme"[18] for each offshore installation setting out the measures to be taken to decommission an installation, along with projected costs and timing.[19] The notice can be served on a number of parties, including the operator of the installation, licensees of the area in which the installation is located, parties to the JOA or parties with any other interest in the installation, and associates of any of the above.[20]

15 Arts 60(3) and 80 of the UN Law of the Sea Convention 1982 21 I.L.M. 1261 ("UNCLOS") and the Oslo and Paris Convention for the Protection of the Marine Environment of the North East Atlantic 1992 ("OSPAR")

16 The standards adopted are the draft Guidelines and Standards for the Removal of Offshore Installations and Structures on the Continental Shelf and in the Exclusive Economic Zone, as adopted by the Assembly of the International Maritime Organisation on 19 October 1989.

17 A decision of the signatories (including the UK) to the Oslo and Paris Convention for the Protection of the Marine Environment of the North East Atlantic 1992 ("OSPAR")

18 The term "abandonment" is used interchangeably with "decommissioning" in this context.

19 Section 29 Petroleum Act 1998

20 Section 30(1) Petroleum Act 1998

In practice, DECC usually serves notice on the licensees shortly after grant of the licence, requesting an abandonment programme at a time to be determined by it at a later date. Where licensees changes through the life of the licence, DECC will usually withdraw the notice and serve a new notice on the incoming licensee.

Once approved, all parties who submitted the abandonment programme bear joint and several liability for carrying it out. If the parties fail to do so, the Secretary can himself arrange for abandonment work to be carried out and recover the cost (plus interest) from the defaulting parties. The Secretary also has the power, whether before or after approval of the abandonment programme, to take such security as is necessary to ensure that sufficient funds are available.

Parties to JOAs are understandably concerned that all other parties have made financial provision for what can be fairly onerous obligations. It is therefore common practice for parties to enter into a decommissioning security agreement, under which parties make regular payments to a separate fund (protected from creditors as far as possible) as security for future decommissioning costs.

TAXATION

Taxation of offshore oil and gas activities is complex and specialist advice should be taken prior to any investment. This complexity is derived largely from successive governments seeking to find a balance between providing financial incentives for exploration and development whilst ensuring the UK economy as a whole derives significant benefit from the country's natural resources.

The main forms of relevant taxation are:

- Petroleum Revenue Tax – applies on a field by field basis to fields given development consent before 16 March 1993;
- Ring-Fenced Corporation Tax – corporation tax payable by all companies with a "ring-fence" around taxable profits from oil and gas extraction so they are not reduced by losses in other activities; and
- Supplementary Charge – an additional levy on ring-fenced profits.

Further details of applicable rates and reliefs can be found on HMRC's website.[21]

21 http://www.hmrc.gov.uk/international/ns-fiscal3.htm#f

CONCLUSION

The UK offshore oil and gas sector offers a wide range of investment opportunities. The experience gained during the last 40 years of exploration and production in the UKCS has given it a dependable regulatory system and a responsive and efficient regulator. The UK Government's stated aim[22] to ensure security of supply through economic extraction of remaining reserves should give confidence to new and existing participants that the environment for further investment will remain favourable for the remaining life of the resource. Interested investors are encouraged to consult their advisers and DECC for further information.

Further information

Government and overview:
https://www.og.decc.gov.uk/upstream/index.htm

Industry:
http://www.oilandgasuk.co.uk/
http://www.cdal.com/
http://www.logic-oil.com/
http://www.masterdeed.com/home.cfm

Environmental:
http://www.ospar.org/
http://www.opol.org.uk/

---

22 See: http://www.decc.gov.uk/en/content/cms/publications/lc_trans_plan/lc_trans_plan.aspx

6.2 LNG, GAS STORAGE AND ACCESS TO INFRA-STRUCTURE

Mark Evans
Watson, Farley & Williams, LLP

INTRODUCTION

At the time of writing (July 2010) the UK's Department for Energy and Climate Change (DECC) has just released key energy data for the first quarter of 2010. Total gas demand in the UK in the first quarter of 2010 was 370.32 TWh, up 13.2% when compared to the first quarter of 2009, Of that, 94.63 TWh was used for electricity generation (up 18.4%) and 158.59 TWh was domestic consumption (up 12.9%). However gas imports to the UK were up 31% to 16.7bn m3 or 183.76 TWh, and North Sea gas production was down 9.2% to 16.6bn m3 (183.35 TWh). The UK therefore imported more than half of its demand in the quarter.

This is probably not a wholly typical situation: gas prices were low during the 2009/10 winter which was a cold one in the UK. As a result, more gas was imported than would otherwise have been the case. Most of the imported gas came from pipelines from Norway and the Netherlands. Liquefied natural gas (LNG) was also imported from Qatar, Trinidad and Algeria and comprised more than 25% (47.94 TWh) of total gas imported – an increase in LNG imports of more than 100% compared to the first quarter of 2009.

Gas is still the predominant fuel used for power generation in the UK: 45.5% of electricity generated in the first quarter of 2010 was generated by gas-fired power plants, compared to 36.8% in the first quarter of 2009. Coal accounted for 31.2% (down from 38.1%), nuclear 16.5% (up from 15.6%) and renewables 6.2% (down from 6.7%).

Regardless of whether the first quarter of 2010 is to be regarded as typical or not, the trends underlying the statistics are clear. North Sea production of gas is gradually tailing off, whilst gas consumption grows; the UK Government anticipates that importation of gas will be an accelerating trend. Concerns about security of energy supply and a shortage of clean power generating stations to enable carbon emission targets to be met means the UK Government has to focus on ensuring that a coherent legal framework is in place to enable the necessary infrastructure to address these concerns to be consented and built, so as to minimise the risk of a tight gas supply/demand balance in the UK in the future. There are a number of areas where the Government is keen to develop investment.

Offshore LNG regasification

LNG is becoming increasingly important to the UK. The UK has three regasification terminals: South Hook LNG and Dragon LNG at Milford Haven in South Wales, and Grain LNG at the Isle of Grain in Kent. In addition to traditional onshore regasification facilities, floating regasification ships, or FSRUs (floating storage and regasification units) are now becoming more common. Excelerate Energy completed the Teesside Gasport in February 2007. Energy Bridge Regasification vessels (i.e. vessels designed by EE using its Energy Bridge regasification technology) are able to load LNG conventionally, sail to the Teesside Gasport, regasify the LNG onboard, and deliver gas to an onshore loading arm. In other applications, delivery can also be made at sea to subsea loading buoys.

Combustible Gas Storage

Gas storage facilities provide obvious benefits: cheap gas can be injected during periods of low demand and expensive gas withdrawn during periods of high demand. They provide security of supply in periods of low supply. The UK currently has approximately 4 bcm (billion cubic metres) of storage capacity, approximately 14 days' worth at average winter gas demand rates. The UK's largest facility is the Rough Field, a partially depleted gas field in the southern North Sea operated by Centrica, the second largest being nine man-made underground salt cavities at Hornsea in Yorkshire. In contrast, many other European countries dependent on gas imports have large strategic storage capacities of up to 80 days on average.

Carbon Capture and Storage (CCS)

The UK has committed to at least an 80% cut in greenhouse gas emissions by 2050 against a 1990 baseline. The Government has a number of policy objectives designed to achieve this: it is promoting the building of new nuclear power stations to replace the currently ageing fleet which is still providing around 16% of the UK's electricity consumption. It is also promoting the building of a range of renewable technologies, including on- and off-shore wind farms, solar farms and biomass fuelled facilities, to name a few. Great store is however set by the possibility of reducing carbon emissions from new, and existing, coal and gas fired power plants, currently accounting for around 75% of the UK's electricity consumption.

CCS technology is still in development but comprises technology to capture carbon emissions at source at power stations, and then pipe the carbon dioxide through land based and off-shore pipelines to safe permanent storage in, in all likelihood, depleted oil and gas fields. The UK Government estimates that CCS could potentially capture around 90% of the CO2 emitted by the burning of fossil fuels to generate electricity and as much as 28% of global CO2 mitigation by 2050. The Government is committed to build a CCS demonstration plant in the UK by 2014, and the Energy Act 2010 granted powers to enable it to provide the financial assistance to achieve that.

THE LEGAL REGULATORY FRAMEWORK: THE ENERGY ACT 2008 (THE ACT)

Each of these technologies: offshore LNG regasification, combustible gas storage and CCS supports key energy objectives of ensuring security of energy supply and at the same time reducing carbon emissions. Each however raises regulatory issues; activities offshore in UK territorial waters need to be licensed and controlled to ensure safe and responsible exploration and development and decommissioning of assets at the end of their useful lives. At the same time, the UK Government wants to ensure that third parties have access to spare capacity in off-shore assets at a fair price, so that projects which do not justify the construction of dedicated infrastructure might nevertheless be economic and realisable, making a further contribution to Government's achieving its energy objectives. The regulatory regime in the UK governing these activities is contained in the Act.

Activities covered by the Act

Relevant legislation in existence prior to the Act was targeted principally at licensing oil and gas production and was not appropriate to new types of offshore gas supply transactions. The Act now simplifies the consents regime. The Act creates two licensing regimes: one for combustible gas storage, recovery and delivery (i.e. not carbon dioxide and therefore not CCS) and a second regime for CCS, which is less developed as a technology and has the unique facet of requiring permanent storage. These regimes are now fully in force in the UK, save insofar as they relate to the unloading of gas into a pipeline and the establishment or maintenance of an installation for that purpose. Provisions relating to these activities are not in force as at July 2010.

The activities to be licensed under the Act are the use of the sea for gas storage or unloading, the recovery of stored gas, the conversion of natural features, eg salt domes, for gas storage, related exploration activities, and the establishment and maintenance of installations (fixed or floating).

The area of sea in question (referred to in the Act as a "controlled place") is any place in, under or over the UK territorial sea (i.e. 12 nautical miles approximately from the coast) and waters in a Gas Importation and Storage Zone (the power to nominate which, within the next 188 nautical miles from the outer edge of the territorial sea, is taken by the Act).

Licensing and model clauses – combustible gas

A licence is required from the Secretary of State for Energy and Climate Change (the Secretary of State) to undertake any of the activities set out above, together with a lease (in respect of activities in the territorial sea) or an authorisation (in the case of activities in the Gas Importation and Storage Zone) from the Crown Estate.

The Offshore Exploration (Petroleum, and Gas Storage and Unloading) (Model Clauses) Regulations 2009 set out the model clauses for exploration licences for gas storage activities (i.e. storage and recovery of combustible gas, conversion of a natural feature for storage of gas and establishment of installations for those purposes) using non-intrusive methods (e.g. seismic and shallow drilling) which the Secretary of State can vary in any particular case. The Offshore Gas Storage and Unloading (Licensing) Regulations 2009 set out the model clauses for gas storage licences themselves (i.e. covering the relevant activity, not exploration for the purposes of the activity).

The two sets of model clauses are very similar to each other. The exploration licence model terms deal with a number of topics including rights to commence drilling wells, obligations to abandon and plug wells, and the Secretary of State's rights to revoke the licence for the licensee's breach or insolvency or change of control.

The gas storage model terms additionally deal with work programmes to be completed under the licence, the requirement to have development plans approved by the Secretary of State, rights to transfer the licence, and the Secretary of State's rights to revoke the licence for a change of control of the licensee.

Where gas is to be recovered from a depleted field which may still contain non-injected petroleum, a question could arise as to whether a petroleum licence (i.e. one to bore for and get petroleum) is required under the Petroleum Act 1998, in addition to a gas storage licence under the Act. The Act deals with this – permitting the Secretary of State to direct that no such licence is required where the volume of petroleum existing in its natural condition is so small that it should properly be disregarded.

Licensing and model clauses – CO2

The Act also provides a framework for storing carbon dioxide (CO2) offshore as part of CCS technology. (There is currently no framework legislation in the UK dealing with the storage of carbon dioxide onshore). The Act creates the power to grant licences, to stipulate who can apply, how the application is to be made, what supporting documents must be provided, and what financial security must be provided in respect of the licensee's obligations relating to licensed activities.

Licences are to be granted by the Secretary of State, or, where the activity is to be carried out in the territorial sea adjacent to Scotland, the Scottish ministers. Licences may set out the obligations of the licencee during the period between closure of the facility (i.e. when it is full) and the subsequent termination of the licence and what financial arrangements (e.g. regarding on-going liability for the closed facility) will then apply. There is no power taken to adopt model clauses for CO2 storage licences.

It should be noted that none of these provisions apply to CO2 being used for the purposes of enhanced petroleum recovery: i.e. injected into a petroleum producing well to increase pressure and thereby the flow of hydrocarbons.

Decommissioning – Petroleum Act 1998 (Part 4)

Decommissioning obligations impose significant financial obligations on those with interests in offshore infrastructure. The relevant obligations are contained in Part 4 Petroleum Act 1998 which is amended by the Act and then applied by it to all installations the subject of combustible gas storage licences and also CO2 licences.

Part 4 requires all offshore installations to be removed to the extent possible after the permanent cessation of the facilities' operations, as set out in a decommissioning programme approved by the Secretary of State. Once a decommissioning programme is approved by the Secretary of State, each person who submitted it has a duty to secure that the programme is carried out and all conditions are complied with. The Secretary of State requires entities to submit a decommissioning programme by serving notice on them.

A wide category of persons can be required to submit a decommissioning programme to the Secretary of State, including a manager of the installation, a person with the right to exploit mineral resources in the area, or to unload, store or recover gas in the area or convert a natural feature in the area for that purpose, a person who has transferred such rights without consent, a person who owns an interest in the installation other than as a lender and a person associated with any of the foregoing.

Due to the potential liabilities attaching to an abandonment programme, the power of the Secretary of State to send notices requiring a party to submit one in respect of an offshore installation, is carefully circumscribed. In particular, generally no notice can be sent to a party which has never benefitted economically or otherwise from the installation. Nor may a notice be sent to an associated party of a liable party if the Secretary of State is satisfied that adequate arrangements for abandonment have been made. A party is entitled to make written representations before being sent a notice by the Secretary of State and, finally, the exercise of discretion by the Secretary of State is subject to challenge on a number of procedural grounds set out in the Act.

The Secretary of State can also require financial security for decommissioning costs at any time, not just at the end of the life of a field, and the Act overrides insolvency law so that funds set aside for decommissioning remain available for that purpose, notwithstanding any insolvency of the provider of the funds.

The Secretary of State is now also given broad powers to request financial information to back up a decommissioning programme, including information on the costs of the programme, predictions of future revenue, and up to date management accounts. fr

THIRD PARTY ACCESS TO INFRASTRUCTURE
Ensuring that third parties are able to access unused capacity in infrastructure, often offshore pipelines, on reasonable commercial terms is essential to ensure that smaller developments, without the economic might to build their own

infrastructure, are able to access markets at a reasonable cost. This is particularly true as the UK Government tries to maximise the economic recovery of the UK's oil and gas.

The concept of mandated third party access is thus enshrined in UK legislation, with the Petroleum Act 1998, the Pipelines Act 1962 and the Gas Act 1995 (all as amended by the Act) now giving the Secretary of State power to intervene in negotiations which have not led to access being granted within a reasonable time and to grant access in respect of all upstream infrastructure.

The Infrastructure Code of Practice, published by Oil and Gas UK and introduced in 2004 in conjunction with DECC sets out principles and procedures to guide parties involved in TPA negotiations. The code sets out overarching principles: for example to uphold infrastructure safety and integrity, protect the environment and follow the Commercial Code of practice for the industry – effectively a good faith and ethics code – and principles: for example to provide meaningful information during negotiations, support negotiated access in a timely manner, and publish key agreed commercial provisions. The code also offers advice on how parties should seek to allocate risks and liabilities in negotiations.

The code deals with the interface between good faith bilateral negotiations and the formal process of seeking Secretary of State determination. After principles have been discussed and information exchanged and negotiations can reasonably be considered to be 6 months away from conclusion, the bona fide enquirer will formally notify the infrastructure owner and the Secretary of State of the process. The code then maps the timetable for negotiations and further applications to the Secretary of State for dispute resolution under his statutory powers.

Note that it is not uncommon for exemptions to be granted from the obligation to provide third-party access, particularly when the financing of an asset depends upon a long-term usage contract.

CONCLUSION

Energy policy in the UK has been slow to respond to the twin threats of aged nuclear and coal power stations and carbon fuelled climate change. Steps taken to reduce carbon emissions have generally not been successful and only recession and reduced demand for electricity has resulted in emission reductions. The Government is clearly focused on ensuring that a stable regulatory regime exists to accommodate the technologies which will be a part of the answer to these threats. An important question now is what else might need to be done to secure the necessary private sector investment in the current economic environment. One way or another, there is likely to be significant investment in offshore infrastructure in UK waters over the long term.

The regulatory regime governing different types of offshore UK infrastructure is complex and this chapter can only give a flavour of that complexity. Investors in the sector, who will generally be well aware of this, will, of course, require detailed advice.

Information:
Please direct any queries to Mark Evans, who is a partner in the Oil and Gas Group at Watson, Farley & Williams – tel: 0207 814 8099; mevans@wfw.com

6.3 SCIENCE PARKS
AND BUSINESS INCUBATORS

Nick Hood
Carter Jonas

THE INVESTMENT RATIONALE FOR SCIENCE PARKS

In our opinion Science Parks should be considered as a separate sector within the property investment market. Factors for investors to consider include:

- consistently high occupancy rates leading to reduced void costs for investors;
- new opportunities for investors to enter the market with the pressure on public sector investment into the sector;
- tenants willing to take long leases leading to security of income;
- technology companies perform well at different times within the wider economic cycle diversifying the risk;
- preliminary evidence that investment returns have been better than office parks over one, three and five years.

These issues and the importance of Incubators are discussed in greater detail in this article.

SCIENCE PARKS

The Science Park movement in the United Kingdom is now 40 years old; Cambridge Science Park celebrated its 40th birthday this year. Herriot Watt Science Park was established when the University relocated from central Edinburgh to a green field site to the west of Edinburgh in 1971. The movement started slowly but gathered momentum in the 1980s and the United Kingdom Science Park Association (UKSPA) was founded in 1984.

Today there are some 65 fully paid up members of UKSPA and they vary in size and composition but all contribute to the promotion of the 'knowledge based economy' in the United Kingdom. UKSPA provides a useful definition of a Science Park as:

"A Science Park is essentially a cluster of knowledge-based businesses, where support and advice are supplied to assist in the growth of the companies. In most instances Science Parks are associated with a centre of technology such as a uni - versity or research institute."

All Science Parks will comply with some aspects of the definition but it is perhaps the human activities in the promotion of business support and interaction, coupled with the proximity and links to a centre of technology, which is the principal differentiator between a Science Park and a more conventional business park. The cluster effect is important and extends beyond the boundaries of an individual park. It is not therefore surprising that the more successful and prosperous Science Parks are located in cities with strong universities and research organisations. Edinburgh, Cambridge, Manchester and Oxford all have strong Science Parks.

Some of the important characteristics of these clusters are:

● Strong academic base in science
● Skilled workforce.
● Effective research and development networks in the region
● Entrepreneurial culture
● Attractive environment so people wish to live in the area
● Good local schools
● Good local support infrastructure; access to finance, legal teams, accountants etc.

BUSINESS INCUBATORS AND INNOVATION CENTRES

Most Science Parks, but not all, will have a Business Incubator as part of their model. A Business Incubator does not necessarily need to be on a Science Park but where it is, it will often be considered a generator of tenants for the wider Science Park. The term Business Incubator or Innovation Centre is widely used but they vary considerably in terms of what they seek to provide and some are actually no more than managed work space.

On a Science Park, a Business Incubator or Innovation Centre will provide small business suites with units of normally less than 100m2 (1,000 sq ft) on short term 'easy in easy out' agreements with common services and meeting rooms as with most business centres. Space will normally be let at market rates but there will be additional business support services provided either directly or through third party partners at often minimal or low cost to the recipient. Indeed, a good Innovation Centre will be delivering these services to a wider area so that tenants do not need to be in the Centre or even on the Park. The Centre will interact with the local business community and regional higher education institutes and research organisations to provide a catalyst for the growth of new and early stage business opportunities in their region. This activity will often be supported by the local authority or regional development agency but some parks will see this activity as the pipeline for future tenants not only for the Incubator but also for the park. A good Innovation Centre or Incubator will act as a Flagship in terms of generating activity and publicity for the benefit of the wider Science Park and will usually be focused on a particular sector or sectors of the technology market place.

The majority of Incubators will provide basic workshop or office specification space, usually with good high speed internet connectivity. A few will offer more specialised space for biotechnology or other laboratory users. Some have been in response to the closure of a research organisation, such as Boots in Nottingham or Roche in Welwyn Garden City. The availability of specialised laboratory space at low or reduced cost, coupled with a skilled workforce, can provide a unique opportunity to create a new broader business base at a time when the potential job losses in the local market place is seen as a major problem.

In contrast, managed workspace will provide simple offices or workshops for small businesses without any additional management support or advice and while they may well serve a useful local need they are not Incubators. Business centres provide an additional level of service and provide active support to their tenants and seek to create a business community within the centre but will not be actively looking to promote economic activity. They are often supported by local authorities and well run centres can thrive in private ownership within a vibrant local economy but are unlikely to be actively supporting business incubation.

Incubators are often considered high risk investments given the short term nature of their agreements and the comparatively poor covenant strength of their tenants. However, they generally charge inclusive rental packages and in well managed centres can, once established, achieve consistently high occupancy rates with the opportunity to generate additional revenue from other activities such that the net rent to the investor can often match or better the income from conventionally let buildings. In twenty years the occupancy of the St John's Innovation Centre in Cambridge very rarely fell below 90% and then usually only when a larger tenant matured and moved on to new premises. If this can generate leads to the wider park, both from indirect marketing and tenants expanding, the centres can provide a positive contribution to a park.

Goodman and Unilever, with some support from the East of England Development Agency, have recently started work on a new £13.7m Business Incubator at Colworth Science Park near Bedford. The Exchange will provide conference and catering facilities in addition to fully serviced laboratories and offices on flexible terms on this 500,000 sq ft park which specialises in food health and wellness.

There are companies running Incubators who will take a direct investment stake into the businesses in their Incubators and will be actively involved in the business. This requires a different business model and is more closely akin to investment into a business rather than a property investment and has been successful in the USA.

OWNERSHIP

The Science Park movement is now reaching maturity and should be considered an investment sector in its own right. The original Science Parks were often funded by academic institutions seeking to promote the growth of businesses utilising the technologies within academia and to foster links between academia and the wider business communities. In general, while they were not considered on strict investment criteria, they were expected to deliver a return to their promoters in the longer term. These parks are generally found close to the major universities; the Surrey Research Park or Herriot Watt would be typical examples.

The success of these first parks encouraged others into the field and the public sector saw the potential benefits in the growth in knowledge based businesses. Local authorities started to encourage Incubators and Science Parks in association with their local higher education institutes and a number of publically funded research organisations also saw the benefit of promoting businesses alongside their own research. This support was further enhanced following the creation of the regional development agencies under the Labour Government. A number of leading Science Parks are joint developments between various stakeholders including local authorities and academic institutions such as Manchester Science Parks whereas Birmingham Science Park at Aston is a local authority initiative.

Today over 50% of Science Parks have a direct investment from an academic institution and a further 20% from publically funded research organisations and over 50% also have some aspect of funding from local authorities and development agencies. In the current economic climate it is difficult to see further public sector initiatives so it is a concern that there are few investment and development companies who have taken an interest in the Science Park movement. At present only about 20% of parks are controlled by the private sector and while some of these will also have public sector funding, they are expected to provide an economic return to their investors. These investment or development companies, such as Aviva or Goodman, have appreciated the potential from Science Parks and can see that proactive management of their parks, coupled with knowledge of the sector(s) in which they are investing, can improve investment performance. Unfortunately there are too few private sector companies who understand the sector or are perhaps even aware of the opportunities it presents.

Sectors

Science Parks encompass a wide variety of uses and the building specifications will reflect this. Many technology companies are engaged in computing and software for which a standard office specification is appropriate, though possibly with enhanced cooling systems for server rooms and most investment companies or developers would be entirely comfortable with the specification. At the other extreme, a fully fitted biotechnology building will have an extensive fit out, probably costing rather more than the basic shell and core building. This requires a different approach by the developer/investor who may choose to simply provide a shell and core building, leaving the occupier to fund the fit out, usually on the basis of a 20 or 25 year lease with a rent geared to a proportion of an office rent. The basic shell and core will itself potentially be more expensive than a similar shell specification for a straightforward office use due to the requirement for the capacity for additional plant and equipment which might include an extra floor just for plant.

A more creative approach by a limited number of developers has been to split the package with a basic rent related to the shell and core building and a further 'rent' related to the fit out of the laboratory where the deal will be more related to a financial package than a traditional property one. Again the package may have different elements relating to the different elements of the fit out and the potential life expectancy of the components. This may give the occupier greater flexibility to modify the fit out as requirements change over time. Churchmanor Estates Company and Aviva Investors at Chesterford Research Park near Cambridge have successfully developed laboratory buildings, most recently for US based Illunina Inc, and have just started development of a new 28,000 sq ft flexible laboratory building capable of occupation as a whole or in up to sixteen separate suites.

The strength of the tenant covenant will pay an important part in the negotiations as a specialised fit out may have limited value should a tenant vacate necessitating an expensive refit before the building is capable of occupation by another company.

Technology companies operate in growth markets often with higher margins than companies in more traditional markets. They are prepared to pay a premium for the right premises in the right location with the appropriate facilities to attract and retain their employees. Company failure rates on Science Parks are reputedly lower than average but this needs substantiation.

There are a few parks where laboratories are provided for early stage businesses but these will generally be to a fairly basic specification, in terms of the fit out, with further adaptation required to meet individual needs of tenants. Babraham Research Campus in Cambridge has successfully developed Bioincubator buildings for early stage biomedical enterprises.

FUNDING

The majority of existing Science Parks have been established through public sector funding in various forms, often working together and including universities, local authorities, regional development agencies and research organisations. While in some instances the initiative may have been in response to economic deprivation, in others it has been to exploit the economic potential of research within the local institutes. In the latter case the private sector can be involved in supporting the initiative as development can be economically viable.

Larger property investment funds will have an exposure to 'out of town business parks' and through these are already likely to have an exposure to science based tenants. These tenants will possibly have located to an area based on the potential 'cluster effect' and parts of the London market, the M4 corridor and Cambridge are typical. The companies are looking for the right environment for their employees and their business and the criteria that make a good business park are equally valid for a science based company. Larger companies will generate their own links with academia and research organisations and will therefore look for the best premises and terms to meet their requirements within a general geographical location. Science Parks should be seeking to provide a better environment to attract these businesses through the provision of services tailored to the specific needs of technology companies.

Technology companies will tend to be in growth sectors and, in our opinion, can often operate to slightly different economic cycles to the reminder of business in a region. If so they should also be considered as a separate asset class offering an opportunity to spread risk within the property sector. However, data is required to support this contention and at present, partly due to the nature of the ownership of a significant number of the parks, this is not available. With Parks which are in private ownership, or even where funds own an individual building on a Science Park, they will be assessing the performance of their assets by reference to the performance of other assets and, in particular, other property funds and as such are likely to provide information to the most widely used benchmark, the IPD Index.

Investment Property Databank (IPD)

At present there is no IPD Index covering the Science Park sector though, from some preliminary work carried out by IPD earlier this year, they have data on some 8 institutional properties within Science Parks and on a further 7 through public/private joint ventures and they have used this to produce Table 6.4.1 below. They have no data for an institutional specialist fund and the data they have will form part of the office park index.

Figure 6.3.1 Annualised total return comparison prepared by IPD

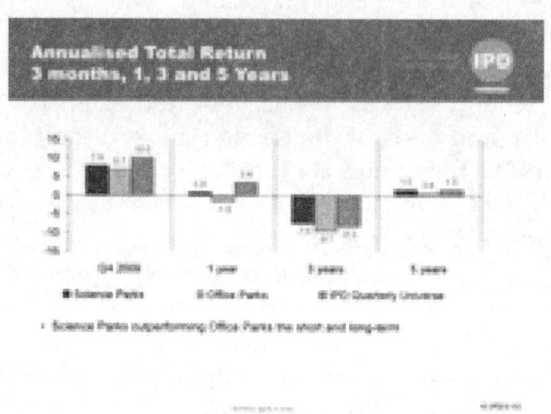

In our opinion, a separate Science Park Index would provide useful information for generating investment into the Science Park sector by showing not only that it can match or better the performance of office parks but that it does operate on a slightly different economic cycle. It will take time to build the necessary data and Science Park owners, particularly those in the public sector, will need to cooperate in the provision of information to IPD. It may also require some education of valuers to understand that there might be a distinction between the parks but that is a discussion that the few institutional owners probably already have with their valuers.

Carter Jonas is looking for one further company to assist in the sponsorship and then, in co-operation with UKSPA, we will be able to implement this initiative with IPD. It is, in our view, important to make the case to institutional investors that the Science Park sector should form a part of their property investment strategy and in doing so sustain investment into this sector which makes an important contribution to the UK economy.

CONCLUSION

Science Parks and Incubators have now reached maturity and with the current tightening of public sector funding will need to attract more private sector funding. At present only a small number of the property investment companies are aware of the sector and the potential it offers. It is essential that Science Parks promote themselves as a complementary sector capable of offering competitive returns to investors and further spreading their risk from regional offices and business parks.

6.4 LONDON: THE LEADING DESTINATION FOR OVERSEAS INVESTMENT

Michael Charlton
Think London

INTRODUCTION

In 2009, London was once again voted the world's number one centre of commerce, its talent, global connectivity and diversity all helping to underpin its success. Our goal is to ensure that London is recognised as the undisputed world capital of business and the continued flow of inward investment over the last year, in spite of the challenging economic conditions being experienced across the globe, has served to underline just how successful this objective has been.

Indeed, London's resilience has played a fundamental part in this success. The city has weathered the economic storm thanks to a stable business environment, access to markets, a wealth of talent, specialist clusters and innovative spirit. Emerging markets may have offered lower costs, but London has become a safe refuge, prompting a 'flight to quality' among overseas companies and maintaining London's status as Europe's leading destination for foreign direct investment for the twelfth year running.[1]

In the throes of a deep recession, Think London has had a buoyant year. Although foreign direct investment into Europe contracted during 2009-10, investment into London has actually risen by more than a third compared to last

1 Ernst and Young 2010 European Attractiveness Survey

year's figures, with 239 companies setting up or expanding in London. And while the recession was expected to slash FDI job prospects, we have created and protected 6,157 jobs, a figure that falls just fractionally short of last year's all-time high.

EXPLORING THE LONDON OPPORTUNITY

There are a number of compelling reasons to have a presence in London. Not only is it a European transportation hub, with easy access to the wider EU market through five international airports, high-speed rail services to mainland Europe, and one of Europe's largest sea freight centres, but with multiple world class business clusters, it is also one of the most cost effective places to do business.

London is essentially a microcosm of Europe, if not the world, which makes it an efficient test-bed and single point of action for business expansion. The capital also pools top talent from all over the world, offering the largest regional workforce in Europe through a labour pool of over nine million people. Finally, the fact that it sits at the centre of the world time zones gives the added benefit of being able to work with both the West Coast of North America and Asia in a single working day.

London's pre-eminent role in the globalisation strategies of companies worldwide has made it a world-class success story. Crucially, London stays ahead of the game in all of the key components that drive business growth. These are:

A global market place

Not only does London have the largest city economy in Europe, but the UK capital is also home to more of the world's largest companies than any other European city. It is the number one destination for European headquarters, having attracted three times more (135) than any other European city since 2003.

London also offers surprising value for money, with 80%[2] of overseas investors agreeing that being based in the city provides them with a premium level of return on investment (ROI). Furthermore, the recent Mercer Cost of Living Survey 2010 highlighted that London's cost of living dropped even lower this year, ranking London 17th in a survey of leading global business cities.

Market opportunities

London is also the largest consumer market in Europe. The city and its surrounding areas constitute the largest urban zone in the EU with a market of almost 12 million consumers.

Top talent

London provides access to world class talent, which is the number one resource for business success. More than half of London's working population (1.9m out of 3.7m; or 53%) is highly qualified, covering senior positions in management, professional and technical occupations, and associate professorships.[3] Furthermore, London boasts access to some of the best graduate talent in the world with more top ranking universities than any city across the globe. And London also boosts executive careers: nearly six out of ten foreign-born executives have been promoted during their time in London;

Resilience, transformation and growth

Finally, London is one of the most resilient business centres in the world. Despite the global recession and its major impact on world business centres, overseas firms in London are increasingly confident about doing business in the capital. According to Think London's FDI Barometer, 62%[4] of business leaders from overseas owned firms in London said they were more confident of the prospects for their business in London over the next 12 months, when compared to the previous 12 months, whilst the majority of respondents anticipated that they will increase their employment levels in the year ahead.

LONDON BY SECTOR

The wealth of opportunity in London, combined with the numerous benefits that come from having a base in the capital, mean that the city boasts some unique sector strengths.

Financial and Business Services

London is Europe's financial capital and a leading centre for all of the professional and business support services upon which a successful business depends from law, accountancy and consulting to IT services and advertising.

Not only this, but half of all European investment banking activity is carried out in London, and the UK capital has more foreign banks than any other centre worldwide. With businesses demanding locations that offer a combination of access to talent and cost attractiveness, London's position at the centre of the world's time zones and proximity to an established financial services cluster has made it a magnet for emerging economy FDI.

2 Ipsos MORI, July 2010
Office for National Statistics, 2007-2008

Creative Industries

The creative industries is an emerging growth sector and London already has a reputation as a leading international centre of creativity, accounting for £21 billion, or 16% of London's annual Gross Value Added (GVA), every year. It is the second largest industry in London after business services and one third of all creative industry jobs are location in London.

Information and Communications Technology

London's ICT sector is the largest in Europe and the leading location for business in terms of IT infrastructure[5] with 19 of the top 25 software and services suppliers having their HQ's in London. The sector is driven by the need to optimise global operations, with companies searching for integrated solutions that will help them cope with increased pressure on costs. London is particularly cost competitive when compared with other Western Europe locations, and the convergence between ICT and other sectors, for example creative industries and financial services, creates some undeniable opportunities for investment.

Environmental

The environmental sector is a major growth area for overseas investment, with approximately 30,000 jobs created globally in 2008. Although production projects for renewable energy have generated the vast majority of jobs so far, as this relatively young sector matures over the coming years, job creation from activities such as R&D will become increasingly prominent.

THE 2012 GAMES

The London 2012 Olympic and Paralympic Games are expected to release £1.7bn worth of contracts, most of them awarded by the end of 2010 and from which will flow numerous supply chain opportunities across a variety of sectors, products and services. This is a huge business opportunity that can be interpreted and capitalised upon in several ways.

From an economic perspective, the Games are worth almost £10bn and are logistically comparable to hosting 26 world championship sports events simultaneously. It is the largest logistical exercise a country can undertake in peace time.

Everything about the Games is on a large scale, from the 205 countries taking part to the 70,000 volunteers needed to manage the event. For international business, the opportunities to play a part in what is deemed to be the "greatest

3 Office for National Statistics, 2007-2008
4 Ipsos MORI, July 2010

show on earth" are therefore immense.

The four-year London 2012 Cultural Olympiad started in September 2008, at the end of the Beijing 2008 Paralympic Games. It is the largest cultural celebration in the history of the modern Olympic and Paralympic Games, designed to give everyone in the UK a chance to be involved with the spectacle of London 2012. The Torch Relay is an important part of this build up to the Games. Celebrating and uniting sport and culture, it will bring the spirit of the Games to the whole of the UK in the months leading up to the Opening Ceremony.

Whilst both of these activities present an opportunity for business involvement, the fact that the 2012 Olympics will be the first ever 'digital games' means that the opportunities for those in the technology, creative or entertainment spaces really stand out.

London has a multi-billion dollar digital media market and is not only the global centre of convergence for the technology and creative industries, but Europe's number one spot for online advertising, digital TV, telecoms and software. It is therefore unsurprising that London has attracted more than twice the number of creative industry greenfield projects than any other city in Europe or the US since 2003.

It is important to remember that 2012 is not just about sport. It will also coincide with the first Diamond Jubilee year of a ruling English monarch since 1897, marking one of the biggest ever series of cultural events in our lifetime. With the benefit of digital technology billions of people will be united in enjoying the experience worldwide.

With the BBC committed to global, national and local coverage, encompassing print, broadcast online, co-operation and collaborative opportunities with companies across the digital and creative spheres will be rife as the BBC works to ensure that its digital media services are fit for purpose.

But from a business perspective, probably one of the most important points is the way in which the staging of the Olympic and Paralympic Games is creating an opportunity to regenerate the East part of London. This was an integral element of London's initial bid to host the Games and the city remains committed to delivering on its promise to ensure that the Olympic Park and the surrounding areas continue to thrive well beyond 2012.

The post-Games vision for London's Olympic Park is to create a unique and inspiring place for events and leisure activities, a major centre for sport and culture, new communities built around family housing with a range of affordability, and a hub for enterprise and innovation. This vision will be delivered through a series of partnerships across the public, private and third sectors, making the most of the right skills and resources to transform the Park into a sustainable model of live, work and play space.

LOOKING TO THE FUTURE

London's economy is projected to grow by £155 billion by 2025,[6] moving it up from 5th to 4th rank of the world's richest cities. Equally, London is transforming itself to accommodate a 1 million growth in population over the next two decades and, to remain Europe's number one place to do business, investing several billion pounds to improve the capital's infrastructure. Alongside the Olympic Park, some of the largest and most exciting development projects that are or will be taking place in London include Crossrail, King's Cross, Stratford City, and the Canary Wharf extension.

As Europe's fastest growing capital city, London will clearly not be standing still. It's clear that in today's changing business environment London must actively seek to develop its unique strengths as a world city in the face of growing global competition and, in light of this fact, Think London commissioned an independent report with IBM and Chatham House, home of the Royal Institute of International Affairs, entitled *London 2020: Competing in a New FDI Era*'.

Multinational organisations are facing an increasing amount of choice in today's global FDI arena, and London needs to ensure that it remains the leading option for overseas companies looking to invest. However, none of this will happen by chance and London must continually evolve in order to take advantage of the changing FDI landscape. Although London is best placed to benefit from the predicted influx of foreign direct investment (FDI), the report identified four key drivers for FDI over the next decade, outlining how these need to be developed for London to retain its position as the world's leading FDI destination:

Efficiency

It is expected that companies will start to reconfigure their global footprints to take advantage of lower operating costs and, with new FDI activity predicted to focus on consolidation and optimisation, it will become important to develop London as the destination of choice for investors wanting efficiency to go hand in hand with global expansion.

International firms will therefore benefit from London's access to a concentration of specialist business clusters, a skilled workforce and new technology – all of which reduces the cost of doing business abroad in multiple countries.

Talent

As workforces become more fragmented, businesses are reshaping their global footprint in order to access talent and facilitate recruitment. London's research establishments and educational institutions are capable of attracting skilled staff and growing the next generation of talent, and it will be essential to ensure the continuation of excellent training and educational opportunities to assist in growing this area.

Innovation

London helps companies create operational efficiencies while being at the heart of world innovation and entrepreneurship. The UK has the fewest barriers to entrepreneurship in the world and should become a hub for innovation, using technology to enhance efficiency and mobility. Smarter buildings, low-carbon transport, greener energy, electric vehicles, dedicated cycle lanes and improved pedestrian thoroughfares will all demonstrate London's forward-thinking culture.

Globalisation

Developing countries will be the main driver for growth over the next decade. To ensure that London remains the key springboard for international expansion and business development, it will become increasingly important to pro-actively target the emerging and rapidly developing markets, as well as continuing to improve the capital's transport infrastructure. London must also develop the global reach of key professional institutions such as the capital's insurance and accountancy organisations, the City of London, trade Guilds and educational establishments.

Case Study

Teasla Motors

Tesla is the world's only manufacture of high-performance electric cars. Founded in 2003 in California, it employs 500 people globally, with 40 people in the UK, employed through a partner's manufacturing plant. There are 15 Tesla showrooms across the US, with others in Monaco, Munich and now London.

Aim

Tesla wanted to raise its global profile and increase sales from its flagship European showroom in London by capitalising on London's consumer spend profile and its status as an international travel hub.

Think London helped with:

- Intelligence: providing data on London consumer perceptions of electric cars and alerts on latest industry developments.
- Industry profile: introductions to electric car legislation and infrastructure policy-makers, including the Greater London Authority (GLA) and Transport for London.
- Publicity: securing a high-profile appearance at Think London's 'Route to 2012' business event — held in San Francisco in 2009 and focusing on sustainability.
- Retail: introductions to Best Buy, a leading eco-product retailer setting up in the UK in 2010; introductions to high net-worth individuals through one of Think London's clients.

Business success

Tesla opened its London showroom in June 2009. By the beginning of 2010 it was selling one of its $100,000 Roadsters a week and attracting visitors from around the world. With Think London's help, it has established itself as a high-profile brand, actively shaping the sustainable transport industry.

6.5 THE UK PROPERTY MARKET

Nasima Ahmed
EMEA Capital Market Research,
Jones Lang LaSalle

BACKGROUND
Property market size

The UK commercial real estate market remains one of the most established and transparent markets in the world, and plays an important role in the UK economy, making a significant contribution to fixed capital investment. The economic deterioration impacted commercial real estate significantly over the last two years. Property values dropped by 26% in 2008 and as a result the IPD Annual Index recorded the lowest total returns ever, with all property returns falling by 22.1%. The financial meltdown in the aftermath of the collapse of Lehman Brothers and the casualties witnessed within the banking and the corporate sectors contributed towards this misery. Since then however, we have observed considerable recovery with all property delivering positive total returns of 3.5% in 2009, with a particular resurgence over the second half of the year. This trend continued into the first half of 2010 with year to date (Jan-May) returns of 8.5%.

Estimating the total size of the UK commercial property investment is not easy. According to the 2009 Pan-European Property Index, the total value for UK commercial investment market was estimated at £210 billion. The substantial fall in values in 2008 reduced the size of the UK investment market by 45%.

The most up to date report on total commercial floorspace was published in 2008 by the Department for Communities and Local Government. The report suggested that there was 596 million sq m of commercial floorspace in England and Wales of which over 60% was in factories and warehouses, with retail accounting for 18% and offices 17% (see Figure 6.5.1 and Figure 6.5.2 below). Office is further split between different uses, with 83% classified as "commercial offices" and the remainder as "other offices".

Figure 6.5.1 Commercial and industrial floorspace, by property type; 1 April 2008

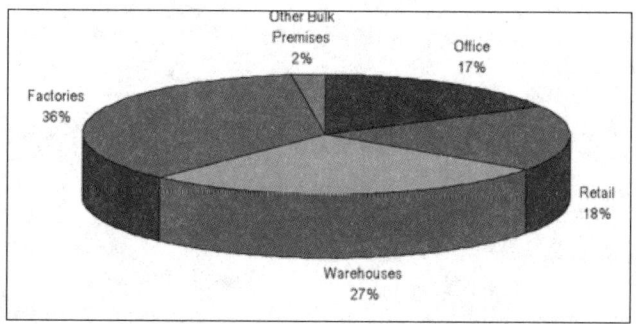

Source: Communities and Local Government

Figure 6.5.2 Commercial and industrial floorspace, by property type, Wales and English regions; 1 April 2008

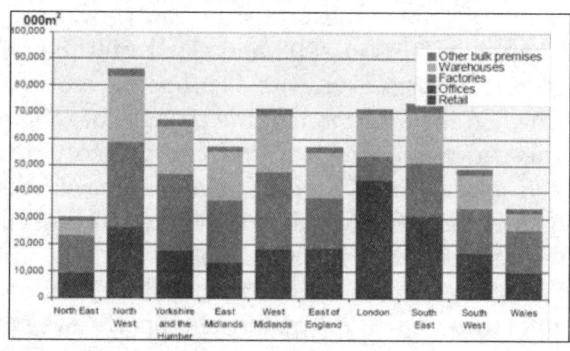

Source: Communities and Local Government

The North West has the highest amount of floorspace and the North East the smallest. The make up of bulk class (property type) also varies across the regions. London has the highest proportion of office floorspace, but also the lowest proportion of factory floorspace.

Structure of the Industry

The UK property industry comprises many professions and organisations, with different disciplines providing advice on a range of activities. Firms engaging in surveying, agency, real estate consultancy and service provision activities represent the backbone of the industry. There are of course other players involved in real estate including financial institutions, planning, legal firms and architectural practices who are regulated by separate organisations and rules. In the UK the main body representing the surveying profession is the Royal Institution of Chartered Surveyors (RICS) who ensure that standards are maintained. Table 6.5.1 below provides a brief summary of the key players in the market place.

Table 6.5.1 Key players involved in the market place

Player	Role
Real estate consultancy firms	These firms, ranging from the multi national firms such as Jones Lang LaSalle, CBRE and other to small independent organisations are the backbone of the profession. These firms provide advice to a variety of organisations on the sale, acquisition and disposal of space. They are also involved in the valuation and management of real estate and also provide investment advice and strategy work for the major pension fund and other institutional investors. Firms also provide holistic advice to major corporate organisations in terms of their occupational requirements and strategies. This advice is backed-up by research based work supplied either in-house or through independent providers. Some of the larger firms also have in-house teams auctioneers, planners and building surveyors.

Auctioneers	Auctioneers, who are surveyors themselves, deal with the sale of property via auctions, as opposed the traditional method of private treaty. Auctions are generally used for the sale of secondary property, especially smaller lot sizes (though not always) to private individuals and property companies.
Planners	Planners oversee and determine applications within their respective areas. They are however also employed within firms of surveyors in advising developers and other parties in the submission and appeals to planning applications.
Property Research Organisations	In recent years there has been an increase in the number of independent research organisations providing both advice on the specific aspects/ investment advice, but also in the provision of market-based data.
Solicitors	Solicitors provide a range of services including advice on transactions, leases, litigation and on the structural form of property investment vehicles.
Banks	Banks (high street, investment and merchant) and building societies provide the funding to investors for the acquisition and development of schemes.
Insurance & pension funds	Insurance and pension funds are key investors in commercial real estate and employ significant teams in the management of these portfolios. Firms may not be restricted to the UK, with a significant number of over seas funds also investing in the UK.
Property Companies	Property companies, both listed and private, are major players in the market, holding land for development opportunities, investment purposes. Given the discount to net asset value many property companies have de-listed and gone private in recent years.

Private individuals	In recent years private individuals have become a significant player in the market, investing and trading in property. While a significant number invest in secondary lower value lot sizes, in recent years they have also become owners of more substantial assets.
Construction companies	Construction companies are important to developers undertaking the construction and fit-out of buildings. Some construction firms may also hold property.

Adapted from Brett 1997

ECONOMY AND THE PROPERTY MARKET
The relationship between the economy and the property market

UK real estate is strongly linked to the economy; thus understanding the dynamics of the economy and its future performance is vital to those involved in both the investment and leasing markets.

Figure 6.5.3 shows a strong relationship between employment growth in Central London and the amount of office space acquired by firms.

Figure 6.5.3 Central London Office Market: Employment Growth and Demand (Take up)

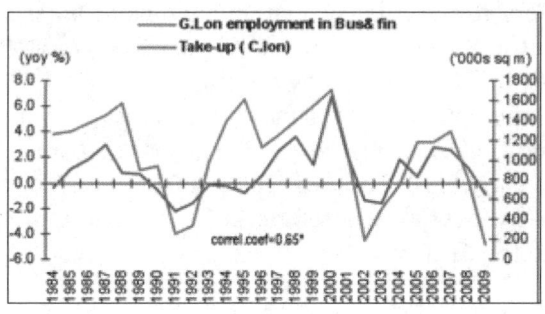

Correlation Coefficient;
Note: Employment refers to employment in financial, business services and public administration in Greater London
Source: Jones Lang LaSalle, Experian Business Strategies (employment data)

Of course, firms may hoard available space or us it more intensively as their employment requirements change. The strength of the relationship signifies the linkages between business activity and employment and demand (take up) for office space.

Retail rents show a close relationship with consumer spending growth, as Figure 6.5.4 illustrates. As consumers increase their spending, so the profitability of retailers and the ability to pay higher rents increases

Figure 6.5.4 UK Retail Property Market: Consumer Spending and Retail Rents

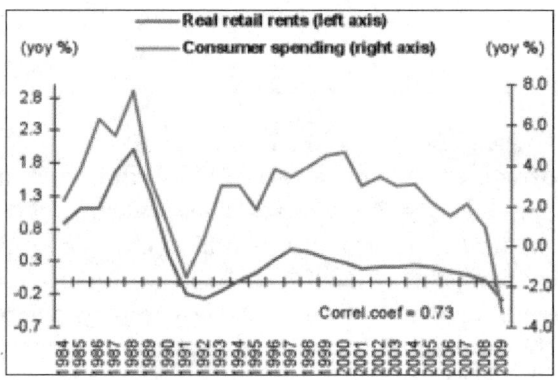

Source: IPD, ONS

The relationship is very strong (the correlation coefficient takes a value of 0.73). We can observe that the slowdown in consumer spending growth last year (2009) is mirrored in a similar trend exhibited by retail rental growth.

Total returns (a combination of rental income from property and the change in the price of property) is closely related to GDP growth. Figure 6.5.5 shows how the recessions of the early 1990s and over 2008-2009 resulted in negative returns from property. Indeed, over this latter period the decline in GDP was much sharper compared to the 1990's.

Figure 6.5.5 UK All Property: GDP and Total Returns

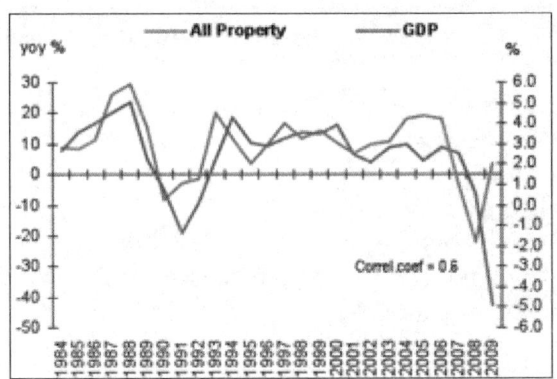

Source: IPD, ONS
Note: A measure of the closeness of a relationship is the correlation coefficient. A value of 1 signi - fies a perfect relationship. The value of 0.65 obtained for employment and office take up repre - sents a strong relationship.

As a consequence, investors lost confidence in the property market which is reflected in the significant fall in total returns in 2008. Since then, however, all property returns have recovered considerably in line with the UK economy, which came out of recession in Q4 2009.

Useful economic data sources

Given the linkages between the economy and property market activity, the avail- ability of data and access to information describing economic activity is essential to investors. In the UK, there is a vast array of economic data published on the economy throughout the year, including both official data provided by the Office of National Statistics (ONS) together with other survey based data provided by var- ious representative and trades bodies, including most notably the Confederation of British Industry (CBI) and the Chartered Institute of Purchasing Supply (CIPS). These databases cover the economy at the national, regional and local levels.

Table 6.5.2 below summarises a number of key pieces of survey data, which are important in understanding the performance of the economy, both immediately and in the future. Much of this data is freely available for current periods, although some historical time-series data is only available by subscription. All official UK statistics are currently available free of charge.

Table 6.5.2 Economic data available for the UK

Data	Comment	Released	Provider	Internet Link
Economic Growth (GDP)	Size and growth of economy and its component sectors	Quarterly	National Statistics	www.statistics.gov.uk
Industrial Production	Index of production showing output in various production/ manufacturing industries	Monthly	National Statistics	www.statistics.gov.uk
Interest Rate	Current bank base rate and background to rate decision	Monthly	Bank of England	www.bankof england.co.uk
Retail Sales	Level of sales	Monthly	National Statistics	www.statistics.gov.uk
Labour market	Levels of employment, unemployment and earnings at UK and regional level	Monthly	National Statistics	www.statistics.gov.uk
Swap rates	Finance rates often used on loans for real estate	Daily	Financial Times	www.ft.com
Inflation	Current rate of inflation and contributory factors	Monthly	National Statistics	www.statistics.gov.uk

Inflation outlook	Inflation report, providing the current outlook for inflation and the UK economy	Quarterly	Bank of England	www.bankof england.co.uk
Treasury Forecasts	Independent forecasts of various economic data over two and four years.	Monthly	HM Treasury	www.hm-treasury.gov.uk
Business Sentiment	Survey data on business activity, including output and employ-ment, for the manufacturing and service sectors	Monthly	Chartered Institute of Purchasing Supply	www.cips.org
Business Sentiment	Survey data on manufacturing, retail and financial services sectors	Monthly and Quarterly	Confeder-ation of British Industry	www.cbi.org.uk
Consumer Confidence	Indicator of confidence on a range of measures	Monthly	Martin Hamblin GFK	www.martinhamblin -gfk.com
Business Activity	Survey data on orders, employment, capacity utilisation, cashflows	Quarterly	British Chambers of Commerce	www.british chambers.org.uk
Financial Stability	Review of the financial stability of the UK economy	Bi-annual	Bank of England	www.bankof england.co.uk

LEASING STRUCTURE OF THE UK PROPERTY MARKET

The UK has a distinctive leasing system that both overseas occupiers and investors need to understand. Leasing products vary, and include fully serviced offices on short term contracts to traditional space on longer term contracts. Some firms may also wish to outsource space needs to a specialist provider, for example, Land Securities. When seeking to secure premises in the UK it is always appropriate to seek advice from a professionally qualified surveyor. The following sections outline the various characteristics of the traditional institutional lease in the UK.

Lease length

Traditionally an occupier will enter into a lease (subject to the legislative framework), which may provide rights for renewal, or other obligations, expressed or otherwise by law. The length of lease will be a matter for negotiation, or could be restricted on the assignment of a lease. In recent years the average length of a typical institutional style lease has fallen from under 20 years to below 15 years. Lease lengths are typically longer for retail property, which retailers traditionally seek, most particularly in order to recoup the cost of their fit-out. The chart below highlights the change in lease lengths over time for the main sectors.

Figure 6.5.6 Changes in lease length for the main sectors (1999 – 2009)

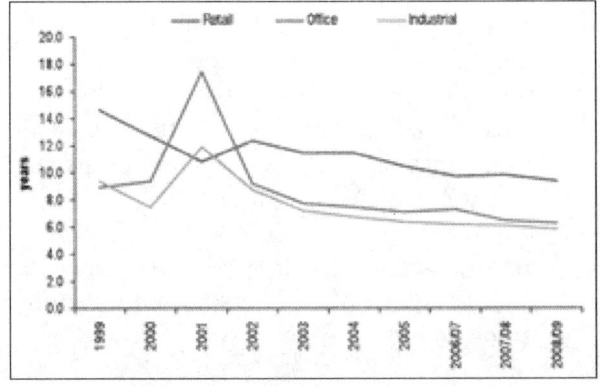

Source: IPD/ BPF

The graph shows that average lease lengths have fallen in all three sectors in response to modern business requirements. The retail sector showed their largest fall in average lease from 14.6 years in 1999 to 9.4 years in 2008/2009. Industrial leases showed the second largest fall from 9.4 to 5.8 years over the same period.

In taking a lease for a long period of time, occupiers need to be aware of the possible restrictions that may arise should they seek to assign a lease. The Landlord and Tenant (Covenants) Act 1995 led to a change in rules regarding "privity of contract". For leases entered into before this act, the obligations between the original landlord and tenant remain enforceable even if the lease has been transferred or assigned. Leases entered into after this Act was introduced are subject to this restriction, releasing the tenant from any future obligations on the transfer or assignment of the lease. Of course, there may be restrictions placed in the terms of the lease in respect of, for example the financial standing of the tenant.

Rent review

Leases will contain provision for rent reviews, the period and nature of review being set out in the terms of the lease as agreed between the landlord and tenant. Traditionally rent reviews in the UK will be every five years to the then open market value, subject to an upwards only clause, preventing the rent from falling below the passing rent (should rents have fallen). The rent at review will be subject to negotiation between the two parties with reference to rents recently agreed (comparables) for similar premises in the open market.

Sometimes the lease will have another basis on which the rent will be reviewed. This could be that rents are reviewed by a fixed percentage, to a certain sum, or are set to rise by the then rate of inflation, possibly with a cap or collar to restrict the level of increase. The exact nature of the review will be specified in the lease. With the length of leases shortening, there are now a higher proportion of leases which are not subject to a rent review.

Turnover rents are becoming very common in the retail sector. Retail tenants who have/are experiencing trading difficulties are requesting linking rent to turnover to reduce liabilities and the risk of void. Anecdotally, over 80% of recent lettings have a turnover element attached and of that, around half are turnover only for at least part of the term. Although this causes fluctuations to the levels of rental income for the landlord, most are happy to move to this type of lease structure to protect value in the short term by eliminating void costs. Full market rental deals are generally limited to value brands and phone shops and this is unlikely to change in the short term.

Repairing obligations

The general obligation to repair is placed on the tenant to undertake, or pay for (often in the case of a multi-tenanted building by way of a service charge) all necessary repairs, even if these pre-date the lease. This is typically referred to as an FRI (Full Repairing and Insuring) lease. Special provisions can be incorporated into the lease which may limit the obligations to keep the property in its initial condition at the time the lease is granted, and a special Schedule of Condition can be attached to the lease. In some limited circumstances the lease may limit repairs to the interior of the property, with the landlord undertaking the external repairs, otherwise referred to as IRI (Internal Repairing and Insuring lease).

Incentives and other obligations

Some leases may contain additional provisions such as the inclusion of a break clause in which one or both of the parties is able to determine the lease at a certain point in time and subject to any penalties agreed between the parties. There may also be a time period specified by which the parties must serve their notice to break the lease.

In addition to break options a lease may contain other incentives such as a rent free period. This is often provided for a short period; say 3-6 months to allow the tenant to undertake fit-out works, although at times when leasing activity is slow the level of rent free may increase dependent on the negotiations.

At the time of signing the lease, the landlord may require the tenant to provide a deposit covering rent for a certain period of time. A guarantee may also be required against the obligations for the term of the lease which may be enforced even if a business fails.

Lease reform

Following the recent government review of leasing practice in the UK, the Government has decided not to take any legislative action against leasing practice for the time being. Nevertheless, some concerns remain and the Government has reiterated that it will continue to monitor practice over the next three years to ensure flexibility continues to be offered and provided. The government also intend to review the law on assignment and subletting, including legislative options, to enhance flexibilities, whilst not jeopardising the investment market.

In addition to the cost of renting and professional fees, occupiers will also have a liability to other occupational and leasing costs, including taxation and running/maintenance charges.

Taxation, Management and Transactions Costs

On taking a lease (or even acquiring premises freehold) stamp duty will be payable on the transfer of the property. The current freehold rates are outlined in Table 6.5.3 below. As of 1st December 2003 new rates came into force for leases, with the rate set at a 1% of the net present value of the rental stream, discounted at a rate of 3.5%. An individual will be exempt from liability where the net present value of the income stream is below £150,000. Further details on stamp duty are available at www.inlandrevenue.gov.uk. It is recommended that professional advice is sought with regard to the tax implications, including value added tax.

Table 6.5.3 Stamp Duty Rates (as at December 2009)

Value band	Rate
Up to £125,000	0
£125,000, no more than £250,000	1%
£250,000, no more than £500,000	3%
Over £500,000	4%

Source: Inland Revenue

If the transaction involves the purchase of a new lease with a substantial rent there may be an additional stamp duty land tax (SDLT) charge to that shown above, based on the rent.

The SDLT tax is a tax on transactions, not documents. When a property or land is purchased, the buyer must fill in a land transaction return (SDLT1) and send it to HMRC. The conveyancer/solicitor acting behalf of the purchaser normally completes the return as part of handling the transaction. But legally, the purchasers are responsible for the information submitted.

There are also further costs. Occupiers are required to pay business rates to provide a contribution to the provision of local services. In simple terms the rates payable are based as follows: (rateable value x multiplier) less any relief. The multiplier, known as the uniform business rate, is set by the rating authorities and increases by the rate of inflation each year. The rateable value is also subject to a five-year review. More specific information on the level of rates, relief, exemptions and reviews can be obtained from the valuation office (www.voa.gov.uk).

Specific running costs on the property (service charges) will also be payable and will vary depending on the location, size and age of building. The provision of air conditioning will also have an impact. The Table 6.5.4 provides an outline of the likely costs (per sq ft) based on both air-conditioned and non air-conditioned buildings in various locations of the UK. In recent years service charge costs have risen above the rate of inflation with maintenance, insurance and security charges adding to the increase. The trend towards shorter leases is also likely to lead to planned maintenance programme over three and five years.

Table 6.5.4 Average Office occupancy costs 2008

	Air Conditioned	Non-Air Conditioned
London – City	7.54	7.04
London – West End	7.98	7.08
Greater London	6.54	5.31
South East	6.40	3.10
Midlands	4.39	4.76
Outer Regions	5.31	4.42
UK Average	6.36	5.28

Units: £s per sq ft
Source: Jones Lang LaSalle, Office Oscar 2008

A further factor which occupiers may wish to consider is the potential impact of the accountancy standards FRS12 which requires companies to list leasehold liabilities on the balance sheet. This could act as an additional driver towards shorter leases.

THE STRUCTURE OF UK PROPERTY INVESTMENT
Investor categories
The UK is by far the largest investment market in Europe accounting for almost

35% of the total European investment volumes. Over the last five years the UK investment market has changed considerably. Direct investment volumes in the UK peaked in 2006 with £63bn transacted. Activity remained healthy in 2007 but since then a significant drop occurred in the wake of the financial crisis with volumes decreasing dramatically. The bottom of the market was reached in Q4 2008, which became the weakest quarter on record. With investor sentiment improving coupled with moderate easing of the debt market, investment demand improved considerably in Q4 2009 particularly for high quality prime stocks. This trend continued into the first half of 2010 and we expect total volumes to be 20% higher for the whole year compared to £23bn recorded in 2009.

The investment market comprises a number of players ranging from the traditional institutional investor to the private individual. The institutions, including funds, are the dominant players and include life, general insurance and pension funds. These include both those based in the UK, but also in Europe, the US and other countries and some examples of UK domiciled funds include Grosvenor, Scottish Widows and Legal and General. Over the last three years institutions and property funds combined accounted for almost 45% of the total investment in the UK (see chart below). In addition there are a number of property companies (quoted and private) who are not only involved in development, but who also hold property for investment purposes. Examples of these include Land Securities, British Land, Hammerson and Quintain. These groups represented nearly 35% of the aggregated investment volumes over 2007-2009. There are also a number of private (high net worth) individuals and other indirect property investment vehicles, such as limited partnerships and property unit trusts which have holdings in commercial real estate. Indeed the proportion of private investment improved dramatically from 3% in 1999 to averaging over 15% in the last three years. The relative proportions of investment by investor type are charted in Figure 6.5.7.

Figure 6.5.7 Investment by Investor Type – 2007-2009

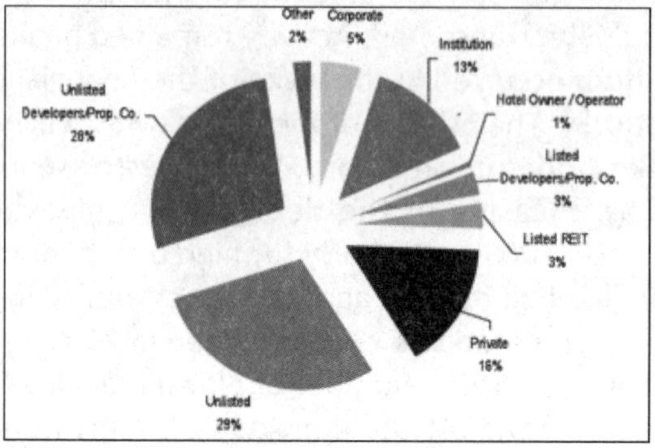

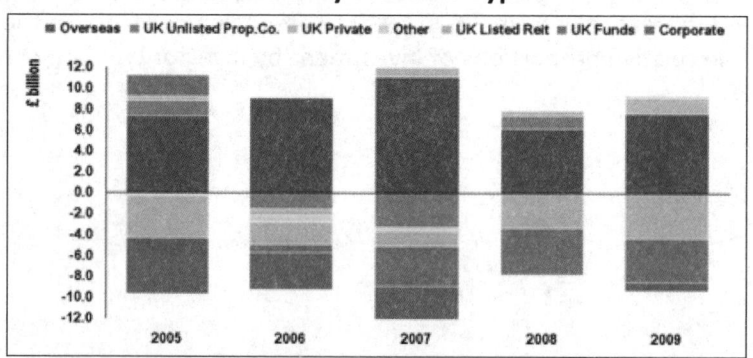

Source: Jones Lang LaSalle

One key trend in recent years has been that of the significant increase in activity from overseas investors within the UK property market. This has been driven by a number of factors, including the performance of alternative assets such as equities, the low cost of finance (although this has increased since 2007) and the diversification benefits of holding real estate in the UK. This trend has continued over the last five years as illustrated by Figure 6.5.8. Overseas investors have injected a significant amount of money into the UK property market with net investment (acquisition – disposals) averaging £8.3bn in the last five years, making them the highest net investors compared to the other investor type.

Figure 6.5.8 Net Investment by Investor Type

Source: Jones Lang LaSalle

One of the reasons has and continues to be the appeal of investing in property compared to other asset classes, with property being the strongest performing asset class over the long term. As illustrated in Figure 6.5.9, all property outperformed equities and gilts over the last ten years with total returns of 6.4%. Comparable returns for gilts were 6.0%, whilst equities produced the weakest returns at 1.6%. Over the short term however equities outperformed other asset classes.

Figure 6.5.9 Property Equities and Gilts – Total Returns

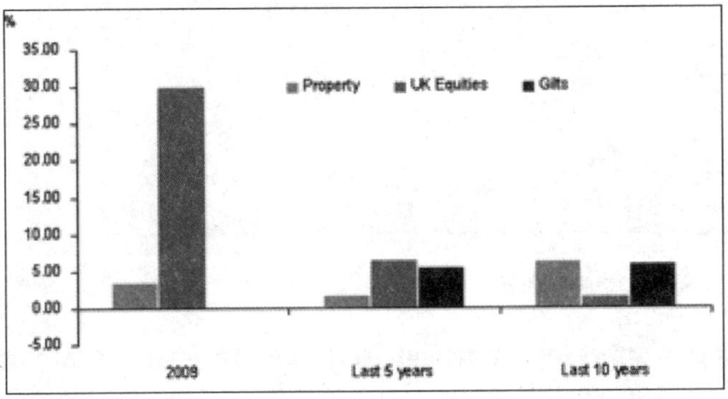

Source: IPD

The low cost of finance and fundability of property, in which the level of returns measured by the yield is greater than the cost of finance, also attracted investors into the commercial real estate market. When the market peaked in 2006-2007, however, this situation changed (as shown in Figure 6.5.10 below). Given the sheer weight of money prime yields compressed to levels below the cost of financing, thus property was no longer self-financing.

The recent credit crisis resulted in pricing across all assets classes re-adjusting considerably in latter part of 2008 and early 2009. Gilt yields and five year swaps fell to record lows. Property yields also increased significantly, particularly in the first half of 2009. As a result the margin between property yields and cost of financing reached a record high (500 basis points for prime and over 600 basis points against secondary yields) making investing in property very attractive, particularly for those with substantial equity as the lending markets were very restrictive. Given the improvement in investment activity over the latter part of 2009 and early 2010 this gap has reduced rapidly. We expect this trend to continue in the medium term as the expected rise in interest rates and gilt yields over this period imply a significant rise in the risk free rate from the current, artificially low, level.

Figure 6.5.10 Property yield gap

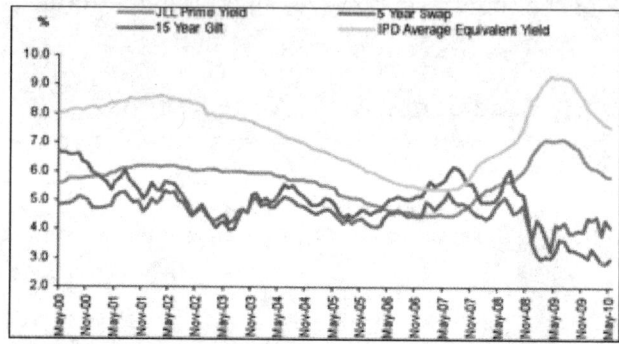

Source: Jones Lang La Salle/ IPD; DataStream

The graph shows that short term financing rates and 15-year gilts are now considerably below the average IPD equivalent yields and prime yields. Over the medium term, however, we expect the margin between property yields and cost of financing to narrow further.

Looking ahead, weaker levels of employment and curtailed domestic spending represent clear risks for commercial property. Investors will look to identify markets where occupational demand will hold up through the period of government retrenchment and will keep an eye as to where quality prime assets are marked down to an extent where clear recovery plays, as in 2008, will present themselves. Prime commercial property could also come to be seen as a relatively safe haven for some given the expected volatility of other asset classes.

It is also worth highlighting the changes to Capital Gains Tax which were announced at the recent 'Emergency Budget'. This clearly has implications for real estate investors.

The following changes affect chargeable gains on or after 23 June 2010:

1.   If your income, less all allowable deductions and reliefs, plus your net chargeable gains are less than the upper limit of the basic rate income tax band, £37,400 for 2010-11, Capital Gains will still be subject to a flat rate of

18%. If higher, a flat rate of 28% will apply to gains, or the part of the gains that cause you to be a higher rate tax payer.

2. If you dispose of qualifying assets on or after 23 June 2010 two aspects of CGT Entrepreneurs' Relief have changed:
    ●   There is a technical change to the way in which the relief is calcu-lated, although effectively a flat rate of 10% will continue to apply, and
    ●   The lifetime gains that can benefit from the relief are increased from £2m to £5m.

Another key trend worth noting is that the UK commercial property market is becoming ever more characterised by a driver towards sustainable buildings, most especially with the corporate occupiers and institutional investors. Although the link between value and sustainable property has yet to be quantifiably proven, recent surveys, such as the Jones Lang LaSalle and Corenet annual survey, point towards an ever increasing number of companies desiring good quality, efficient and sustainable space for their operations. The UK's legislative environment is also pushing in this direction with buildings now needing Energy Performance Certificates (EPCs) to transact and an ever growing plethora of regulation. Any investor in UK property either directly or through leasing activity should be aware of future regulatory drivers.

PROPERTY LENDING

The level of lending to real estate increased significantly since the mid-1990s reflecting not only the demand from individuals and institutional investors at a time of strong investment performance, but also the willingness of banks and other financial institutions to lend. Figure 6.5.11 below shows the level of lending based on figures from the Bank of England, in which the total amount outstand-ing to real estate topped over £246bn by the end of the first quarter 2010. This compares to £41bn at the time of the last peak (September 1999). Although the latest Bank of England lending data showed continued growth in lending to real estate, it is worth highlighting that bank lending in sterling to real estate fell over Q3 and Q4 09, the first fall since December 1997. Total lending dropped by £2bn to £242bn (including lending by building societies) compared to a £2bn growth over the same period in 2008. The year on year growth in the volume of real estate lending has fallen considerably, from £26bn in Dec 2008 to only £1.3bn in

Dec 2009, the lowest growth recorded since March 1997. Indeed the lending market was very restricted in the aftermath of the banking crisis up until the second half of 2009.

Figure 6.5.11 Bank lending to real estate

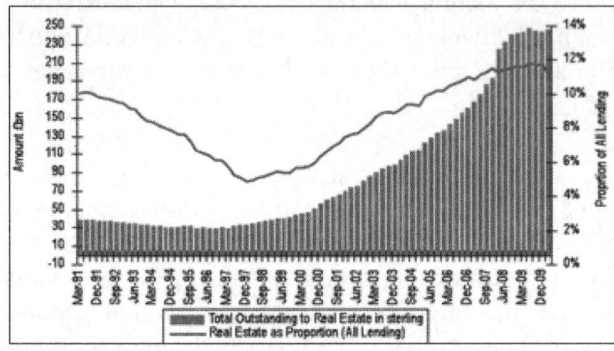

Source: Bank of England

Whilst the Q1 2010 lending data showed some improvement in Bank lending, the issue of major balance-sheet lenders' distressed loan books caused by the credit crisis remains a significant obstacle to any return to true normality in both the UK banking and real estate markets. The slight increase in bank lending is indicative of the continued caution in the lending market and suggests that the expected wave of bank-led property disposals has not commenced. Most banks are restructuring where possible, in following a policy of 'extend and amend'. Where loans are at risk of not fully repaying at their scheduled maturity date, but the sponsors are still servicing their interest, lenders are simply extending loan maturity dates in return for a quid pro quo, such as an increased margin or additional back-end fees. Lenders may also seek to claim a share in any upside in acknowledgment of their new position of increased risk.

Over the first half of 2010 we have seen evidence of active competition between banks for new lending especially for strong cash flows. Competition has forced down margins for prime investments. LTV (loan-to-value) pressures are generally being resisted by most banks. The appetite for lending on developments is still very limited and we expect this to continue over the medium term.

References

Brett, M. (1997), *Property & Money*, Estates Gazette, London

Floorspace and rateable value of commercial and industrial properties 1 April 2008, (England & Wales), Department for Communities and Local Government.

Global Transparency Index 2008 – Jones Lang LaSalle

OSCAR 2008 – Jones Lang LaSalle

BPF IPD Annual Lease Review 2009 – IPD and British Property Foundation

IPD Annual Index 2010 – IPD

Freemans Guide to the Property Industry, Freemans Publishing 2000

Understanding Commercial Property Investment; A Guide for Financial Advisers (2003) Seven Dials Consulting (and sponsored by IPF, RICS and BPF).

6.6 AGRICULTURAL PROPERTY INVESTMENT

Richard Binning
Savills

Historically farmland is regarded as a safe haven in times of economic uncertainty; this proved to be the case during 2009 and 2010. In addition, trading and owning land has tax benefits quite apart from the windfalls that strategically located farmland can produce by way of future development. Land also has obvious life style attractions and a more positive sentiment in the amenity and country house markets in the second half of 2009 and early 2010, gave additional support to farmland values.

Many private and institutional land owners have recognised land as a spectacularly good investment and, for many, this has been the case over the last 25 and 50 years. For others, the story has been more mundane. What makes the difference?

TIMING

Farmland can be a very good investment if done for the right reasons and with the right land. However, as with all investments, timing of trading makes a huge difference to short- and medium-term performance.

The high demand for a relatively fixed stock of farmhouses has boosted the investment performance of farms and the provision of land for development can be an extremely profitable activity. Total investment returns from high performance commercial farming of arable land, including growth in capital value, averaged just over 10 per cent per annum over the 30 years to December 2006. This compares favourably with the return from equities and commercial property. Recent turbulence has amplified the changes as the investment return over 3 years is over 20% compared to commercial property at -5%. The comparison is highly sensitive to the timing of investment, a 2 per cent return is shown over 10 years to December 2006.

In 2004, 42% of the farms over 100 acres handled by Savills were bought by 'lifestyle buyers' from outside farming. In 2009 this has shrunk to 21% and institutions / corporate buyers had dipped to make up 4% of purchasers from 10% in 2006.

THE MARKET CONDITION

The volume of publicly traded farmland has been shrinking since 1945 as shown in Figure 6.6.1 below. The value of land publically traded this year is likely to be very low, comparable to the year Foot & Mouth Disease struck in the UK (2000) and the last Common Agricultural Policy (CAP) review (2005).

Figure 6.6.1 The volume of publicly traded farmland since 1945

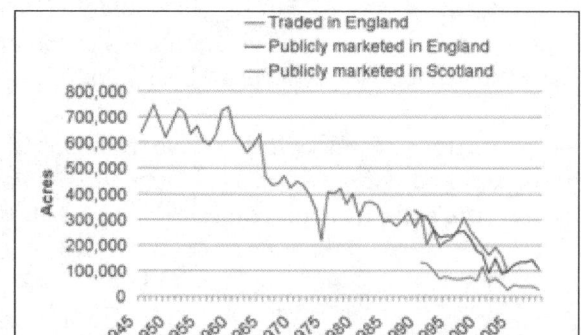

The demand for land remains strong and Savills have over £7.5 billion worth potential waiting to be spent on UK farmland. However, not all of this money will actually be invested in land as some buyers, frustrated by lack of opportunities to find what they are after, will look to other investments which are more easily accessible in the volumes required for modern day trading.

The surges in values seen through recent years have stabilised in 2009/2010, although Savills research shows increases from 2004 to 2010 of 122%.

We have researched the effect of recession on land values. Values tend to grow or remain strong through recession, as the attraction of safe assets prevents sales and increases demand. As the economy picks up (as shown in the early 90's), more land tends to come to the market as Capital is withdrawn to fund other investment opportunities. Figure 6.6.2 charts the fluctuations in land and wheat prices since 1970.

Figure 6.6.2 Land and wheat price (at current prices)

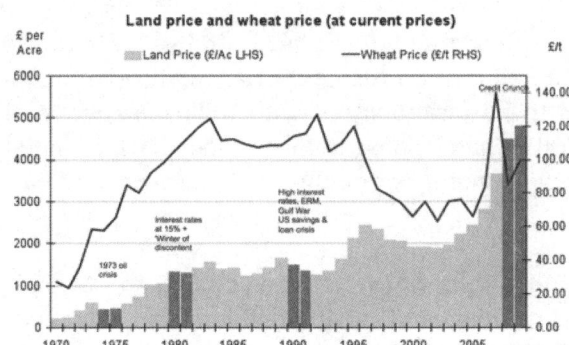

Tenure

Let land portfolios generated a return of about 17 per cent per annum to investors over ten years to December 2009, and total returns this year are likely to be around 10%. This follows a period when returns averaged around 12 per cent per annum over twenty years as initial yields have dropped. This is a niche market with generally low turnover and wide variation in the nature of the asset. Initial income yields vary in a range of less than one to four per cent. Mis-pricing is a hazard for the uninformed in such a market, so buyers and sellers should trade with care.

INITIAL LET YIELDS (INCOME AND CAPITAL)

Yields from let land are compared with yields from let residential property, gilts and indexes for farming's top 25%, commercial property, forestry and equities in Figure 6.6.3.

Figure 6.6.3 Initial let yields (income and capital)

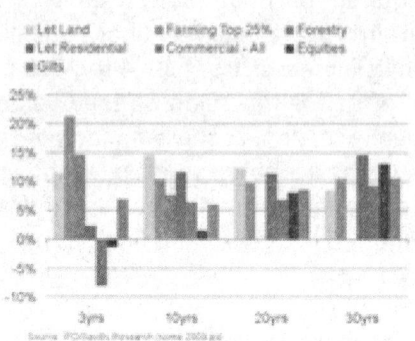

Those pension and life funds that bought farmland heavily in the late 1970s in a rising market (only to be part of a rush out of agriculture in the mid-1980s in a falling market) tend to be disappointed with their experience of agricultural investment. On the other hand, some of those funds have retained a reserve of strategic land with development hope value, which has paid off handsomely.

Development

With agricultural land typically worth between £5,000 and £6,000 per acre and greenfield residential building land worth anything from £200,000 to £2 million per acre depending on location, the provision of land for development can be an extremely profitable pastime. It is also an increasingly complicated activity, with the new government steering new housing development towards 'brownfield' land (i.e. previously developed land) and looking to secure a proportion of affordable housing within the development mix.

Glossy syndicated offerings of land with development potential are increasingly common. Buyers beware – planning permission is the principal constraint and without it your new investment is highly unlikely to be one of the top performers of the next 25 years!

Tax

Taxation advantages tend to be a significant secondary reason for holding land. 100% relief from Inheritance Tax after a qualifying period of ownership, which can be two years, is a valuable means of passing wealth to the next generation. For instance, if land is held for 10 years before death then this could add more than three per cent a year to the effective investment return from land, although other ways of avoiding tax are possible. There have been rumours that this tax position could be reviewed.

The value in rolling over capital gains into farmland, thus deferring Capital Gains Tax, will again become an important factor following the increase in CGT in the last Budget.

CONCLUSION

All in all, there are many good reasons to own a slice of the British countryside, with lifestyle motives tending to be *high* amongst them. From an investment perspective, there has been, and will continue to be, great variation in the returns from land ownership, depending on its location and characteristics. As ever, stock selection is the key to good investment return.

Appendix I
Contributors' Contacts

Artaius Ltd
Southgate House
St. George's Way
Stevenage SG1 1HG
Tel: +44 (0) 1438 758 100
Contact: Melanie Troiano
e-mail: Melanie.troiano@artaius.com

British Design Innovation (BDI)
9 Pavilion Parade
Brighton BN2 1RA
Tel: +44 (0) 1273 675 317
Contact: Maxine J. Horn
Mobile: +44 (0) 7803 2907 150
e-mail: Maxine@britishdesigninnovation.org

Business Leaders Network (BLN)
Citylife Enterprise Centre
182-190 Newmarket Rd
Cambridge CB5 8HE
Contact: Mark Littlewood
Direct line: +44 (0) 7760 171 929
e-mail: Mark@The BLN.com

Cairn Financial Advisers LLP
61 Cheapside
London EC2V 6AV
Tel: +44 (0) 20 7148 7900
Contacts:
Tony Rawlinson
e-mail: tony.rawlinson@cairnfin.com
Simon Sacerdoti
e-mail: simon.sacerdoti@cairnfin.com

Carter Jonas
6 Hills Road
Cambridge CB2 1NH

Tel: +44 (0) 1223 368 771
Fax: +44 (0) 1223 369550
Contact: Nick Hood
Direct line: +44 (0) 1223 346 607
e-mail: nick.hood@carterjonas.co.uk

Chemical Industries Association (CIA)
King's Building
16 Smith Square
London SW1P 3JJ
Tel: +44 (20) 7834 3399
Contacts:
Neil Harvey
e-mail: HarveyN@cia.org.uk
Alan Eastwood
e-mail: EastwoodA
e-mail: EastwoodA@cia.org.uk

HSBC Bank plc
Level 33
8 Canada Square
Canary Wharf
London E14 5HQ

Inward Investment
Contacts:
Anne Marnat
Tel: +44 (0) 20 7992 1638
e-mail: anne1.marnat@hswbc.com
Sarah McCourtie
Tel: +44 (0) 20 207 991 8515
e-mail: sarahmccourtie@hsbc.com
James Roberts
Tel: +44 (0) 207 991 3707
e-mail: jamesroberts@hsbc.com
General Enquiries
Tel: +44 (0) 20 7991 0538
e-mail: inwardinvestmentuk@hsbc.com

Jones Lang LaSalle
EMEA Capital Market Research

25 Bank Street
London E14 5EG
Tel: +44 (0) 20 3147 1211
Fax: +44 (0) 20 3147 1730
Contact: Nasima Ahmed
e-mail: nasima.ahmed@eu.jll.com

Legend Business
2 London Wall Buildings
London EC2M 5UU
Tel: +44 (0) 7448 5137
Contacts:
Tom Chalmers
Direct line: +44 (0) 7448 5162
e-mail: tomchalmers@legend-paperbooks.co.uk
Jonathan Reuvid
Direct line: +44 (0) 1295 738 070
e-mail: jreuvidembooks@aol.com

One Nucleus
UCB Building
Granta Park
Cambridge CB21 6GS
Tel: +44 (0) 1223 896 450
Contact: Belinda Clarke
e-mail: Belinda@onenucleus.com

PNO Consultants Limited
Dunham House
Brooke Court
Lower Meadow Road
Wilmslow
Cheshire SK9 3ND
Tel: +44 (0) 161 488 3488
Fax: +44 (0) 161 488 3489
Contact: Chris Wilshaw
e-mail: chris.wilshaw@pnoconsultants.com

Savills (L & P) Limited
Wytham Court
11 West Way

Oxford OX2 0QL
Tel: +44 (0) 1865 269 000
Contact: Richard Binning
e-mail: rbinning@savills.com
website: www.ssavills.com

The SourcingSolutions Ltd
7200 The Quorum
Oxford Business Park North
Garsington Road
Oxford OX4 2JZ
Tel: +44 (0) 1865 497 150
Fax: +44 (0) 1865 481 482
Contact: Mark Norcliffe
Direct line: +44 (0) 1304 830 509
e-mail: mnorcliffe@thesourcingsolutions.com

Think London
Level 35, 25 Canada Square
Canary Wharf
London E14 5LQ
Tel: +44 (0) 7718 5400
Contact: Michael Charlton
e-mail: michael.charlton@thinklondon.com

Watson, Farley and Williams LLP
15 Appold Street
London EC2A 2HB
Tel: +44 (0) 20 7814
Contacts:
Christina Howard
Direct line: +44 (0) 20 7814 8182
e-mail: CHoward@wfw.com
Asha Kumar
Direct line: +44 (0) 20 7814 8182
e-mail: AKumar@wfw.com

Wilder Coe LLP
223-237 Old Marylebone Road
London NW1 5QL
Tel: +44 (0) 20 7724 6060
Contact: Robert Coe
e-mail: Robert.coe@wilderce.co.uk
website: www.wildercoe.co.uk

Appendix II
Useful Contacts and Websites

UK TRADE & INVESTMENT - GLOBAL NETWORK
UNITED KINGDOM
London Headquarters
e-mail: inward.investment@ukti.gsi.gov.uk
Tel: +44 (0) 20 7215 8000
www.ukti.gov.uk
Director for Investment
Andrew Levi
Tel: +44 (0) 20 7215 8719
e-mail: andrew.levi@ukti.gsi.gov.uk
Deputy Director for Investment – Strategy
Jane Eardley
Tel: +44 (0) 20 7215 4686
e-mail: jane.eardley@ukti.gsi.gov.uk
Deputy Director for Investment – Projects
Martin Phelan
Tel: +44 (0) 20 7215 4926
e-mail: martin.phelan@ukti.gsi.gov.uk
Head of Global Entrepreneur Programme
Derek Goodwin
Tel: +44 (0) 20 7215 8349
e-mail: Derek.goodwin@ukti.gsi.gov.uk
Regional Investment Contacts
East
East of England International
www.eedainvest@org.uk

East Midlands
East Midlands Development Agency
www.emda.org.uk

London
Think London
www.thinklondon.com

North East
One North East
www.onenortheast.co.uk

North West
Northwest Regional Development Agency
www.nwda.co.uk

Northern Ireland
Invest Northern Ireland
www.investni.com

Scotland
Scottish Development International
www.sdi.co.uk

South East
South East England Development Agency
www.seeda.co.uk

South West
South West of England Regional
Development Agency
www.southwestrda.org.uk
Wales
International Business Wales
www.internationalbusinesswales.com

West Midlands
Advantage West Midlands
www.advantagewm.co.uk

Yorkshire & Humber
Yorkshire Forward
www.yorkshire-forward.com

ASIA PACIFIC AND AFRICA
AUSTRALIA
Sydney
Paul Noon, British Consulate-General
Tel: +61 2 8247 2207
e-mail: paul.noon@fco.gov.uk

CHINA
Shanghai
David Percival, British Consulate-General
Tel: +61 21 3279 2021
e-mail: david.percival@fco.gov.uk

CHINA – HONG KONG AND REGIONAL HEADQUARTERS
Hong Kong
Tony Collingridge, British Consulate-General
Tel: +852 2901 3265
e-mail: tony.collingridge@fco.gov.uk

INDIA
New Delhi
Paul Grey, British High Commission
Tel: +91 11 2419 2504
e-mail: paul.grey@fco.gov.uk

JAPAN
Tokyo
Ben Chesson, British Embassy
Tel: +81 3 5211 1140
e-mail: ben.chesson@fco.gov.uk

KOREA
Seoul
Tom Matlock, British Embassy
Tel: +822 3210 5610
e-mail: tom.matlock@fco.gov.uk

MALAYSIA
Kuala Lumpur
Matthew Smith, British High Commission
Tel: +603 2170 2232
e-mail: m.smith@fco.gov.uk

NEW ZEALAND
Auckland
John Waugh, British Consulate-General
Tel: +64 9 303 5010
e-mail: john.waugh@fco.gov.uk

SOUTH AFRICA
Johannesburg
Corin Wilson, British Consulate-General
Tel +27 11 537 7209
e-mail: corin.wilson@fco.gov.uk

TAIWAN
Taipei
Stephen Metti, British Trade and Cultural Office
Tel: +886 2 8758 2066
e-mail: stephen.metti@fco.gov.uk

EUROPE
AUSTRIA
Vienna
Jane Spegel, British Embassy
Tel: +43 1 716 136 250
e-mail: jane.spiegel@fco.gov.uk

BELGIUM
Brussels
Inge Haeldermans, British Embassy
Tel: +32 2 287 6276
e-mail: inge.haeldermans@fco.gov.uk

DENMARK
Copenhagen
Christina Liaos, British Embassy
Tel; +45 35 44 5103
e-mail: christina.liaos@fco.gov.uk

ESTONIA
Tallin
Annely Lautre, British Embassy
Tel: +372 667 4736
e-mail: annele.lautre@fco.gov.uk

FINLAND
Helsinki
Kari Luukkonen

Tel: +358 9 2286 5229
e-mail: kari.luukkonen@fco.gov.uk

FRANCE
Paris
Andrew Holt, British Embassy
Tel: +33 1 4451 3169
e-mail: andrew.holt@fco.gov.uk

GERMANY
Düsseldorf
Ulrich Marthaler, British Consulate-General
Tel; +49 211 9448 207
e-mail: ulrich.marthaler@fco.gov.uk

ICELAND
Reykjavik
Petur Stefansson, British Embassy
Tel: =354 550 5123
e-mail: petur.stefansson@fco.gov.uk

ISRAEL
Tel Aviv
Richard Salt, British Embassy
Tel: +972 3725 1231
e-mail: richard.salt@fco.gov.uk

ITALY
Milan
Danielle Allen, British Consulate-General
Tel: +39 02 723 00222
e-mail: danielle.allen@fco.gov.uk

LUXEMBOURG
Luxembourg
Thomas Flammant, British Embassy
Tel: +352 22 9864 2216
e-mail: thomas.flammant@fco.gov.uk

NETHERLANDS
The Hague
Michiel Veldhuizen, British Embassy
Tel: +31 70 427 0211
e-mail: michiel.veldhuizen@fco.gov.uk

NORWAY
Oslo
Roy Kristiansen, British Embassy
Tel: +47 2313 2765
e-mail: roy.kristansen@fco.gov.ik

PORTUGAL
Lisbon
Ana-Cristina Abreu, British Embassy
Tel: +35 1 21 392 4065
e-mail: ana.abreu@fco.gov.uk

SPAIN
Madrid
Justine Winterburn, British Embassy
Tel: +34 91 714 6330
e-mail: justine.winterburn@fco.gov.uk

SWEDEN
Slotckholm
Anna Lindberg
Tel: +46 8 671 3067
e-mail: anna.lindberg@fco.gov.uk

SWITZERLAND
Berne
Ian Gavin, British Embassy
Tel: +41 31 359 7751
e-mail: ian.gavin@fco.gov.uk

TURKEY
Istanbul
Taclan Topal, British Consulate-General
Tel: +90 212 334 6441
e-mail: toclan.topal@fco.gov.uk

AMERICAS
BRAZIL
Sao Paulo
Richard Turner, British Consulate-General
Tel: +55 11 3094 2713
e-mail: richard.turner@fco.gov.uk

CANADA
Calgary
Stacie Symington, UKTI Office
Tel: +1 403 539 2234
e-mail: stacie@btoalberta.com

Montreal
Jeremy Mackenzie=Lee, British Consulate-General
Tel: +1 514 866 5863
e-mail: jeremy.lee@fco.gov.uk

Toronto
Matthew Hobbs, British Consulate-General
Tel: +1 416 593 1290
e-mail: matthew.hobbs@fco.gov.uk

Vancouver
Andrea Morgan, British Consulate-General
Tel: +1 604 683 4421
e-mail: andrea.morgan@fco.gov.uk

MEXICO
Mexico City
Isaac Vargas, British Embassy
Tel: +52 55 1670 3245
e-mail: isaac.vargas@fco.org.uk

USA
New York
Fiona MacLeod, British Consulate-General
Tel: +1 212 745 0458
e-mail: fiona.macleodny@fco.gov.uk

Boston
Kirsten Chambers, British Consulate-General
Tel: +1 617 245 4509
e-mail: kirsten.chambers@fco.gov.uk

Chicago
Colette Buscemi, Consulate-General
Tel: +1 312 970 3845
e-mail: colette.buscemi@fco.gov.uk

Houston
Emma Briggs (Interim), Consulate-General
Tel: +1 312 970 3801

Los Angeles
Andrew Lewis, Consulate-General
Tel: +1 310 996 3024
e-mail: andrew.lewis@fco.gov.uk

Miami
Rebecca Mowat, British Consulate-General
Tel: +1 305 374 1522
e-mail: rebecca.mowat@fco.gov.uk

San Francisco
Jaclyn Mason, British Consulate-General
Tel: +1 415 617 1360
e-mail: jaclyn.mason@fco.gov.uk

Washington DC
Melinda Goforth, British Embassy
Tel: +1 202 588 6864
e-mail: melinda.gofoth@fco.org.uk